THE
TYPEWRITER
REPAIR
MANUAL

Other TAB books by the author:

No. 941 *Mimeograph Operation, Maintenance & Repair*
No. 1163 *The Complete Handbook of Sewing Machine Repair*
No. 1208 *Make Your Own Gemstone Jewelry*

THE
TYPEWRITER
REPAIR
MANUAL

BY HOWARD HUTCHISON

TAB BOOKS Inc.
BLUE RIDGE SUMMIT, PA. 17214

FIRST EDITION

FIRST PRINTING

Library of Congress Cataloging in Publication Data

Hutchison, Howard.
    The typewriter repair manual.

    Includes index.
    1. Typewriters—Maintenance and repair—Handbooks, man-
uals, etc.   I. Title.
Z49.H954   652.3   81-9195
ISBN 0-8306-0034-5   AACR2
ISBN 0-8306-1336-6 (pbk.)

Contents

Preface   **7**

1 Definition and an Overview of Typewriter Controls   **11**
Good Communications—Service Manual—Manual and Electric Typewriters—Keybutton or Key—Typebars and Typebar Heads—Typebar Typewriter—Single Element Typewriter—Standard Typewriter—Pitch of a Typewriter—Pica and Elite—Proportional Spacing Typewriter—Typewriter Ribbons—Platen—Carriage—Paper Table-Feed Rolls—Overview of Control Buttons and Levers—IBM Selectric II Controls—Summary

2 Manual Typewriter Mechanisms   **44**
Typing Mechanism—Spacing Mechanism—Escapement Mechanism—Back Space Mechanism—Margin Stop Mechanism—Margin Release Mechanism—Shift Mechanism—Shift Lock Mechanism—Vertical Line Spacing Mechanism—Paper Feed—Paper Release Mechanism—Ribbon Feed (or Transport) Mechanism—Ribbon Lift Mechanism—Tabulation Mechanism—Tab Set-Clear Mechanism—Carriage Release—Platen Release Mechanism—Summary

3 Electric Typewriter Mechanisms   **86**
Power Roll—Electrical System—Driving Mechanism—Switch Mechanism—Typing Mechanisms—Escapement Mechanism—Shift Mechanism—Half Space Mechanism—Space Mechanisms—Back Space Mechanisms—Tab Set and Clear Mechanisms—Color Change and Ribbon Lift Mechanism—Ribbon Feed Mechanism—Ribbon Cartridge Mechanism—Line Space Mechanism—Paper Feed and Release Mechanism—Carriage Release Mechanism—Correction Mechanism—Platen Release—Summary

4 Practical Tips for the Beginning Typewriter Repairman   **134**
Sticky, Dirty Typewriters—Thoroughly Cleaning and Lubing a Typewriter—Giving a Typewriter a Superficial Cleaning and Lubing—Cosmetic Cleaning—Selecting Tools—Designing a Workshop—Securing Technical Information on Typewriters—Getting Service Manuals and Parts Catalogs From IBM—Reconditioned Platens—Adjusting the Pressure on Individual Typebars—Removing Typewriter Covers—Stocking an Assortment of Ribbons—Giving a Customer an Estimate—Summary

5 Making Repairs and Adjustments on the Olympia Model B-12 **172**

Parts of the Olympia Model B-12—Developing the Right Mental Attitude to Repair and Adjust Typewriters—Cleaning and Oiling the Olympia Model B-12—The Back Space Doesn't Work—The Carriage Binds—The Shift Binds—The Shift-Lock Fails to Lock—The Escapement Malfunctions—The Carriage Fails to Line Lock—The Line Space Fails to Space or Is Irregular—The Paper Feed Doesn't Feed or Feeds Erratically—The Paper Release Will Not Release the Paper When the Paper Release Lever Is Pulled—The Margin Fails to Release When the Margin Release Button Is Depressed—The Tab Set-Clear Fails to Clear—The Tabulator Fails to Tab—The Carriage Moves When Tabbing But Fails to Stop at a Preset Stop—The Typebar Fails to Print When Activated—The Machine Fails to Space When the Space Bar Is Tapped—The Repeat-Space Fails to Repeat—The Ribbon Lift Will Not Place the Ribbon Fully Between the Typeface and Platen During Typing—The Ribbon Is Not Fed—The Ribbon Fails to Reverse—The Variable Line Spacer Fails to Operate—Adjustments—Removal of Covers, Components and Mechanisms of the Olympia Model B-12—Blow-Up Drawings With Accompanying Parts Numbers and Name-Number Lists for the Olympia Model B-12—Summary

6 Adjustment and Repair Procedures for the Brother Model JP8 **250**

Removing the Covers—Removing the Motor—Adjusting the Belt Tension—The Switch Mechanism—The Printing Mechanism—The Space Bar Mechanism—The Escapement Mechanism—Back Space Mechanism—The Shift Mechanism—The Tabulator Mechanism—The Color Change and the Ribbon Lifting Mechanism—The Ribbon Feed and Reverse Mechanism—The Margin Release and Margin Stop Mechanism—The Spring Drum—The Paper Feed Mechanism—The Paper Release Mechanism—The Line Space Mechanism—The Carriage Release—Adjustment of the Warning Bell—The Repeat Space Mechanism—Removing the Upper Cover and Left Platen Knob—The Shift Mechanism—The Carriage Return Mechanism—The Return Clutch—The Return Jamming Release—The Carriage Release Mechanism—Line Space Mechanism—Parts Blow-Ups and Parts Names and Numbers for the Brother Models 3,000, 1,000 and XL-4,000—Parts Blow-Ups and Parts Names and Numbers for the Brother Model 3500—Mechanism Removal Procedures—Summary

Appendix: Typewriter Manufacturers and/or Distributors **349**

Index **350**

Preface

One of the great mysteries of machine repair, from the layman's viewpoint, has been in the field of typewriters. Probably once or twice in your life you have had problems with a typewriter, taken it to the repair shop, and been informed that there was a "flat fee" for minimum service to the machine, and anything beyond minimum service would be subject to an hourly rate. The unfortunate aspect of this information was that the "flat fee" turned out to be about the equivalent of a day's wages on your factory or secretarial job, and the hourly rate (if you had the nerve to ask) was about two or three times your own hourly rate. Then, when the machine was returned to you (you picked it up, of course, to save additional charges), you looked it over to find that it was now nice and clean looking, and the problem had been solved. But a nagging mystery remained. How much work did the repairman actually do, and how much time did he actually put in doing it? Maybe—just *maybe*—all he did was wipe the machine off on the outside, reach in and rehook a spring, and then make out the ticket for $92.50—which was about twice the resale value of the machine—and then took his coffee break.

On the other hand, the professional repairman could argue that he is not duty-bound to explain exactly what he did, largely on the premise that the average layman wouldn't understand it anyway. And he might also argue—rightly enough—that, like lawyers and other professional people, the customers must ultimately pay for the education and training that allows him to find the spring that needs rehooking.

The above scenario is more true in the field of typewriter repair than in, say, auto repair, in which a lot of do-it-yourselfers have learned to reline their own brakes, tune up their own engines and even make major overhauls, largely as a matter of survival. Many of these amateur mechanics learn to do competent work, and many more of them go on to become professionals. Why isn't this the case in the field of typewriter repair?

One answer to this question is that, in most cases, if professional help isn't affordable, it turns out to be more practical to relegate a typewriter to the closet than it would be to put the family car on blocks. Individuals with only moderate mechanical knowledge venture forth to fix their cars, and find that it isn't nearly as difficult as their friendly neighborhood garageman told them it would be.

The other answer is that the mechanisms of a typewriter look truly formidable, largely because bookshelves of libraries and bookstores aren't stocked with typewriter repair manuals, as they are with auto repair manuals. Manuals, such as the one you are holding in your hand, are a tremendous help in making these mechanisms look less formidable. And if the manual is written exclusively for laymen—*as this one is*—you'll find that not only do the illustrations do much to clarify the operation, functions, and working sequences of and tolerances between various parts, but also, the text is written so clearly that all those things that professionals know (but are apparently sworn never to divulge) are clearly spelled out. In other words, once you know how, it's infinitely easier to equalize the typing pressure on the typebars of that older IBM typewriter than to change the spark plugs on your VW Super Beetle. It is easier to change a platen, and know when and why it should be changed, than to rotate the tires on your station wagon.

You may argue that this is all very well, but the fact is that the three auto parts stores in your small town all vie with each other for the privilege of selling you spark plugs. Where in the world would you find a new typewriter platen? It has been my own, long-held opinion that a great shortcoming of some do-it-yourself books is that they don't spell out precisely how and where unusual or specialized parts are obtained. Yes, there are sources of typewriter supplies and parts, with apparently enough to go around throughout the United States, but obtaining them requires just a slightly different approach than just walking into your neighborhood store. In this book I will spell out in great detail how to get typewriter supplies and parts.

Then there is the question of obtaining service manuals for specific typewriters. I have been told—more than once and quite emphatically—that it would be impossible to compile all the technical information on every conceivable typewriter brand/model still in use in the United States between the covers of one book. Of course I had to admit—and a moment's reflection will tell you—that this is true, and that the best that I could possibly do would be to provide illustrations and clearly written textual descriptions of representative typewriter mechanisms and, to translate this into practicality, provide detailed and comprehensive procedures for repairing a few specific brand/models, in both electric and manual machines. In other words, if your goal is to repair/maintain one typewriter, and that particular machine is described in this book, you will have all the information you need. Beyond that, this book should provide you with an excellent grounding in basic mechanisms, as well as a thorough understanding of how and why they do what they do. If your particular machine is not represented herein, you will have already been instructed on how and where to get service manuals and parts catalogs that are so necessary for making an effective repair.

If, on the other hand, your goal is to start a part-time or full-time typewriter repair business, there is enough information in this book to get you on that track. These are not just vague generalities applicable to "business in general," but concrete, specific steps to take—such as making supplier contacts, planning a workshop, buying equipment, etc.—for a typewriter repair business. As a matter of fact, if you can combine business acumen, an attribute you probably can't acquire from a book, with the step-by-step instructions in this book, I don't believe you could fail in such a business.

Typewriter manufacturer/distributors who cooperated or in some way helped in compiling the information for this book were IBM, OLYMPIA USA INC, and *Brother International Corporation*. For example, an IBM representative spent considerable time explaining how to get IBM service manuals and parts Catalogs—as well as restrictions on their republication—and a regional IBM engineer provided me with a wealth of information regarding the IBM Model numbering system, which I am passing along with other IBM information. My *Olympia* contact was pleased with the Olympia chapter. Brother International was extremely cooperative in all ways.

The *Ames Supply Company*, a major supplier of typewriter supplies and parts, was extremely helpful and cooperative in providing information for an entire chapter of this book.

I should say that there are innumerable possibilities for errors to creep into a book containing as much technical data as this one. To avoid this, I have submitted the various chapters to the service departments of the previously mentioned companies. The chapters were read for accuracy by their technicians. They were all pleased with the results and agreed that this should make a useful manual for the layman or beginning professional.

Finally, to possibly belabor a point I tried to make earlier, I would suggest that you read this book not as an encyclopedic volume of technical data but more as a textbook. I truly believe that, when used in this manner, it is the most useful typewriter repair book ever compiled for the layman or beginning professional.

Howard Hutchison

Chapter 1
Definitions and an Overview of Typewriter Controls

When you begin to make a typical home repair (let's say repairing a broken window), your job is made relatively easy. Do-it-yourselfers have been repairing their own windows for so many years that neighborhood hardware and building supply stores, which are oriented to this kind of trade, are willing and eager to furnish all the materials. Your building supply dealer will be easy to talk to, and even if you don't know the difference between single-strength and double-strength glass, he'll be eager to explain the difference and make worthwhile recommendations and suggestions. If you happen to live in a small town, he might even offer to lend you a ladder.

However, when you undertake the repair of your own typewriter, you're pretty much on your own. First of all, living in a small town will be a disadvantage because there may not be a local repairman with whom you can discuss your problem, as you do with your home repair dealer. If there is indeed a local typewriter repairman, or even if the town is burgeoning with them, you'll probably be greeted with some skepticism when you state your intention of repairing your own typewriter. Speaking realistically, I'd even suggest that some sort of professional jealously may enter the picture, since trained, professional repairmen look upon their work as too difficult for a layman to "pick up" in a short time. Therefore, if the success of your repair project depends to any extent upon the cooperation of a professional repairman (such as in the ordering of parts, which will be discussed in more detail in a subsequent chapter), you'll have to be convincing and persistent—and it won't hurt your cause to be knowledgeable.

Moreoever, the problem will be considerably compounded if it becomes necessary to correspond with out-of-town distributors. This is the situation in which knowledge—together with good communications—is mandatory.

GOOD COMMUNICATIONS

To explain what I mean by good communications, let me relate a story. Two elderly spinsters lived across the street from each other. Every day, day in and day out, they stood on their respective porches and argued back and forth across the street. A newcomer, observing this phenomenon, asked an old-timer in town: "Why can't the ladies ever agree on anything?"

"Because," replied the old-timer, "they're arguing from different *premises*."

The key word of that story is, of course, *premises*, which is ambiguous when taken out of context. If you think that's a little silly, let me tell you a more relevant story. I recently corresponded with a certain typewriter company, requesting a service manual for a particular typewriter model which that company manufactures and distributes. The reply came back, "We no longer manufacture manual typewriters."

To get back to my case for good communications, the point I've tried to make here is that some words are ambiguous when taken out of context. Other words are just inherently ambiguous and can't be used carelessly. When you get into the really technical words and terms of typewriter repair, a lot of confusion will result if you don't use the words correctly. Finally, the professional will have more respect for your capability, and *might* as a result be more cooperative, if you use the correct word or term to describe the part, mechanism or function you're really talking about.

It might be argued that there is no universal agreement as to what certain parts and functions are to be called, but in most cases common usage is a determining factor. In a few cases, especially where inner mechanisms are concerned, terminology may vary slightly from machine brand to brand and, consequently, from service dealer to dealer, depending upon which brands he has spent the most time working with.

SERVICE MANUAL

Alone, the word *manual* is usually taken to mean a book, prepared by the technical department of the typewriter manufacturer. If it is an *operator's manual*, it will only describe a few superficial procedures that the average, non-technical person needs to know about operating the machine. It will have extremely scant, if any, technical or repair information. If you want repair and adjustment information, be sure, therefore, not to ask for an operator's manual but rather for a *service manual*. Since most (but not all) service manuals are compiled for individual models, be sure and specify the brand and model (and any pertinent information that you think might help) of the machine for which you are requesting the service manual.

Apart from being quite specific about what you want in the way of a service manual, it may also be a good idea to state in your initial letter of request that you only intend to use the manual to repair your own machine (in case the dealer maintains franchised repair centers), and that you won't run it through a copier. Most companies are quite sensitive about the unauthorized reproducing of their publications.

MANUAL AND ELECTRIC TYPEWRITERS

A manual typewriter (Fig. 1-1) is one on which the majority of operations are performed manually—that is, without the aid of electrically actuated mechanisms. A true manual typewriter is in fact equipped with no electrical components; however, even the true manual typewriter may have some functions which emulate

Fig. 1-1. This Brother manual portable typewriter will perform essentially the same functions as an electric machine, but with less ease and convenience (courtesy of Brother International Corporation).

power, with the power source being the tension of a spring which is rewound every time the operator performs a certain operation.

On some machines that are electrical-manual hybrids, every operation is performed manually except the return of the carriage to the left-hand margin, which is performed electrically.

An electric typewriter (Fig. 1-2) is one on which the majority of operations are performed by mechanisms which are electrically actuated when the typist touches the appropriate keybutton, control button or lever.

KEYBUTTON OR KEY

The words "keybuttons" and "keys" are almost synonymous (IBM uses the word "keybutton" most extensively, however) to denote the plastic buttons (Fig. 1-3), which are arranged in a standardized format on the keyboard of the typewriter. However, if you use the word "key," some ambiguity may arise, because in common (but erroneous) usage the word "key" is sometimes taken to mean the *typebar head* that strikes the paper (for example, it is often said that the "keys are dirty," when in fact it is the typebar heads that need attention).

TYPEBARS AND TYPEBAR HEADS

First and foremost, typebars and typebar heads are found only on typebar machines—as in contrast to the more advanced

Fig. 1-2. This Brother electric, Model 4512, typewriter takes the work out of typing. Through electrically actuated mechanisms, it maintains even typing pressure on all typebars, regardless of the strength of the finger that pushes the keybutton (courtesy of Brother International Corporation).

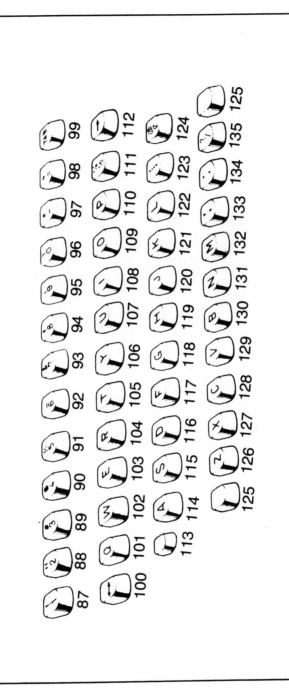

Fig. 1-3. To avoid misunderstanding, you'll be on the safe side to call these items keybuttons (courtesy of Brother International Corporation).

typewriters, which are equipped with spherical elements (these are called *single element* typewriters and will be explained later). However, there are still many typebar machines in use. Typebar machines are still being manufactured. When a keybutton is depressed, the corresponding typebar swings up in an arc, and the typebar head strikes the ribbon/paper. Since the typebar and typebar head make up a solid part, most companies simply call the complete part a *typebar* (Fig. 1-4).

TYPEBAR TYPEWRITER

As I said, there are *typebar* typewriters (Fig. 1-5) and *single element* typewriters. For many years, typebar typewriters dominated the typewriter market. *International Business Machines (IBM)* put the first single element machine on the market in the 1960s and even thereafter, until the mid- and late-1970s. Typebar machines continued to dominate the American market, presumably because IBM held exclusive rights to the patent on the single element mechanism, and wouldn't or couldn't inundate the market with this advanced model (meanwhile, however, IBM itself continued to also manufacture and market typebar machines until, in the late 1970s—I am told by an IBM representative—this company discontinued manufacturing them).

On the typebar machine, the individual typebars—one typebar for every letter, number or character that can be typed on the machine—are arranged in a sort of semi-circle, so that each individual typebar swings up in an arc to make an impression on the paper when the corresponding keybutton is depressed. Sometimes, the complete assembly of typebars, together with the segment in which they pivot, is called a *typebasket*.

The primary advantage of typebar machines is *reliability*, since they have been in production for many years. A disadvantage is that the operator is restricted to one type style and type size per machine, because removing and replacing the typebar assembly is too difficult to do routinely. Another disadvantage, which has nothing to do with maintenance or repair, is that it requires excellent typing skills to avoid occasionally clashing and locking up two or three typebars, when typing speed outruns coordination. This can't happen on a single element typewriter.

SINGLE ELEMENT TYPEWRITER

On the single element typewriter (Fig. 1-6), a spherical piece, with the die-impressed letters, numbers and characters arranged

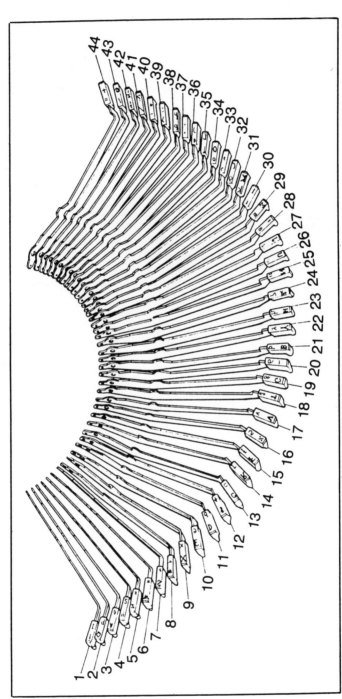

Fig. 1-4. Apart from nomenclature value, this illustration shows a numbering system for typebars which is fairly well standardized in the industry (courtesy of Brother International Corporation).

Fig. 1-5. This old IBM Model A machine is typical of older typebar machines, dating back to the 1950s.

around it, takes the place of the typebars of the older models (Fig. 1-7). The spherical piece is variously called an "element," "type head," or "type font" by the various companies which now manufacture single element typewriters and/or "elements."

Logic would seem to dictate that the term "single element" is a misnomer, since the element can be easily removed and replaced (Fig. 1-8) or, more importantly, replaced by an element containing a different type style or type size. Since the advent of the early single element IBM models of the 1960s, single element machines have become more and more sophisticated and versatile in their functions.

Because the only "old" single element machines in use today are the old IBM models, single element machines are looked upon as too advanced and innovative for do-it-yourself repair jobs and, accordingly, it is next to impossible to get service manuals on them. The exception to this general rule is that IBM sells IBM service manuals (Fig. 1-9) to anyone requesting them, and you would be able to obtain one for your specific single element IBM model.

STANDARD TYPEWRITER

Within some typewriter brands, it is important to indicate whether or not your machine is a *standard* typewriter. In IBMs,

18

Fig. 1-6. This IBM Selectric II, with the cover swing back for a view of the ribbon cartridge and typing element, is typical of the many single element machines now on the market, which will probably eventually replace typebar machines. Removing and replacing the element with a different one is as easy and fast as turning the machine on.

and other brands as well, a standard typewriter is one on which each character takes up the same amount of space as any other character, with the implied distinction being between this and the

Fig. 1-7. This photo of the same machine as that of Fig. 1-6 has the ribbon cartridge removed for a better view of the element. In the case of IBM, each element is a distinctly different type style/size. Each has its own name and number for identification (interestingly enough—in the case of IBM elements— the number that identifies the element to IBM servicemen is not the one plainly stamped on the plastic top of the element, but the extremely small number stamped into the element itself, next to the plastic top).

19

Fig. 1-8. If it were conceivable that a typing format would call for six different type style/sizes, these six elements, at a total cost of around $100, would take the place of six typewriters. One might ask, however, why these machines are called "single element" machines.

machine generally used for specialized purposes, such as typesetting, on which different characters take up different unit widths (the generic term for this latter machine is *proportional spacing* typewriter). Thus, the primary difference, from the repairman's point of view, between standard and proportional spacing typewriters is in the *escapement mechanism*.

Various companies that manufacture the proportional spacing typewriters identify them with their own trade names. For example, while IBM still manufactured typebar machines, its proportional spacer went by the name of *Executive* (Fig. 1-10).

With the advent of single element machines, the terminology has changed somewhat. When making the distinction between standard typewriters and machines for typesetting, it would be well to have some understanding of *pitch*.

PITCH OF A TYPEWRITER

On a standard typewriter, the word *pitch* means the distance between two characters as they are typed on the paper. Tradition-

Fig. 1-9. This array of IBM service manuals and parts manuals does not indicate that I have the inside track with IBM, but simply the I had the modest means to purchase them. You can do the same. The simplest way to do it is to begin by calling the toll-free number given in this chapter, where you will be given information on how to contact your regional IBM engineering representative.

Fig. 1-10. If you've recently shopped for used typewriters, you may have seen a few similar to this one in the displays. It is an excellent typewriter, but with several disadvantages for general typing, the most notable being that the various characters take up various amounts of linear space, making back spacing for corrections confusing in the beginning. However, if your typing format calls for an even right-hand margin, on a low budget, this machine will do the job excellently, Providing it has a carbon ribbon and that it is in good condition. Otherwise avoid it.

21

ally, standard typewriters have been either 10-pitch (10 character/spaces to the inch) or 12-pitch (12 character/spaces to the inch). On the typebar typewriters the pitch is established in the escapement mechanism and is inalterable without changing inner mechanisms. However, on the *more advanced* single element machines, either 10-pitch or 12-pitch can be obtained in the same machine. On yet more advanced single element typewriters, 10-pitch, 12-pitch and a modified form of proportional spacing can be obtained on the same machine.

When pitch is fixed, as on typebar machines and some older single element machines, it is generally assumed that the appropriate type *size* for a 10-pitch machine is *pica* and for a 12-pitch machine, *elite*. However, in the single element machines this is no longer strictly true.

PICA AND ELITE

On the older typebar machines, the word *pica* indicated a 10-pitch machine, with a type that was approximately 12-point in size; and *elite* indicated a 12-pitch machine, with a type that was approximately 10-point in size. (The point system of measuring type is widely used in the printing trade, but in my opinion it has only a tenuous connection to the typewritten copy from standard typewriters.)

PROPORTIONAL SPACING TYPEWRITER

As explained previously, a proportional spacing typewriter is one on which each character is assigned its own unit width (Fig. 1-11), and the carriage is made to move that distance when the corresponding keybutton is depressed. The appeal of such a machine is twofold. Since the characters don't line up under each other like posts in a fence row, the copy has a "printed look." By

```
This is a line of 10-pitch standard

This is a line of 12-pitch standard type

This is a line of proportional spacing type
```

Fig. 1-11. These three lines of type illustrate the differences between the various escapement mechanisms. It may not be immediately obvious to the casual observer that the line of proportional spacing type has any unique characteristics; however, you'll see that certain characters take up less space than others, while on the lines of standard type this is not true.

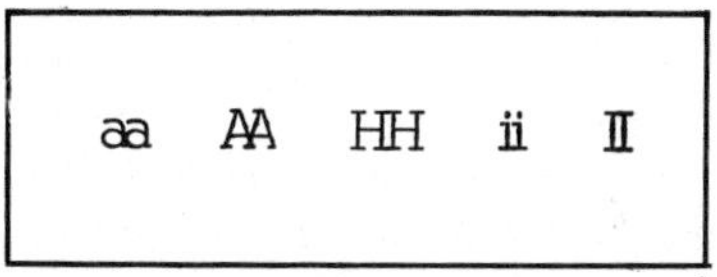

Fig. 1-12. Type any character on a proportional spacing machine. Tap the back space button once. Retype the character, and the result will be something like this.

following a certain procedure in typing, the right-hand margin can be typed even—or *justified*—to give an even more printed look (The right-hand margin can also be justified with a standard typewriter, but the printed look is not quite achieved because of the inherent typed look produced by a standard typewriter).

Unless you have a specific need for a typesetting machine, it is not advisable to buy one of the older model proportional spacers with a view to maintaining it yourself. They are not only complicated to adjust and repair, but relatively complicated to operate as well.

If you have a recently acquired but older machine and don't know whether it is a standard or proportional spacer, make the following test. Type one character (any character). Then tap the back space keybutton and retype the same character. If the second typing does not superimpose (register) exactly on the first typing (Fig. 1-12), it is a proportional spacing machine. Thus, if you think about repairing or adjusting this machine, you should be aware that the mechanism that moves the carriage during typing (called the *escapement*) is relatively complicated. Moreover, be sure to get the appropriate service information for this kind of machine, which may outwardly look like other, standard models.

TYPEWRITER RIBBONS

A typewriter ribbon is essentially the carrier for the medium that creates the impression on the paper when the type head or element strikes it. The two kinds of ribbon in common usage are *fabric ribbons* and *carbon ribbons*.

A fabric ribbon may be either cotton, silk or nylon—with the latter being preferable—impregnated with an ink of the chosen, available color. The ink spreads through the fabric by capillary action. When ink is taken from one small area (as in typing a character), the ink in that area is replenished—until the ink of the total ribbon is depleted through repeated use, or through drying out. Thus, the inking capacity of the ribbon remains about uniform throughout its entire length and width. The entire length of the fabric ribbon is used repeatedly, made possible by a mechanism in the machine that winds and rewinds the ribbon from reel to reel (or *spool* to *spool*, if you prefer). This procedure can be repeated over and over until the ribbon is so depleted of ink that it no longer makes a dark impression. As compared to the carbon ribbon, the fabric ribbon has some distinct disadvantages, only slightly offset by some minor advantages.

Loosely speaking, carbon ribbons have somewhat the same characteristics as carbon paper, with a "plain" side and a "coated" side. The coated side contains the carbon that is deposited on the paper when the ribbon is struck by the type head. However, speaking more correctly, I should say that there are currently a variety of ribbons that are called carbon ribbons. Not all of them are constructed the same way; nor do they react quite the same. However, the one feature that various so-called carbon ribbons share in common is that they are one-time ribbons—that is, when the ribbon is used long enough to empty the original reel, the ribbon is used up and must be discarded.

The primary advantage of a carbon ribbon over the fabric ribbon is that it makes a uniformly dark, crisp impression throughout its life, while the impression of the fabric ribbon gets progressively dimmer as the ribbon is used repeatedly. The fact that a carbon ribbon must be disposed of after one use is offset by the fact that it is initially fairly inexpensive. However, typing with a carbon ribbon turns out to be more expensive than with a fabric ribbon. If you run out of ribbon when using a carbon ribbon, you can't type any more until you purchase a new ribbon, while a fabric ribbon can be used beyond its optimum life (and often is). Finally, a carbon ribbon deposits negligible residue on the typebar or element, whereas inked fabric ribbons leave so much residue of ink—which tends to collect dust and lint—that type heads should be cleaned after several hours of typing.

And what, you may ask, does a lengthy discussion of typewriter ribbons have to do with typewriters *per se*? First, ribbons are an extremely important link in the total typing process, with regard to the quality of type produced by a machine. Second, if you don't understand the capabilities of a given ribbon, you may be misled to think the typewriter doesn't work correctly. Here are a few tips.

Helpful Tips

As a general rule, a typewriter is designed to use *either* a fabric ribbon *or* a carbon ribbon, but not both. There are a few exceptions to this rule, however.

If a typewriter is designed to use *only* a fabric ribbon, there is extremely little chance that you can substitute a carbon ribbon. You probably won't be able to find a carbon ribbon of a *width* to match that of the fabric ribbon. Also, you probably won't be able to find a carbon ribbon wound on a reel, or in a cartridge, that would be accepted by the mechanism of your fabric ribbon machine.

Assuming that you could get around these obstacles, you would find that the one-time carbon ribbon would not make a distinct impression. The mechanism that moves the ribbon through the machine is designed to move the inked ribbon only a fraction of the distance occupied by a character. This works all right on fabric ribbons which are inked by capillary action, but not on one-time ribbons, on which the medium of the ribbon is totally depleted when struck by the type head (thus, the slight overlapping of characters on the ribbon will cause indistinct areas in the typed impressions).

There are available certain kinds of so-called "reusable" carbon ribbons (the word "reusable" is a misnomer, however) that purport to ameliorate the problem of one-time use, which will allow an overlapping of characters. However, it is difficult, if at all possible, to find one of these ribbons that can be substituted on a fabric ribbon machine.

As a general rule, your choices in selecting a ribbon for a given machine are limited by the fact that you're almost forced to use whatever ribbon is wound on a reel that will fit your machine. This is even more true in the case of ribbons loaded into cartridges, since the cartridge must fit the machine. However, the tendency is that some choices are available in cartridge ribbons. For example, a few cartridge ribbon machines are designed to take either fabric or carbon ribbons, with cartridges being supplied accordingly.

Most of the advanced single element typewriters use cartridge ribbons. Generally speaking (and *always*, in the case of IBM *Selectric IIs*), the available ribbon is either one that is transported the full width of a character each time the ribbon is struck (i.e., each time the escapement mechanism and ribbon transporting mechanism is activated) or one that allows some overlapping of characters. In IBM terminology, the former ribbon is called *high yield correctable film ribbon* (Fig. 1-13), and the latter is called *Tech III* (Fig. 1-14). The term "high yield" in the case of the former ribbon is misleading because this ribbon actually yields a significantly lower number of characters than the Tech III ribbon. Moreover, the use of the term Tech III is also a poor choice of

Fig. 1-13. The IBM high yield correctable film ribbon cartridge is specially designed to interact with the ribbon transport of the IBM Selectric II in such a manner that characters do not overlap each other as the element strikes the ribbon. The term "high yield" is sales puff to indicate that this ribbon yields more characters than an earlier IBM correctable film ribbon, primarily because there is more ribbon—not because of any special characteristics of the ribbon.

words because this cartridge is to be used on the Selectric II typewriter. Both, incidentally, are *correctable*, though by different methods.

Suppliers that are not affiliated with IBM, but who supply cartridges for IBM machines, do not use the IBM terminology to describe the ribbons. They designate the ribbon that is comparable to *film* as *pink*—or sometimes *orange* or *red*—core, and the ribbon comparable to the Tech III as *blue core*.

In using either the film or Tech III cartridges, you should understand that the construction of each cartridge determines how it will contact the machine mechanism, and therefore determines the rate at which the ribbon will be transported (Fig. 1-15).

Apart from the kind and quality of the ribbon, the kind of typing paper used affects the quality of the typed impression. With either a fabric or carbon ribbon, a hard-surfaced paper tends to dim the impression and dull its crispness. Moreover, the impression from an inked ribbon tends to smear on a hard-surfaced paper. Some hard-surfaced papers will not accept carbon ribbon impressions at all. Ordinary typing paper is always suitable to be used with either a fabric or carbon ribbon. Other suitable papers are mimeograph bond, duplicator bond and *Xerographic* (the latter, which is plain paper used in Xerox and other plain paper copiers, is less suitable because it is fairly slick; however, it does take an impression). It is

Fig. 1-14. The IBM Tech III ribbon cartridge is designed to interact with the ribbon transporting mechanism of the Selectric II in such a manner that character overlapping is possible. Moreover, this ribbon has certain characteristics which differ from those of the film ribbon. This is an extremely long-lasting cartridge.

important, when choosing a paper to be printed as letterheads, that the paper is compatible (i.e., accepts a dark, crisp impression) with your particular ribbon—especially in the case of the carbon ribbon.

Ribbon Problems

The following are some possible problems arising from ribbons, and their causes:

Problem: The impression is too light (i.e., not dark enough).

Cause #1: The typing pressure is not correct.

Solution: Typing pressure will be discussed later.

Cause #2: Incorrect paper is being used.

Solution: Use the kinds of paper described previously. Sometimes a backup sheet behind the original provides a cushioning effect and makes a darker impression. Avoid hard-surfaced or glossy paper.

Cause #3: In the case of a fabric ribbon, the ribbon is either depleted through use or is shelf-worn.

Solution: Replace the old ribbon with a new one. To avoid the problem of shelf-worn ribbons, buy from dealers who have a rapid turnover of stock.

Cause #4: The multiple-copy control is incorrectly set.

Solution: Most typewriters have multiple copy controls, the purpose of which is to make compensations in the striking pressure of the typing head when several sheets of paper are rolled into the machine. Generally, this is accomplished through a mechanism which backs the platen slightly away from the reach of the typing heads, activated by a lever which is usually calibrated in the letters

A, B, C, D, E, etc., with the highest pressure being represented by A, the next lower pressure by B, etc. Generally, for up to two sheets of paper-plus-carbon, this lever should be set at the maximum pressure (understand, however, that this mechanism does not regulate typing pressure *per se*, but moves the platen away from the typing head, and the more likely result of an incorrect setting of the mutiple-copy control is irregular impressions, rather than consistently light impressions).

Cause #5: In the case of carbon (or ribbons comparable to carbon), the ribbon may be shelf-worn or simply inferior. At the risk of sounding laudatory about "brand names," I would suggest that you always use brand name ribbons that correspond to the brand name of your typewriter (IBM ribbons for IBM machines and the like). This rule does not always hold true, and you may find some "off-brand" ribbons to be superior to brand-name products; however, this has not been my own experience. While some company executives deny that carbon ribbons can become shelf-worn, at least a few repairmen suggest that the shelf life of carbon ribbons is between six months and a year.

Fig. 1-15. Look at these two cartridges closely and you'll see a significant difference in their construction (note the hollow stud in the upper cartridge, which is the Tech III cartridge). This determines the rate at which the ribbon is transported through the machine.

Problem: Characters are clipped off, on either the bottom or top.

Cause #1: In the case of some single-element machines, this is caused by an incorrect adjustment of the mechanism that lifts the element during typing.

Cause #2: In any case, a too-narrow ribbon will cause the top or the bottom of the characters to be clipped off.

Problem: There are light areas in otherwise dark impressions.

Cause #1: In the case of inked ribbons, this could be caused by dirty type heads or shelf-worn ribbons.

Cause #2: In the case of carbon ribbons, this may be caused by shelf-worn ribbons or more generally by a ribbon transporting mechanism that transports the one-time carbon ribbon an incremental distance that is too short, causing overlapping of characters.

Solutions: Most solutions are self-evident—clean typing heads, etc. In the case of the carbon ribbon, be sure you're not trying to use a one-time carbon ribbon in a mechanism designed for an inked ribbon. In the case of some single element machines (IBM Selectric II, for example) the depression/disengagement of a gear in the ribbon transport mechanism, *only* when the Tech III cartridge is installed, causes the ribbon to be transported slowly. Therefore, if for any reason this gear remains disengaged when the *film* ribbon cartridge is installed, the *film* ribbon will not be transported appropriately to produce a uniformly dark impression.

PLATEN

The *platen* is the long, cylindrical roll, with a hand knob on either end, against which the typing head strikes when it is actuated (Fig. 1-16). The platen serves the dual purpose of providing a striking surface behind the paper; and it works in conjunction with feed rolls to feed the paper through the typewriter. To serve this latter purpose, it is equipped on one end with a *ratchet wheel*, which engages with a push pawl to move the platen a specified distance.

On most older typewriters, the platen is rubber—or perhaps synthetic rubber—which, when new, is resilient to provide a cushioning effect. As the typewriter gets older, and regardless of the amount of use it gets, the rubber of the platen hardens, causing two problems to develop gradually. The type heads cut through the paper (this is particularly problematic when typing on mimeograph

Fig. 1-16. Here the platen has been removed from the old IBM, Model A, and is lying in front of it. This particular platen was resilient when new, but is now hard and should be replaced. That's a minor job.

stencils) and, in extreme cases, the non-resilience of the platen may cause a typebar to break. A hardened platen should be replaced with a new one.

Another problem that can develop gradually is that of the platen surface, which was smooth in the beginning, becoming ridged, with the ridges running around the circumference of the platen as spaces equal to the pitch of the typewriter. This causes an uneven impression. In the early stages of ridging, the effects can be ameliorated by using a backup sheet of paper behind the original sheet. Later, the platen can be resurfaced. Resurfacing requires special equipment, but it is a relatively inexpensive procedure.

On some typewriters, the platens are easily removed, while on others they are removed with more difficulty. Removing platens will be discussed for certain models later in this book.

CARRIAGE

On typebar machines, a *carriage* moves leftward during typing to allow the line of type to progress rightward on the paper. On manuals—and generally speaking, electrics as well—the carriage is pulled along by the tension of a spring, and at the end of the predetermined travel the carriage is pushed rightward to align with the left-hand margin of the paper. On a manual typewriter, the carriage is pushed by hand, whereas on most electrics the carriage is returned under power. In any case, the carriage rides on tracks. The entire carriage assembly includes the platen and paper table and feed rolls (Fig. 1-17).

On single element typewriters, the platen remains stationary. The typing element is transported from left to right during typing.

PAPER TABLE-FEED ROLLS

The *paper table*, which may also be called the *paper pan*, is a curved metal table (or pan), directly underneath the platen. It has a highly polished surface and is fitted with feed rolls (see parts 30-31, Fig. 1-17) which contact the platen in such a manner that when the platen is turned, the paper, which is gripped between platen and feed rolls, slides over the polished surface of the paper table and is fed through the typewriter. The tension between the platen and the paper table-feed rolls can be eliminated—so the paper can be quickly removed—by a *paper release* mechanism. This mechanism will be described more fully later in this chapter.

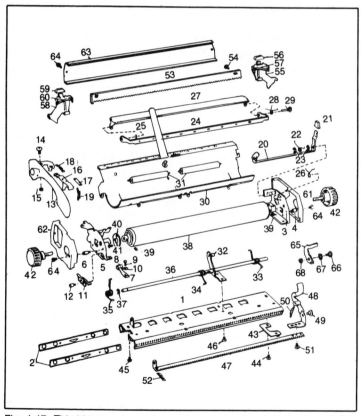

Fig. 1-17. This blow-up shows the carriage parts of certain Brother Models (courtesy of Brother International Corporation).

The *paper bail* is a cylindrical rod, the length of the platen, and is equipped with rolls that swing down against the platen. Its purpose is to hold the paper snug against the platen.

OVERVIEW OF CONTROL BUTTONS AND LEVERS

Typewriter control buttons, levers, knobs, etc., allow the typist to control certain inner mechanisms from an external, convenient position. In some cases these controls are easily identifiable because they are marked; in other cases they are not marked and, in a few cases, reference to an operator's manual is about the only way to identify them. In any case, proper identification of these controls, and the use of the most appropriate terminology to describe them, is important when discussing problems with suppliers and professional repairmen.

Space Bar

Apart from controlling the actions of the typebars through the keybuttons, other operations of the typewriter are controlled through various control buttons and levers. The *space bar* (Fig. 1-18, Item 1) is located directly below the keybutton assembly, in a

Fig. 1-18. This is the Olympia Model B-12, manual portable typewriter. By the time you read this entire chapter you will understand what all the numbers refer to (courtesy of OLYMPIA USA INC.).

Fig. 1-19. This close-up photo shows the two space bars of the proportional spacing IBM typewriter shown earlier in this chapter. Depressing the space bar marked "3" will move the carriage three units of space; depressing the space bar marked "2" will move the carriage two units of space. This provides a means of varying line lengths to fit certain typing formats.

position where it can be touched by the typist's thumb. Most generally, a light touch on the space bar causes the carriage (or typing element, in the case of single element machines) to be moved one "space," which on standard typewriters is always exactly equal to the movement when a character is typed. On certain machines, a constant pressure on the space bar causes the carriage or element to move and continue moving (i.e., "repeat spacing") until the pressure is released (on the machine of Fig. 1-18, repeat spacing is accomplished by depressing the bar indicated as Item 2). If there are two space bars, their functions will depend upon whether the machine is a standard typewriter or a proportional spacer.

The Second Space Bar On The Standard Typewriter. The second space bar (usually on the left) on a standard typewriter may be either a repeat space bar (as in Fig. 1-18) or half-space bar.

The Second Space Bar On The Proportional Spacing Typewriter. Speaking primarily of the IBM *Executive*, the two space bars, from left to right, will be numbered "3" and "2" (Fig. 1-19). The space bar to use for normal typing is the "2" space bar, which moves the carriage leftward a distance of two units of width. The space to use for other purposes—such as modifying line lengths if desired—is the "3" space bar, which moves the carriage leftward by a distance of three units of width. These two space bars are used in conjunction with the back space key, which moves the carriage rightward (that is, *back*) by a distance of one unit of width, to adjust the length of lines of type. A constant pressure on the "3" space bar will cause repeat spacing.

On-Off Control Button

The *on-off control button* is, of course, present only on electric machines (Fig. 1-20), upper left corner of the keyboard. Generally speaking, if it is found in an obvious place, close to the keybutton format, it will be clearly marked with the words on and off. If it is not found near the keybutton panel, it may be found on the side, or underneath, the keybutton panel, in which case the words on and off may be indicated by a pointer or displayed through a small window.

Frequently, the on-off control button is not embodied in the switch itself, but is connected to the switch through a linkage. Sometimes a misadjustment in this linkage can cause switching problems; therefore, when discussing switching problems, be sure and make the distinction between the switch itself, the on-off control button and the linkage—if there is a linkage.

Shift and Shift Lock Control Buttons

In the lower left and lower right corners of the keybutton panel are located the *shift* control buttons (Fig. 1-18, Item 3). Directly above the shift control button in the left corner is the *Shift-Lock* control button (Fig. 1-18, Item 4).

On a typebar machine, depressing either of the shift control buttons will cause the complete typebar assembly to be lowered in such a manner that the *upper portions* of the type heads, which contain capital letters and other "upper case" characters, will strike the platen. Similarly, on a single element machine, the upper case characters will strike the platen, but in this case it is accomplished by rotating the typing element 180 degrees, since one hemisphere of the element contains the lower case characters while the opposite hemisphere contains the upper case characters. The typebar assembly or element returns to its lower case position when the shift control button is released. Depressing the lock control button will lock the assembly or element in position for continuous upper case typing, and can be released by depressing and releasing either of the shift control buttons.

Carriage Return Control Button or Lever

On a manual typewriter, the carriage is returned to its starting position at the left-hand margin manually (by arm power), when the

Fig. 1-20. This is the Brother electric, Model JP10. On this particular machine, the on-off switch is clearly marked, but this is not the case on all machines (courtesy of Brother International Corporation).

operator pushes against a lever (Fig. 1-18, Item 12) that extends outward from the left end of the carriage. This lever is also called a *line space lever* because it also controls the mechanism that turns the platen.

On electric typewriters, the carriage is generally, but not always, returned under power through an electrically actuated mechanism when the operator depresses the *return* control button, located on the right-hand end and about halfway up the keybutton panel.

Simultaneously as the carriage returns, the platen will turn to achieve vertical line-spacing between lines of type. The line spacing mechanism will be explained in the next two chapters.

Tab Set and Clear Control Buttons

Tab set and *tab clear* may be one control button, which rocks back and forth (Fig. 1-18, Item 10), or two separate control buttons. While the location varies from machine to machine, it is generally found near the keybutton panel. Depressing the tab set engages a mechanism which sets a tabular stop wherever the carriage or element happens to be located at the time of setting. Depressing the tab clear will eliminate or "clear" previously set tabular stops, providing the carriage/element is tabbed to that stop before depressing the tab clear control button. Actual tabbing (i.e., tabulating) is done through a tab control button.

Tab Control Button

The word tab means tabular stop and even the oldest of typewriters was equipped with these stops which, when appropriately set, would allow the carriage to move in one uninterrupted motion and stop at the preset position. Depressing the tab control button (Fig. 1-18, Item 17) activates a mechanism which momentarily releases the carriage from the escapement mechanism, allowing it to move leftward under spring tension until the first tab stop is reached, where the carriage will stop. Depressing the tab control button subsequent times causes the carriage to move to subsequent preset tabular stops in a series. The mechanism that accomplishes this will be discussed more fully in the next chapter.

Margin Set Control Button(s) or Lever

If the setting of the left-hand and right-hand margins is accomplished through a control button, it will be marked *mar set*—or some similar marking. If it is accomplished through levers located on the paper scale (Fig. 1-18, Item 14), they may not be marked, but their positions make their functions obvious. In the case of a mar set control button, there may be only one control button, with which to set both the left-hand and right-hand margin stops. This is usually accomplished by moving the carriage to the margin that you wish to eliminate, depressing the *mar stop* button simultaneously with the *carriage release* control button, moving the carriage by hand to the new position, and simultaneously releasing both mar stop and carriage release control buttons. On the other hand, if there are two margin stop levers located on the paper scale, margin setting is accomplished by depressing the appropriate level (i.e., left-hand lever for the left-hand margin stop, etc.) to disengage it from a locked position, and simply sliding it to the new position, where it is allowed to lock in place.

There may be considerable variations from these methods of margin setting, from machine to machine. However, it's usually not difficult to figure out how to set margin stops, even on unfamiliar machines. Here are some points to remember about margin setting.

☐ On any properly operating typewriter, either standard or proportional spacer, the carriage will always stop at the present left-hand margin when the carriage is returned.

☐ On various standard typewriters, the right-hand margin stop may only stop the carriage when characters are being typed, but not when spacing or tabbing. On some proportional spacing machines, setting the right-hand margin does nothing but set the position of a warning bell. It does not actually set a stop that will stop the carriage in its leftward travel.

The actual mechanism of the carriage stops is simple and straightforward and most generally easily visible and accessible. There will be more about this in later chapters.

Mar Rel (Margin Release) Keybutton

A margin release keybutton (Fig. 1-18, Item 5), usually located on the left end of the keyboard, allows the typist to move the carriage beyond the preset left-hand or right-hand margin stops, without the necessity of resetting the stops. Then, when the carriage is again moved between these two limiting stops, the stops are again effective, unless and until the margin release keybutton is again depressed. The mechanism that is activated by the margin release keybutton will be discussed in the next chapter.

Carriage Release Control Buttons

Carriage release control buttons are generally not so marked, but they can be identified by their locations at either end of the platen (Fig. 1-18, Item 19)—generally between the ends of the platen and the platen knobs. The reason for two control buttons is for the convenience of being able to release the carriage with either hand. It is not necessary to depress these control buttons in order to move the carriage rightward, but it is necessary to move the carriage leftward—or the direction it travels during typing.

The feature of being able to move the carriage (and thus the type heads in relation to the platen surface) by hand is unique to typebar machines, as the element carriage of the single element machines cannot be released. Therefore, nothing comparable to the carriage release control buttons is to be found on single element typewriters.

Ribbon Position Control Button

In normal operation, each time a keybutton is depressed to type a character, a mechanism lifts the ribbon into position to be struck by the type head. When the typebar completes its cycle, the ribbon is lowered. This results in an up-and-down motion of the ribbon during typing. On fabric ribbon machines, the *ribbon position* (or *color control*) button is used to put the ribbon in position where either its top half is presented on the up cycle, or its bottom half. This provides a means of switching from the black portion of the ribbon to the red portion or, in the case of a correcting ribbon, from the typing portion to the correcting portion. Moreover, depressing the ribbon position control button still further will completely disengage the ribbon lift mechanism so that no surface of the ribbon is presented for typing. Thus, with the type head missing the ribbon completely, no printed impression is made when the type head strikes the paper/platen. This is the position used for typing mimeograph stencils. On fabric ribbon machines, the ribbon position control button is located near the keybutton panel, usually on the left side of the panel (it is on the right side of the machine in Fig. 1-18, however).

On certain single element machines (again, notably the IBM Selectric II and comparable machines) there is no color control because, to date, there are no dual-colored ribbons (there are, however, ribbons of various colors, interchangeable simply by changing the cartridge). However, there is a provision, on the element carriage, to disengage the ribbon lift mechanism so that a mimeograph stencil can be typed. Never type on a mimeograph stencil that is not covered with the protective film sheet. If this film is not supplied with the stencil, leaving the ribbon in normal typing position, rather than disengaging the ribbon lift, will keep the element from becoming clogged with the collodion of the stencil.

Touch Control Lever or Control Button

Touch control (also called *touch regulation* and other similar names) keybuttons or levers are found on manual typewriters, for the purpose of regulating the amount of pressure that must be applied to a keybutton to activate the typebar. This is to compensate for the different typing pressures that different people inherently exert when typing. Through this compensation, the pressure with which the typebars strike the platen is indirectly regulated. Touch control is also available on some electric machines.

Typing Pressure Regulation

On some electric typewriters, the pressure with which the type head strikes the platen can be regulated by a pressure regulating mechanism. The button that actuates the mechanism is sometimes called an *impression regulator*, and is often marked with + and − symbols (see Fig. 1-20, the control directly below the on-off switch).

Typing pressure control is not the same as touch control, inasmuch as it does not regulate the amount of manual pressure that must be applied to a keybutton.

On most electric typewriters, in addition to overall typing pressure regulation, the pressures of individual typebars can be regulated through individual screw adjustments, found either underneath the machine or under the top cover of the machine. This procedure will be described more fully in the chapter on adjustments.

Back Space Keybutton

The *back space* keybutton (Fig. 1-18, Item 9) is almost always located directly above the return control button. Depressing it actuates a mechanism that causes the carriage to move backward. The distance of this movement on standard typewriters is one character space. On some machines, a constant pressure on the back space keybutton will cause the carriage to keep moving back until the keybutton is released or the carriage is stopped against the left margin stop; this is the feature of repeat spacing.

On some proportional spacing typewriters, the back space keybutton is found in the traditional location. Rather than moving the carriage backward by the distance of a character, it moves it backward only one unit of measurement, which is inherent to the machine and always less than a character width.

Multiple Copy Control Lever

On most electric machines, the platen can be moved slightly back from the striking reach of the type heads to compensate for the larger effective circumference of the platen when several sheets of paper are inserted. This is accomplished by moving a multiple copy control lever (which may not be marked as such), which may be calibrated in either letters or numbers. This lever will usually be found on top of the typewriter, in the area of the platen, but it may sometimes be found nearer the keybutton panel.

Paper Release Lever

To facilitate straightening the paper after it has been rolled into the typewriter, the paper table and feed rolls can be backed away from the platen, until the platen and feed rolls no longer touch each other. This is accomplished through a paper release lever, usually found on top of and on the right-hand end of the typewriter (Fig. 1-18, Item 20).

Line Space Selector Lever

As I said earlier, when the carriage or element is returned to the left-hand margin stop, a push pawl engaging in the platen ratchet wheel turns the platen by some predetermined number of line spaces. This predetermined number is set through a line space selector lever (not to be confused with the carriage return lever—which doubles as a line space lever—on manual machines), which is generally found on top of the machine, on either the right-hand or left-hand end (Fig. 1-18, Item 13). On some machines, line spacing is available in single-spacing, double-spacing and triple-spacing, and the line space selector lever will be calibrated with the numbers "1," "2" and "3." On other machines, line-spacing is available in single-spacing, one-and-a-half-spacing, double-spacing, and—sometimes but not always—triple-spacing. As a general rule, the line space selector lever will be located on the end where the platen ratchet is found.

Platen Release Knob

The ratchet of the platen can be disengaged from the push pawl, causing the platen to turn freely. This is accomplished by pushing inward on a button in the center of the platen knob (usually found on the left-hand knob only—Fig. 1-18, Item 11), while simultaneously turning the platen knob. On some machines the platen is released by pushing inward on the platen knob itself. In any case, the knob returns to its normal position under spring pressure, re-engaging the ratchet wheel with the pawl as soon as you quit pushing it.

Keybuttons

Keybutton formats on U.S. typewriters are for the most part standardized, with each keybutton actuating either a lower case or upper case character. However, this format can vary widely among special purpose typewriters—such as those used for advertising layout, etc. Insofar as standard typewriters—and especially typebar typewriters—are concerned, there may be some slight variations in keybutton format from one machine to the other, with most variations occurring in symbols, numbers and punctuation marks.

The variation of keybutton format from one single element machine to the other is slightly greater than on typebar machines, and these variations introduce the problem of selecting the appropriate typing elements for a given machine. Within the IBM single element line, for example, some keyboards are designated as "88 character," while others are designated as "96 character." Typing elements will not interchange between these two IBM models (namely the IBM Selectric II and IBM Selectric III). Of course, there are slight keyboard format differences—with corresponding differences in the typing elements—between the various typewriter brands.

Despite small variations in keyboard format, the variations are never so radical as to cause typing disorientation. A typical variation would be the inclusion of some mathematical symbol on one machine that is not present on another machine, but generally this new keybutton will not usurp the place of one that is traditionally found on typewriters. Everything said here in regard to keybutton format applies to U.S. standard typewriters.

IBM SELECTRIC II CONTROLS

In addition to the foregoing list of commonly found keybuttons and control levers, some typewriters have others. For example, the IBM Selectric II—as well as comparable single element machines—have innovative functions, for which control buttons and levers must be provided. On the Selectric II you would find the following.

Depressing and holding the *index* keybutton turns the platen the number of vertical line spaces at which the line space selector lever is set, while the carriage (i.e., the element, of course) remains stationary.

Depressing and holding the *express (EXP)* keybutton returns the element leftward, until the keybutton is released or the element reaches the left-hand margin stop, without the platen's turning. Thus, element return can be accomplished without line spacing, if desired.

In the lower-right-hand corner of the keybutton panel is a keybutton marked with the symbol X, enclosed by an arrow pointing leftward. This is the correcting back space keybutton which, when momentarily depressed, back spaces the element one space, while simultaneously engaging a mechanism which will hold the element in position while one character is typed. When a second character is typed, the keybuttons are back in normal operating mode, and the element moves rightward during typing.

On the inside of the right-hand platen knob of the Selectric II is a free-turning dial, calibrated in numbers from 0 to 4. This dial is not connected to any mechanism of the machine, and is simply used to give the operator an indication that the end of the page is being reached (the IBM operator's manual refers to this dial as the *page-end indicator*). It is an unnecessary convenience feature and serves no useful purpose.

On the right-hand end and almost directly over the platen, on the Selectric II, is an unmarked lever which, when pulled out of its normal position and toward the typist, disengages the platen ratchet in such a manner that when the ratchet is later re-engaged—after turning the platen any number of turns—the lever can be moved to its normal position, re-engaging the ratchet. Line spacing will register exactly as it was before the platen was moved. The IBM operator's manual refers to this lever as the *line finder*.

On the left-hand end of the Selectric II and almost directly over the platen is another unmarked lever. The normal position of this lever is toward the rear of the machine, where it is held by spring tension. Pulling it toward the typist and *holding it* activates a mechanism which moves the element back one-half space. The typewriter can be operated while this lever is held back, to provide one-half or 1½ spaces between words. The IBM operator's manual refers to this lever as the half back space lever.

SUMMARY

What I have attempted to do in this chapter is familiarize you with typewriter terminology and to give you a description of the locations, names and purposes of the various controls found on typewriters. This is to help you learn the proper language, so you can be on speaking terms with professional repairmen, manufacturers and distributors. It is extremely helpful to call parts, functions, control levers, etc., by their technically correct names. This can save you some delay and frustration when seeking advice, ordering parts or service manuals. In the next chapter I will talk about the internal mechanisms which these external controls activate.

Chapter 2
Manual
Typewriter
Mechanisms

New manual typewriters are still available. While it may be an overstatement to say that they are an important segment of the industry, it is fair to say that they have been present in the consumer market in sufficient amounts and for enough years that many of the machines seen by professional repairmen are manual typewriters.

While the mechanism descriptions in this chapter are intended to be representative of a fairly large cross-section of machines, the illustrations are those of well-known and popular brands, taken from service manuals supplied by manufacturers. However, the textual descriptions, together with the illustrations, should help you to understand the underlying principles of the mechanisms of just about any manual typewriter.

The part names in the textual descriptions do not always match the ones that I have suggested because, as I explained in the first chapter, there is some variance in terminology between manufacturers. The names were used as they appeared in the service manuals, to make your reference easier.

TYPING MECHANISM

The *typing mechanism* causes a typebar to swing up and strike the platen when a keybutton in depressed. Refer to Fig. 2-1. When the keybutton (key) is depressed down, the key lever pushes down on the bell crank. Since the bell crank is connected to the typebar

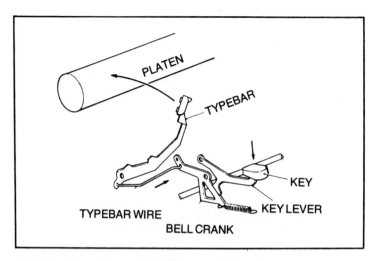

Fig. 2-1. In this illustration, one typebar is isolated from the assembly to clarify the process (courtesy of Brother International Corporation).

by the typebar wire, the bottom end of the typebar is pulled in the direction of the key, and the head of the typebar strikes the platen.

As a further illustration of the typing mechanism principle, refer now to Fig. 2-2. When the key is pushed down, the key lever pulls the typebar wire in the direction of the key, which causes the typebar to swing in an arc toward the platen. Note that in this particular illustration, it is the lower character that strikes the platen, and that the upper character is above the curvature of the platen. This is the positional relationship between the typebar head and platen when the typewriter is set to type lower case characters.

To see yet another illustration of a typing mechanism, refer to Fig. 2-3. When the key lever (1) is depressed, the key lever link (4) is pulled around making the key lever shaft (3) the center of revolution. Because of the movement of the key lever link (4), the sub lever (6) is rotated, with the sub lever shaft (5) being the center of revolution. The typebar link (8) is pulled by this movement, and the typebar (9) swings up and strikes the platen (10). Lastly, the key lever (1) and typebar (9) are returned to normal position by the tension of the sub lever spring (7).

SPACING MECHANISM

The *spacing mechanism* causes the carriage to move one character space when the space bar is depressed. Refer to Fig. 2-4.

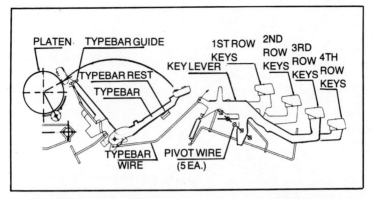

Fig. 2-2. This typing mechanism, from the Brother Model JP7, further illustrates typing mechanism principles (courtesy of Brother International Corporation).

When the space bar is depressed, the space rod is moved in the direction of the arrow, escape crank B moves, and this movement is transmitted to the half space ratchet, which in turn moves the carriage. Releasing the space bar completes the spacing.

To look at yet another representative space mechanism, refer to Fig. 2-5. When the space key (1) is depressed, the space link (3a) pushes a connection (4), which in turn pushes the loose dog (5a), which pushes the fixed dog (6a). This removes the fixed dog (6) from the escapement wheel (7), and the carriage moves one space. Finally, when the space key (1) is no longer depressed by the operator, it—together with the space link (3)—is returned to home position by the tension of spring (8).

ESCAPEMENT MECHANISM

The *escapement mechanism* causes the carriage to move one space when a keybutton is depressed (i.e., when a character is typed). Referring to Fig. 2-6, when the character key is depressed, the escape crank (rear—F-42) will be rotated in the direction of the arrow, by an escape crank (front—F-40). The escape crank (rear—F-42) will shift the half space ratchet (F-48) to the plate where F-48 is engaged with the space ratchet wheel (F-37), via escape crank (rear—F-42).

The half space ratchet (F-48) will be pushed into the inside of the addendum of the space ratchet wheel (F-37). Meanwhile, the space ratchet (F-47) will be disengaged from F-37. In this condition, the carriage will be shifted a half space, by the tension of the spring drum.

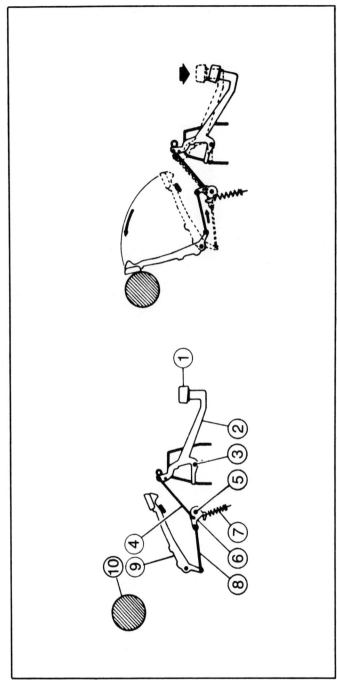

Fig. 2-3. This typing mechanism, taken from the service manual of the Olympia Model B-12, does not differ in any appreciable way from previously shown mechanisms, but further serves to illustrate the basic principle of moving the typebar against the platen (courtesy of OLYMPIA USA INC.).

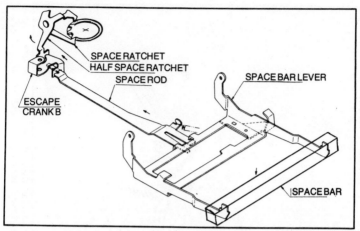

Fig. 2-4. This spacing mechanism, taken from the Brother Model JP7 service manual, shows how spacing is accomplished (courtesy of Brother International Corporation).

F-48 and F-47 will return to the original position by spring action, while simultaneously F-40 will return to its original position, and the carriage will shift another half space. A full space shifting of the carriage has been accomplished.

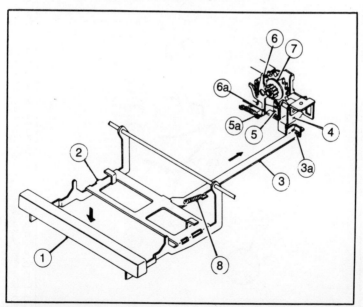

Fig. 2-5. This is the spacing mechanism of the Olympia Model B-12 (courtesy of OLYMPIA USA INC.).

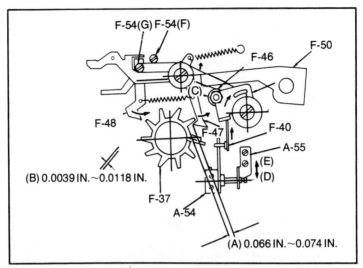

Fig. 2-6. This escapement mechanism is from the service manual of the Brother Model M-100. The adjustment tolerances that are shown here will be discussed in a later chapter (courtesy of Brother International Corporation).

To see another escapement mechanism, refer to Fig. 2-7. When a keybutton is depressed, the typebar (not shown) pushes the escapement drive plate, which moves the escape crank A and

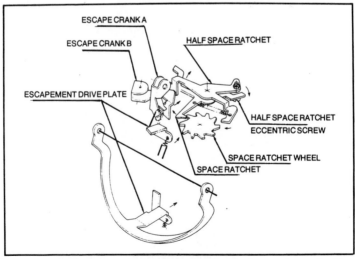

Fig. 2-7. This escapement mechanism is from the Brother service manual for the Brother Model JP7. It's easy to understand if you read the text carefully (courtesy of Brother International Corporation).

also escape crank B, the half space ratchet and space ratchet, which removes the space ratchet from the space ratchet wheel.

For yet another escapement mechanism, see Fig. 2-8. When the key lever is depressed, the typebar is operated in the direction of the platen, and then the side (b) of the typebar pushes the side face (4a) of the segment universal bar. The tip of the bottom part (4b) of the segment universal pushes the connection (5), and then

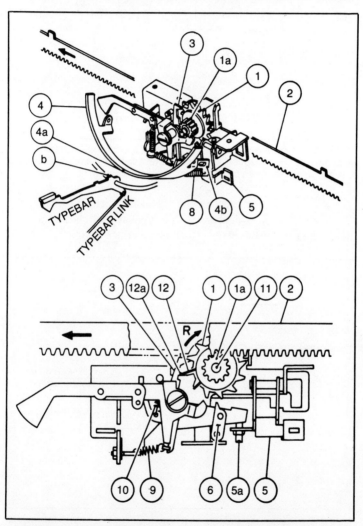

Fig. 2-8. This is the escapement mechanism of the Olympia Model B-12, taken from the Olympia service manual (courtesy of OLYMPIA USA INC.).

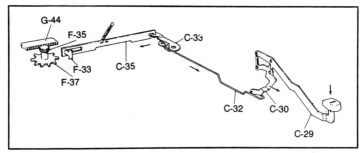

Fig. 2-9. This back space mechanism is of the Brother M-100, taken from the Brother service manual (courtesy of Brother International Corporation).

the setscrew (5a) of the connection pushes the loose dog (6) in the upper direction. The fixed dog (3) leaves the star wheel (1) in accordance with the movement of the loose dog (6).

The carriage moves in the direction shown with an arrow, by the force of the main spring. Then the revolution of the star wheel (1) is stopped by the loose dog (6), and the movement of the carriage stops.

Finally, when the key lever is no longer depressed, the typebar is returned to home position by the sub-lever spring and universal spring (8). The loose dog (6) is released from the star wheel (1) by the loose dog spring (9), and the carriage completes its movement in the direction shown with the arrow, by spring tension. The revolution of the star wheel (1) is discontinued by the fixed dog (3), and the carriage stops.

Incorporated in this mechanism is a "silent return" feature, which operates as follows. The silent return (12) is pivoted on the shaft (11) of the escapement wheel, held friction-tight against the wheel by a special spring. When the carriage is moved from left to right, the wheel (1) turns in the direction shown by the arrow (R), dragging the silent return in the same direction. The arm (12a) of the silent return pushes away the fixed dog (3), which normally rides over the teeth of the wheel. When the carriage resumes its normal forward movement, the silent return returns to home position by the help of the wheel.

BACK SPACE MECHANISM

The *back space mechanism* causes the carriage to move back one space when the back space keybutton is depressed and released. Referring to Fig. 2-9, when the back space key is depressed, the back space lever (C-30) pulls the back space wire

(C-32) in the direction of the arrow. The back space link (C-33) is rotated by the back space wire (C-32), following the arrow direction, and the backspace bar (C-35) is moved by the back space link (C-33), pushing the space ratchet wheel (F-37). Since the ratchet wheel (F-37) is an integral part of the space pinion (F-35), with the latter being engaged in the carriage escapement, the carriage rack (G-44) is moved back one space.

To see another backspace mechanism, refer to Fig. 2-10. When the back space key is depressed, this action is transmitted through the back space key lever to the back space rod, which is moved in the direction of the arrow. This moves the back space crank, which moves the back space pawl and, thus, the space ratchet wheel, which is engaged in the carriage escapement. Note that all the connecting levers, as well as the key lever, are returned to home positions by the tension of a spring.

Another backspace mechanism is illustrated in Fig. 2-11. When the backspace key (1) is depressed, the back space latch plate (5) is pulled by the movement of the back space link (3) and back space crank (4). Thus, the position (5a) is engaged with the escapement wheel (6), which moves the carriage back one space. When the operator no longer depresses the back space key (1), the tension of back space spring (7) returns the back space key to its original position.

MARGIN STOP MECHANISM

The border spaces on the paper, on the left-hand and right-hand edges of the line of type, are called the left and right margins. Normally, the left-hand margin is maintained even, since the carriage automatically comes to rest at the same position on each successive return of the carriage. However, the evenness of the right-hand margin is only approximate, since it is not determined by automatic stopping, but rather by a combination of the preset margin stop and the typist's discretion, with final stopping achieved only when the typist types past the discretionary point. When this happens, the carriage will ultimately stop against the preset right margin stop. Referring to Fig. 2-12, the left and right margins are determined by the position of margin stoppers G-52 and G-55 (G-55 is not shown), and the margin rack (G-57). Carriage travel is limited when the margin stoppers strike the carriage stoppers (F-13). Locking of the carriage at the preset right margin is accomplished as follows.

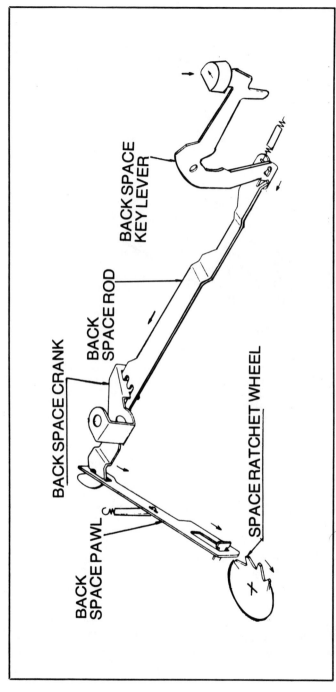

BACK SPACE KEY LEVER

BACK SPACE ROD

BACK SPACE CRANK

BACK SPACE PAWL

SPACE RATCHET WHEEL

Fig. 2-10. This is the back space mechanism of the Brother Model JP7. As always read the text to understand it more fully (courtesy of Brother International Corporation).

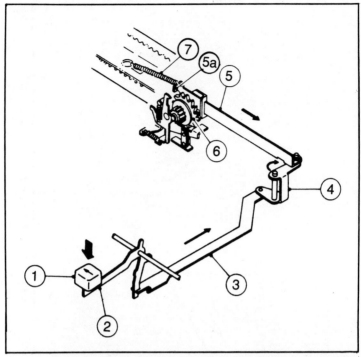

Fig. 2-11. This is the Olympia Model B-12 back space mechanism, as shown in the Olympia service manual. By now it should be evident that the carriage is literally pushed back through manual power as it works through the various levers and linkages, since the natural tendency of the carriage is to move rightward with the tension of the spring drum (courtesy of OLYMPIA USA INC.).

When the last character is typed, that is, when the last typing key prior to margin locking is depressed, the margin stop (G-52) pushes the carriage stopper (F-13) a half space to the left to activate the margin release bar unit (C-23), which is also pushed to the left. The margin release bar unit (C-23) is pivoted at (A), activating the ribbon drive crank (D-16) to the right, drawing the (B) portion of the margin release bar unit (C-23) against the ribbon drive crank (D-16) at the moment the key lever is released. As the key lever is released, the carriage moves the remaining half space. The (B) portion is sprung into locking position, and the key type is locked.

Another margin stop mechanism is shown in Fig. 2-13. The typing key is depressed. The right margin stopper is pushed against the carriage stopper. The escape stopper is pushed in such

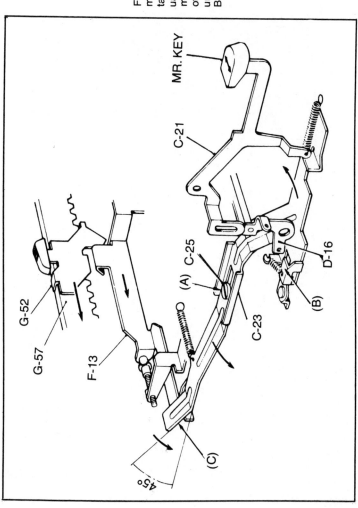

Fig. 2-12. This is the margin stop mechanism of the Brother M-100, taken from the Brother service manual. The operator controls of this mechanism are G-52 and mr. key; other parts of the mechanism are under the covers (courtesy of Brother International Corporation).

55

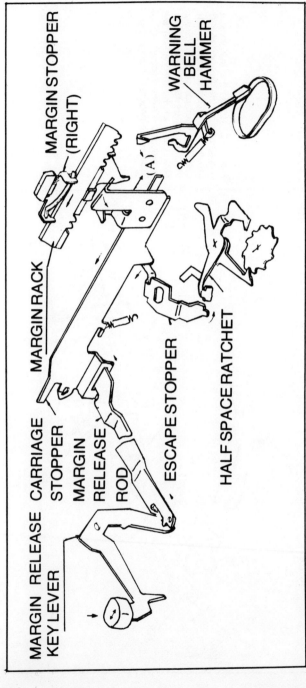

MARGIN RELEASE KEY LEVER · CARRIAGE STOPPER · MARGIN RACK · MARGIN STOPPER (RIGHT) · WARNING BELL HAMMER · MARGIN RELEASE ROD · ESCAPE STOPPER · HALF SPACE RATCHET

Fig. 2-13. This is the margin stop and release mechanism of the Brother Model JP7, taken from the Brother service manual. Note that margin stopping and margin releasing are two different operations, working into the same mechanism. Margin releasing is described fully in the text (courtesy of Brother International Corporation).

a manner that it swings against the half space ratchet, making it impossible for the half space ratchet to disengage from the ratchet wheel. The carriage is locked so that typing is no longer possible.

Yet another margin stop mechanism is shown in Fig. 2-14. The left margin stop (10) is set where the typing line should begin, and the right margin stop (12) is set where the carriage should stop—or the typing line should maximally end. When the carriage moves toward this latter position by actual typing, the right margin stop (12a) touches the carriage stopper (5a), and, simultaneously, the stopper (5c) touches the back frame (20a). This stops the movement of the carriage stopper (5), and the carriage is stopped.

MARGIN RELEASE MECHANISM

If it is necessary to begin a line of type ahead of the left-hand margin, or finish a line of type past the right-hand margin, a *margin*

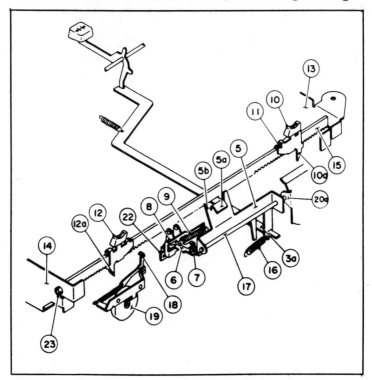

Fig. 2-14. This is the margin stop and margin release mechanism of the Olympia Model B-12, taken from the Olympia service manual (courtesy of OLYMPIA USA INC.).

release mechanism can be activated by depressing the margin release keybutton (usually marked "MR"). The margin release works as follows (see Fig. 2-13 again). When the margin release key is depressed, the margin release rod moves in the direction of the arrow, causing the carriage stopper to come off the margin stopper, at which time it returns in the direction A, allowing the escape stopper to come back, which in turn allows the escapement mechanism to function. It is possible to type through the preset position.

To study yet another margin release mechanism, see Fig. 2-15. When the margin release keybutton (1) is depressed, the margin link (3a) moves in the direction of the arrow to push the carriage stopper (5), and thus (5a) is released from the margin stop

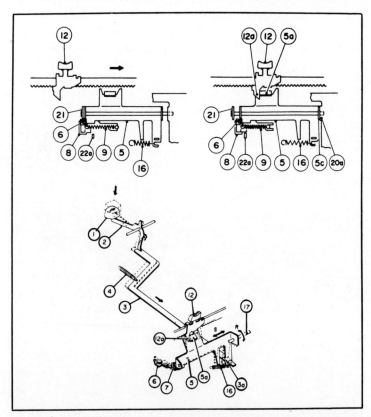

Fig. 2-15. Here, Olympia explains more fully the operation and principle of the margin release mechanism—read the text (courtesy of OLYMPIA USA INC.).

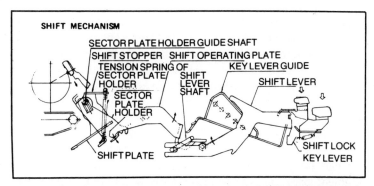

Fig. 2-16. This Brother shift mechanism, taken from the Brother service manual, is fairly typical of those mechanisms which shift the typebar sector; however, later in this book you will see mechanisms that shift the carriage up and down. In either case the typebar strikes the platen on an arc of the curve of the platen in such a manner that the slightly curved typeface hits the platen (courtesy of Brother International Corporation).

(12a). When the typist releases the margin release keybutton (1), the tension of the spring (4) pulls the margin link (3) back, thus returning both the margin link (3) and margin release keybutton (1) to their original positions.

SHIFT MECHANISM

The *shift mechanism* raises and lowers the typebar assembly, so that the appropriate upper- or lower-case characters will strike the platen, while the inappropriate ones will not touch the platen because they are either above or below the curvature of the platen. See Fig. 2-16. When the shift keybutton (the keybutton to the right in the illustration) is pushed down, the shift lever pivots to push the *shift operating plate* in the direction of the arrow, causing the other end of the shift operating plate to move downward in the direction of the arrow, thus lowering the *sector plate holder*. This allows the upper case characters to strike the platen when a typing keybutton is depressed (note that in Fig. 2-16, the mechanism is holding the typebars in lower case position—that is, the shift keybutton is not depressed).

In the context of this discussion, lower case means the characters on the lower half of the type head, which strike the platen when the typebar is *up*. Some service manuals refer to this position of the segment as upper case, presumably on the premise that the segment is in the uppermost position. However, common usage (and strict definition as well) would seem to dictate that the lower case condition is when the segment is *up*, and lower case characters (as opposed to capitals, etc.) are typed.

To see another shifting mechanism, refer to Fig. 2-17. When the shifting keybutton (1) is pushed down, the shift lever (3) rotates, its pivot point being the key lever shaft (C). This rotates the torsion bar (4), which is retained at the left and right side frames by the shift center (6) and nut (7). Note that the torsion bar is connected to the shift lever (3) by a torsion bar part (4a), and also to the segment hanger shaft (5) and segment base (9) by the torsion bar part (4b). Thus, since the segment (10) is mounted on the segment base (9), the segment base is lowered, placing the typebars in upper case position. When the typist no longer depresses the shift keybutton (1), the torsion bar (4) is returned to its home position by the tension of shift spring (8); and the shift lever (3) and segment base (9) are likewise returned to their home positions.

SHIFT LOCK MECHANISM

When it is necessary to place the typebar assembly in its lower position for continuous upper case typing, the typist may depress a *shift lock* (usually marked lock) keybutton, which holds the segment down. See Fig. 2-18. When the shift lock button (2) is depressed, the tip of the shift lock lever (22) is locked at the shift lock fitting (21).

The shift lock can be released, allowing the segment to return to its normal position, as follows (still referring to Fig. 2-18). When the shift button (1) is depressed slightly more than its locked position, the torsion bar (4b) is rotated by just the pitch of "S" (see inset drawing) of the oval shaped hole (D) of the torsion bar part (4b). This causes the shift lever (3) to lower by the length of stroke S, thus releasing the shift lock lever (22) from the shift lock fitting (21).

VERTICAL LINE SPACING MECHANISM

Vertical line spacing means the vertical space between lines, which is standardized at 1/6 inch (six lines to the inch) on standard typewriters.

The distance of vertical line spacing may differ on special purpose typewriters. For example, on the IBM *Executive* proportional spacer, the vertical distance between single-spaced lines is 3/16 inch.

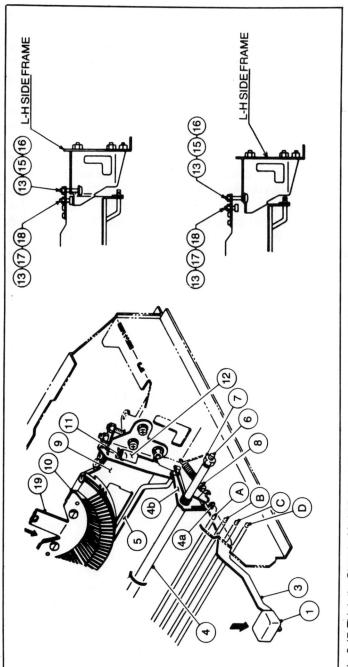

Fig. 2-17. This is the Olympia, Model B-12, shifting mechanism (courtesy of OLYMPIA USA INC.).

On standard, manual typewriters, line spacing is actually accomplished simultaneously with the return of the carriage, even though the carriage return is, strictly speaking, an operation independent of line spacing. However, the lever that is used to return the carriage serves the dual purpose of line space lever. See Fig. 2-19. When the line space lever is pushed, it moves against the line space lever plate, which moves the line space pawl in the direction of the arrow, causing the line space ratchet wheel to rotate. Since the line space ratchet wheel and platen are integral to each other, the platen rolls the appropriate amount, determined by the number of teeth in the ratchet wheel. The paper, which is gripped between the platen and feed rolls, moves a corresponding amount. In this particular mechanism, single-spacing, one-and-a-half-spacing and double-spacing is determined by which ratchet wheel tooth the pawl slides into, which is typist regulated by moving the line space adjusting cam (see Fig. 2-20). This latter mechanism will be explained more fully in the chapter on adjustments.

To see another vertical line spacing mechanism, refer to Fig. 2-21. When the line space lever (1) is operated, the feed arm (3) is rotated by the line space link (2). The line space feed pawl (4a) slides along the cam (6c) of the line space selector (6); thus, the feed pawl (4a) is engaged with a tooth of the line space ratchet (5). Since the line space ratchet is integral to the platen, the platen is turned by an amount corresponding to the travel of the pawl as it slides into a ratchet tooth. The line spacing is restricted by the touch of the feed pawl (4), with a stopper pin (12). The line space lever is returned to its home position by a spring (11).

PAPER FEED

Paper is fed through the typewriter when the platen turns, because the paper is gripped between the platen and a set of small feed rolls (the feed rolls are turned by the rolling of the platen, not vice versa). See Fig. 2-22. When the platen is correctly installed, and the paper release lever (not shown) is in normal position, the platen and paper feed rollers are in spring-tensioned contact. Thus, when a piece of paper is inserted, the back set of paper feed rollers, which are in contact with the platen, catches the paper and rolls it toward the front set of the paper feed rollers. The paper feed plate (the curved plate between the feed rollers, in the illustration) is curved upward on the outfeed side in such a manner as to deflect the paper upward, around the platen. This is an extremely simple

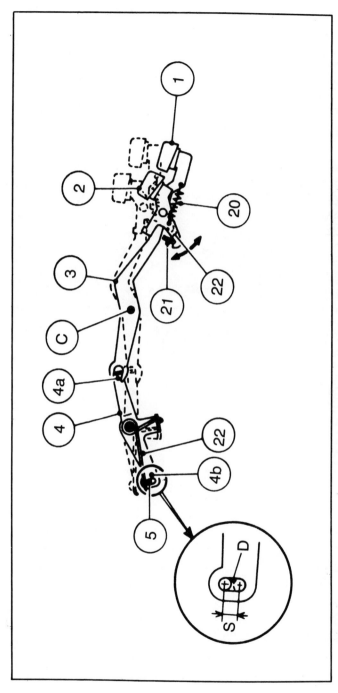

Fig. 2-18. This shift lock mechanism is from the Olympia Model B-12 Service Manual. The dotted lines represent the unshifted position; the solid lines the shifted position (courtesy of OLYMPIA USA INC.).

63

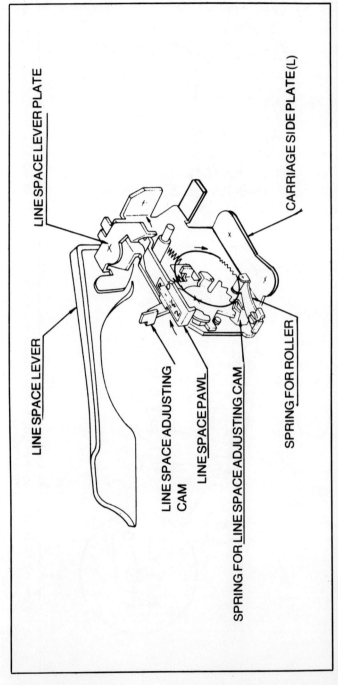

LINE SPACE LEVER PLATE

LINE SPACE LEVER

CARRIAGE SIDE PLATE(L)

LINE SPACE ADJUSTING CAM

LINE SPACE PAWL

SPRING FOR LINE SPACE ADJUSTING CAM

SPRING FOR ROLLER

Fig. 2-19. Vertical line spacing is accomplished when the handle (line space lever in the drawing) is pushed sideways to return the carriage. Study this illustration and read the text to understand how (courtesy of Brother International Corporation).

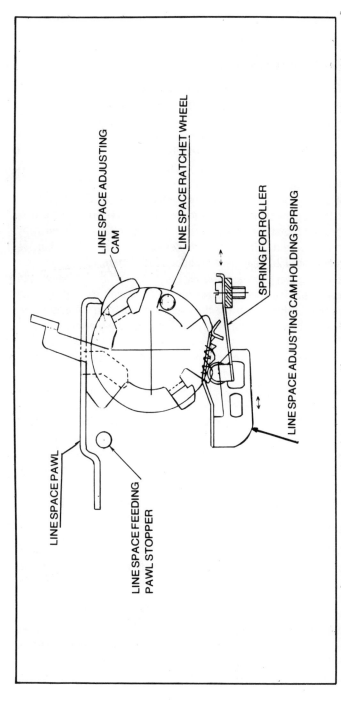

Fig. 2-20. This illustration shows how single, one-and-a-half, and double line spacing is accomplished on the Brother Model JP7 (courtesy of Brother International Corporation).

LINE SPACE PAWL

LINE SPACE FEEDING PAWL STOPPER

LINE SPACE ADJUSTING CAM

LINE SPACE RATCHET WHEEL

SPRING FOR ROLLER

LINE SPACE ADJUSTING CAM HOLDING SPRING

LINE SPACE ADJUSTING CAM

mechanism and one that is easy to work on (provided that the platen is easily removed, which is not *always* the case).

PAPER RELEASE MECHANISM

The *paper release mechanism* releases the contact pressure between the platen and feed rolls, simultaneously backing the paper pan away from the platen. This releases the paper and allows the typist to quickly remove the paper without the need for turning the platen knob, and/or straighten the paper, in case it was rolled into the typewriter crookedly, without the need to remove and reinsert the paper. The mechanism is activated through a lever on top of the typewriter (the lever is often unmarked). See Fig. 2-23. When the paper release lever is moved in the direction of the arrow (toward the typist in actual practice), the paper pan is pushed away from the platen. Since the movement of the paper pan is interconnected to that of the paper feed rollers (the paper pan usually rests on the feed roll assembly), moving the paper pan downward also moves the paper feed rolls downward—away from the platen. In this condition, the paper is freed from the grip of the feed rolls, as well as from the drag between the platen and paper pan.

For a view of yet another paper release mechanism, see Fig. 2-24. Normally (that is, when the mechanism is set to feed paper through the typewriter), the L-shaft arm (2a) pushes the paper pan (7) toward the platen side by the tension of the spring (3).

When the paper release lever (1) is depressed, the release pin (1b) pushes against the L-shaft arm (2), causing the L-shaft (2a) to move away from the paper pan (7). In the illustrated mechanism, depressing the paper release lever (1) releases the paper bail scale arm (5—connected to 6, the paper bail) by pushing it up. This convenience feature facilitates moving or removing the paper.

RIBBON FEED (OR TRANSPORT) MECHANISM

The *ribbon feed mechanism* causes the ribbon to be fed through the typewriter one small increment each time a character is typed. When the ribbon has passed from one reel to another, the mechanism reverses the direction of the ribbon feed, so that it is fed back to the recently emptied reel. See Fig. 2-25. When a keybutton is depressed, the bell crank will push the ribbon drive crank (D-16), which will push the ribbon feed pawl (right—D-40). The ribbon feed wheel (right—E-2) is rotated in the direction of the arrow by the ribbon feed pawl (right—D-40).

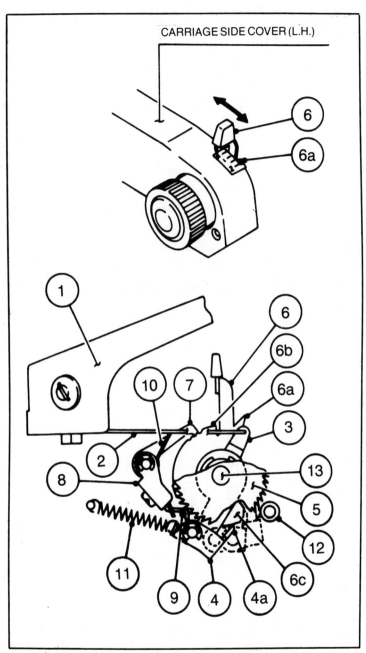

CARRIAGE SIDE COVER (L.H.)

Fig. 2-21. This is the line spacing mechanism for the Olympia Model B-12, taken from the Olympia service manual (courtesy of OLYMPIA USA INC.).

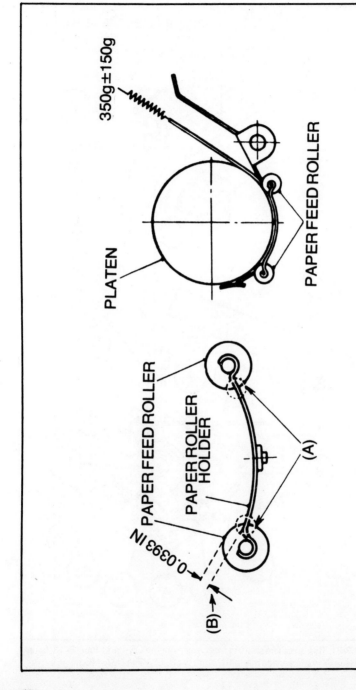

350g ±150g

PLATEN

PAPER FEED ROLLER

PAPER FEED ROLLER

PAPER ROLLER HOLDER

0.0393 IN

(A)

(B)

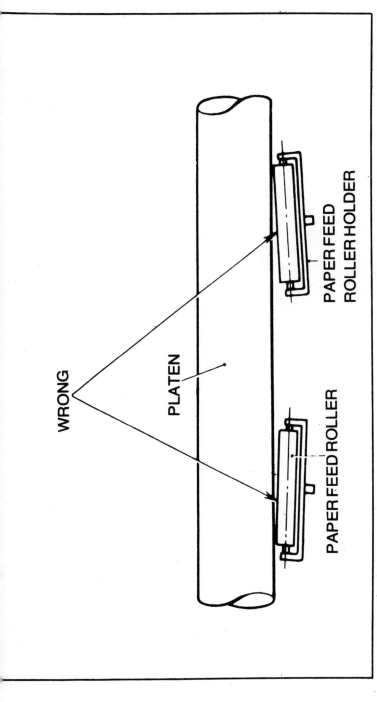

WRONG

PLATEN

PAPER FEED ROLLER

PAPER FEED ROLLER HOLDER

Fig. 2-22. This is the paper feed mechanism of the Brother M-100, taken from the Brother International Corporation).

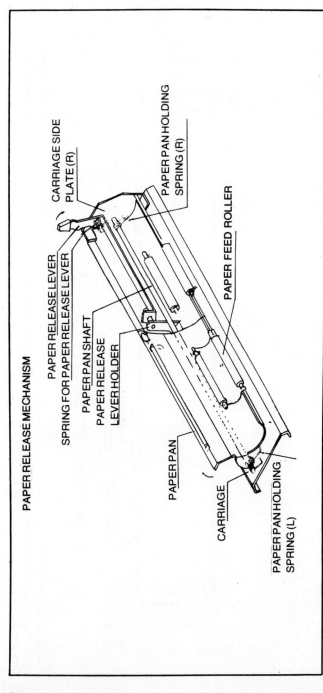

PAPER RELEASE MECHANISM

PAPER RELEASE LEVER
SPRING FOR PAPER RELEASE LEVER

CARRIAGE SIDE PLATE (R)

PAPER PAN HOLDING SPRING (R)

PAPER PAN SHAFT
PAPER RELEASE LEVER HOLDER

PAPER FEED ROLLER

PAPER PAN

CARRIAGE

PAPER PAN HOLDING SPRING (L)

Fig. 2-23. Since the feed rolls are connected to the paper pan, moving the latter away from the platen also moves the rolls, and the paper will be free to move around (courtesy of Brother International Corporation).

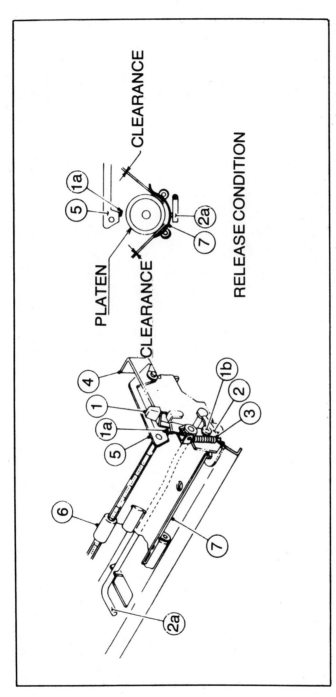

Fig. 2-24. This paper release mechanism is from the Olympia Model B-12, taken from the Olympia service manual (courtesy of OLYMPIA USA INC.).

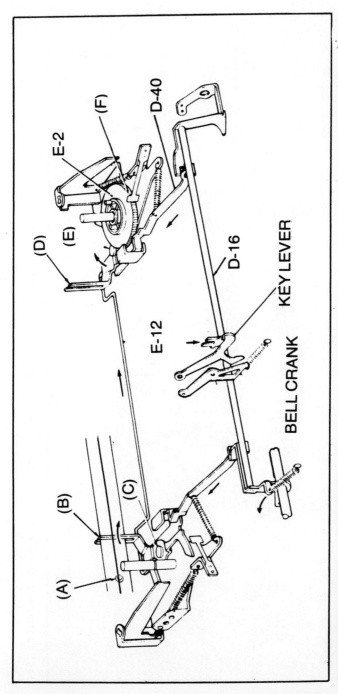

Fig. 2-25. This ribbon feed mechanism, taken from the Brother service manual for the Model JP7, shows how the ribbon is fed from one spool to the other—and then back (courtesy of Brother International Corporation).

When the ribbon is wound all the way on the right reel, the eyelet (A) of the ribbon pulls (B) in the direction of the arrow, with (C) being the fulcrum of the motion. This causes the ribbon reverse wire (E-12) to move in the direction of the arrow, moving (D) clockwise on its fulcrum (E), throwing the ribbon feed pawl (D-40) and stopper plate (E) out of mesh with the ribbon feed wheel (E-2). As a result, the ribbon travel will be reversed and it will be wound to the left side.

Yet another ribbon feed mechanism is shown in Fig. 2-26. When the key lever (1) is operated, the ribbon universal bar (2) pulls the ribbon feed link (4) and also the ribbon feed lever (3). By this pulling operation, the gear feed pawl (5) is engaged with the ribbon ratchet gear (6), causing the ribbon ratchet gear (6) to rotate. The direction of the ribbon winding is reversed as follows.

When the eyelet hole (9a) of the ribbon tape (9) pulls the reverse lever (8) inward, a change of ribbon winding direction is automatically made. Both reverse levers (left—8 and right—7) are

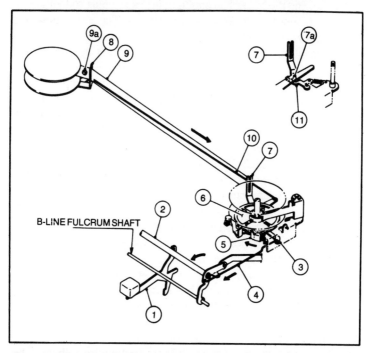

Fig. 2-26. This Olympia ribbon feeding mechanism, taken from the Olympia service manual, shows how the ribbon is fed and reversed (courtesy of OLYMPIA USA INC.).

retained at certain positions by the reverse lever pin (right—7a) and the reverse ring (10). The gear retaining pawl is mounted on the reverse lever (7) and is engaged with the ribbon ratchet gear (6) in order to prevent rewinding. At the same time, the ribbon feed system on the opposite side becomes free, being pushed by the reverse ring (10).

RIBBON LIFT MECHANISM

The *ribbon lift mechanism* causes the ribbon to vibrate up and down, in synchronization with the actions of the typebars, so that the type heads contact either the upper or lower half of the ribbon. When the ribbon lift mechanism is disengaged, the ribbon will not be lifted when a character is typed, causing the type head to miss the ribbon completely as it strikes the platen. This enables the typist to type on a mimeograph stencil without the ribbon acting as a barrier. Since the total height of the ribbon lift is made variable, one-half of a ribbon can serve one purpose (typing black, for instance), and the lower half another purpose (typing red, or laying down a correcting substance, for instance). Thus, in typewriter terminology, "ribbon lift" and "color change" work in conjunction with each other. See Fig. 2-27. When the typist operates (i.e., moves up or down) the color change lever, the motion is transmitted to the color change selector, changing the position of the RV wire against the RV operating plate. The color change stopper moves and the lift and lifting positions of the ribbon are changed.

For a view of yet another ribbon lift and color change mechanism, see Fig. 2-28. When the color selector (1) is operated, the cam lever (3) is rotated around the shaft (4) by the color selector link (2). The cam lever (3) is provided with three cams (3a, 3b and 3c). Position 3a corresponds with "red," position 3b with "black," and 3c with "stencil." The cam lever (3) is retained at the "color-selected" position by the color select detent spring (11).

The mechanism works when a keybutton is pushed down, as follows. As the key (10) is pushed down, both the ribbon lift link (6) and ribbon lift bar (7) are pulled by the ribbon universal bar (5). The ribbon lift crank (8) is rotated, making the shaft (4) the center of revolution, and the vibrator (9) rises. Since the ribbon is threaded through the vibrator, the ribbon rises with it.

The actual amount of ribbon lift is determined as follows. The ribbon lift crank (8) is rotated by the ribbon lift bar (7), being guided by the cam lever (3). If the preset position of the cam lever (3) is

74

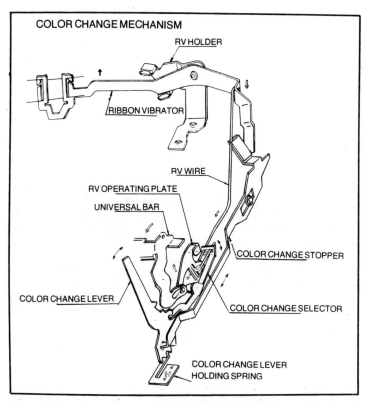

COLOR CHANGE MECHANISM

RV HOLDER

RIBBON VIBRATOR

RV WIRE

RV OPERATING PLATE

UNIVERSAL BAR

COLOR CHANGE STOPPER

COLOR CHANGE LEVER

COLOR CHANGE SELECTOR

COLOR CHANGE LEVER
HOLDING SPRING

Fig. 2-27. As explained in the text, "ribbon lift" means the distance of the up and down motion (vibration) of the ribbon during typing; and "color change" means varying that distance so that certain portions of the ribbon are used while other portions are missed. If the color change selector is set for "stencil," the ribbon vibrator is (generally) moved downward slightly, where it remains stationary, so it is missed by the typebar (courtesy of Brother International Corporation).

changed by the color selector (1), the revolving angle of the ribbon lift crank (8) around the shaft (4) varies. Thus, the degree of lift of the ribbon vibrator (9) becomes variable.

TABULATION MECHANISM

The *tabulation mechanism* makes it possible to move the carriage leftward, in one continuous, freewheeling movement to a preset position, where it will automatically stop. The typist accomplishes this by presetting tab stops and, thereafter, simply depressing the tab button until the carriage reaches the desired stop. See Fig. 2-29. When the tab key is pushed down (in the arrow direction), the tab operating crank (F-3) is rotated through the

75

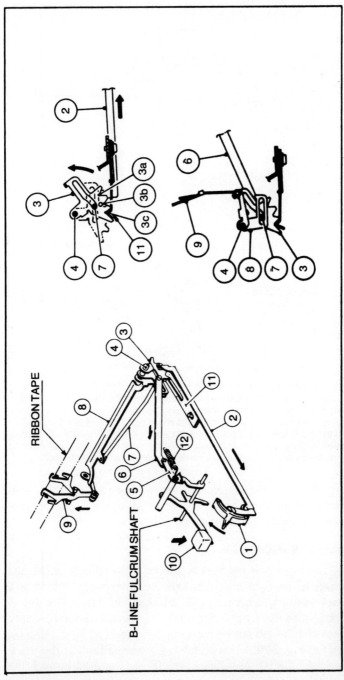

RIBBON TAPE

B-LINE FULCRUM SHAFT

Fig. 2-28. Here is yet another view of a ribbon lift and color change mechanism (courtesy of OLYMPIA USA INC.).

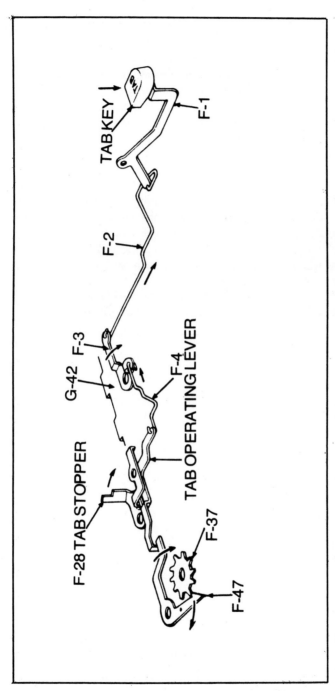

TAB KEY

F-1

F-2

G-42 F-3

F-4

TAB OPERATING LEVER

F-28 TAB STOPPER

F-37

F-47

Fig. 2-29. It may be a little difficult to orient this tabulator mechanism to one in a machine, since only the essential parts are shown. However, a tab mechanism is fairly easily examined in the machine (courtesy of Brother International Corporation).

medium of the tab operating wire (front—F-2). The revolution of the tab operating crank (F-3) rotates the *tab operating lever* through the medium of the tab operating wire (rear—F-4). The revolution of the tab operating lever shall first rotate the tab stopper to the arrow direction, and the tip end of the tab stopper will be engaged with the tab stop pawl (G-42). At the same time the tab operating lever will push the space ratchet (F-47) by its tip, disengaging F-47 from the space ratchet wheel (F-37). When F-47 is disengaged from F-37, the carriage is free to move leftward, through the tension of the spring drum, until the tab stopper contacts with G-42.

For a view of yet another tabulation mechanism, see Fig. 2-30. When the tab key is pushed, the tab rod moves in the direction of the arrow, turning the tab operating lever, which turns the tab stopper. The space ratchet is disengaged from the space ratchet wheel. This allows the carriage to move leftward, until the tab pawl hits the tab stopper and stops.

Another tabulator mechanism is shown in Fig. 2-31. When the tab key (1) is depressed, the tabulator main bar (5) is rotated by the

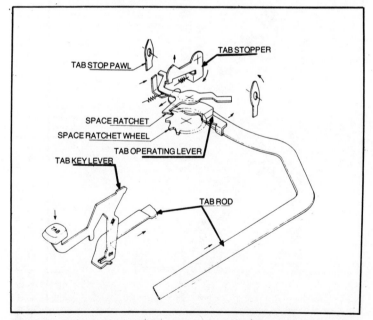

Fig. 2-30. This tab operating mechanism is out of the Brother Model JP7 service manual. Be sure and make the distinction between tab operation and tab set-clear (courtesy of Brother International Corporation).

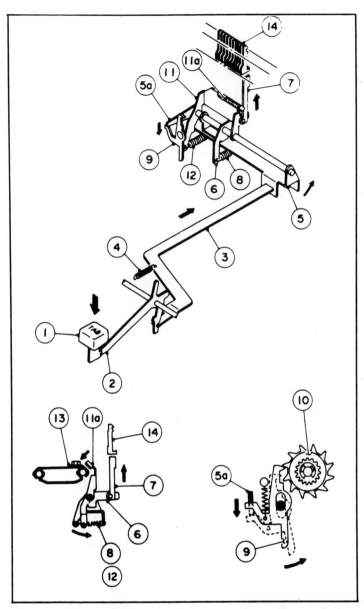

Fig. 2-31. This is an Olympia tab operating mechanism, from the Olympia service manual. The fact that the drawing differs somewhat from that of the Brother mechanism does not mean that the mechanisms are radically different; for example, here you see the tab chips (14), which are not shown in the Brother illustrations but are present in the actual mechanism (courtesy of OLYMPIA USA INC.).

movement of the tabulator link (3). The rotation of the tab stopper lift crank (6), caused from the spring (8), results in the rise of the tab stopper (7).

When the fixed dog (9) is rotated by the tabulator main bar (5a), the fixed dog (9) is released from the escapement wheel (10). This releases the carriage and it moves leftward under the tension of its spring. The tab chip (14), which was preset for tab 1, touches the tab stopper (7).

When the tab key (1) is released by the typist, the tab stopper (7) leaves the tab chip (14), and then the carriage moves leftward. The return of the fixed dog (5a) to its home position causes the rotation of the escapement wheel (10) to stop. The carriage stops at a position where the tab was originally set. In this particular mechanism, there is a braking operation on the carriage, which works as follows.

There is a brake shoe (11a) glued to the brake arm (11). When the tabulator main bar (5) is rotated, the brake arm (11) is rotated by the spring (12) and touches the carriage rail, which results in the stopping of the carriage. Because of this mechanism, the carriage can be released only after both the tab stopper (7) and brake shoe (11a) are set.

TAB SET-CLEAR MECHANISM

The *tab set-clear mechanism* allows the typist to set tab stops at preset positions, from an external control (namely, from the tab set-clear lever, which is usually distinctly separate from the tab keybutton itself). See Fig. 2-32. To use this mechanism, the carriage should be moved to the position at which a tab stop is to be set. This can be done by either tapping the space bar or using the carriage release control, until the carriage is in the correct place. The tab set lever (1) is then moved to set (+), and this movement is transmitted through the linkages to the tab set finger (5), which sets the tab chip (6), through contact with 5a—also see the inset drawing. Consecutive tab chips can be set by moving the carriage to the desired preset position and moving the tab set lever (1) to set (+).

When tab stops are no longer required for a given typing format, their presence becomes a nuisance. They can be removed or "cleared," as follows (still referring to Fig. 2-32). To clear an individual tab chip, the typist must first tab to that stop. The tab set lever (1) is moved to (−). When the carriage moves leftward, the tab chip (6), which was previously set, is returned to the individual

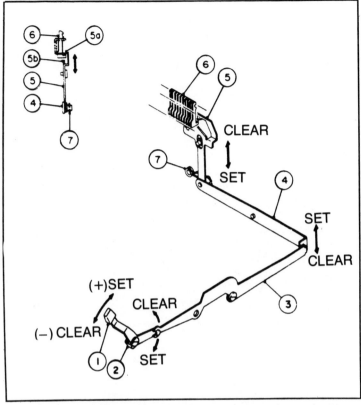

Fig. 2-32. This is a tab set-clear mechanism of the Olympia Model B-12, as taken from the Olympia service manual. About the only thing this mechanism has in common with the tab operating mechanism is its contact with the tab chips (6), which will determine where carriage will stop when a tab keybutton is pushed (courtesy of OLYMPIA USA INC.).

home position by the tab set finger (5b—shown in the inset illustration with Fig. 2-32).

The tab set lever is returned to an intermediate, or neutral, position through the tension of the torsion spring (7) when the typist releases it.

CARRIAGE RELEASE

The carriage is normally held in whatever position it happens to be in, through the engagement of the teeth of the escapement rack with the ratchet wheel. Since it is desirable to occasionally move the carriage leftward from its locked position without the necessity of typing or using the spacing bar, a carriage release

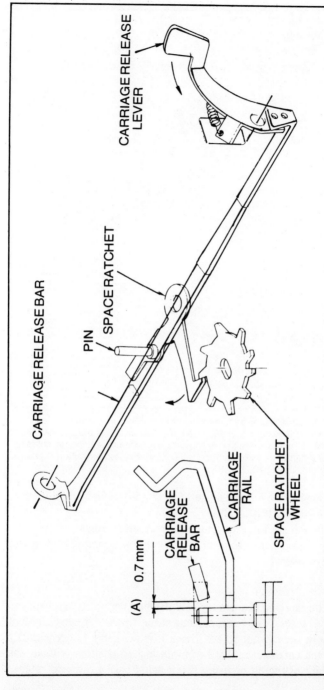

Fig. 2-33. This, the carriage release mechanism of the Brother Model JP7, allows the carriage to move leftward through the tension of the spring drum and is analagous to putting a car "out of gear" (courtesy of Brother International Corporation).

CARRIAGE RELEASE LEVER

CARRIAGE RELEASE BAR

SPACE RATCHET

PIN

SPACE RATCHET WHEEL

CARRIAGE RAIL

CARRIAGE RELEASE BAR

0.7 mm

(A)

mechanism allows the typist to move the carriage leftward, rather rapidly, by hand. See Fig. 2-33. When the carriage release lever is moved, the movement is transmitted to the space ratchet, which moves clockwise (in the direction of the arrow), disengaging from the space ratchet wheel. The carriage is then free of the escapement to "freewheel" leftward.

Another carriage release mechanism is shown in Fig. 2-34. When the carriage release button (1) is depressed, the rack bracket (4) is pushed by both the carriage release lever (2) and release lever pin (2a). The carriage rack (6) is released from the escape pinion gear (7), swinging at the fulcrum of rack bracket retaining screws (5 and 8). The mechanism is returned to its original status by a release spring (3).

PLATEN RELEASE MECHANISM

The *platen release mechanism* enables the typist to disengage the platen ratchet wheel, so the platen can be turned freely. See Fig. 2-35. The platen knob (7), variable ratchet (7-1) and platen shaft (8) are connected. The push rod (5) is inserted into the push

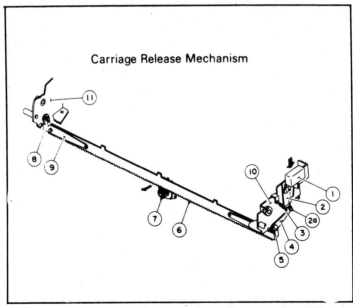

Fig. 2-34. If you study this drawing carefully, you will see a significant difference in its principle of operation, from that of the previous illustration; however, the end result is the same—the carriage is released (courtesy of OLYMPIA USA INC.).

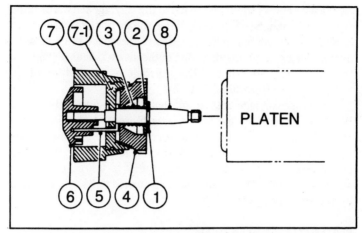

Fig. 2-35. This is a cutaway illustration of the platen disengaging mechanism, which allows the platen to be turned (by hand) in a freewheeling motion. Part (6) is the central button in the platen knob which, when pushed, releases the platen (courtesy of OLYMPIA USA INC.).

button (6). The variable ratchet wheel (4) is engaged with the variable ratchet (7-1) by a spring (3). The part indicated with (1) is the E-ring, and the part indicated with (5) pushes the variable ratchet wheel (4), which is released from the variable ratchet (7-1). Thus, the platen is freed to roll without the drag of the ratchet.

SUMMARY

As you will remember, this chapter was intended simply as an overview of the mechanisms found on manually operated typewriters. Generally speaking, there is little similarity between these and the mechanisms of electric typewriters, the general exceptions being those mechanisms in which the moving of an external lever directly changes the position of an internal part or lever as, for example, the paper release, tab set-clear, margin stops, carriage release and platen release.

Some points to remember are:

☐ The power to pull the carriage leftward is the tension of spring drum.

☐ Absolutely uniform typing impressions are almost impossible to achieve on a manual typewriter, since the density of impressions depends upon muscle coordination.

☐ Since the carriage is always returned (*slammed*, that is) back to the left-hand margin by arm power, most manuals have an irritating way of moving around on the typing table.

☐ For the reasons listed, and also because manual typewriters do not command a high resale value, the purchase of a manual typewriter as a "fixer-upper" is probably not a good investment. However, an inexpensive one would provide a good machine for the novice repairman to work on. In later chapters I will give repair and adjustment information for specific manual typewriter models. In the next chapter I will discuss the mechanisms generally found on electric typewriters.

Chapter 3
Electric
Typewriter
Mechanisms

Several of the operations that are performed manually on manual typewriters are performed by electrically powered mechanisms on electric typewriters, with the mechanism activated when the typist depresses the appropriate keybutton. In essence, the keybutton and its connecting linkages act as an engaging mechanism by contacting a continuously turning power roll, through which the action is transmitted to such mechanisms as typing, carriage return, etc.

POWER ROLL

A major component of the electric typewriter is the *power roll*, which is usually a cylindrical roll of about the same physical size as the platen, and usually located underneath most of the operating mechanisms. On many typewriters, the power roll is rubber—or perhaps some synthetic rubber-like material, with about the same resilience and surface characteristics as the platen (any comparison between the power roll and platen is only superficial, since their purposes are totally different, however). On some typewriters, the power roll is constructed of harder material, somewhat similar in appearance to *bakelite*, with parallel ridges running along its length.

The purpose of the power roll is to transmit its motion to the appropriate mechanism when contacted with a cam—or cam-like part—which, on the rubber rolls, is accomplished by the friction between the cam and power roll. On the ridged power rolls, the cam-like part actually makes positive contact with the ridges of the roll.

It would seem that any value judgment between the two types of power rolls is inappropriate. However, I might say that one shortcoming of the rubber roll is its sensitivity to oil, which necessitates its removal when the typewriter is to be cleaned and oiled. Regarding the quality of operation of the two types of power rolls, though, many other factors enter into the total picture.

To understand the basic principles of the operation of electric typewriters, it is probably helpful to understand that most conventional electric typewriters aren't "electronic," in the sense that each individual mechanism works through an electrical relay. On the contrary, the action is simply transmitted through the continuously turning power roll to the mechanisms.

A few operations are still performed manually in electric typewriters. Some of those mechanisms will also be described in this chapter.

ELECTRICAL SYSTEM

The first and most obvious difference between electric and manual machines is that the electric has electrical components, such as the motor and necessary wiring, including capacitors, etc. See Fig. 3-1. The motor of this particular machine is a capacitor motor, with a no-load rpm of 3,400, to operate on U.S. voltage of 115 volts, 60 Hz frequency (this is standard voltage and frequency in all but a few isolated areas of the United States). Since the power roll must rotate at a considerably slower speed (on the order of 500-600 rpm for the power roll that is driven by this particular electrical system) than the motor, the motor is belted to the power roll through reduction pulleys.

DRIVING MECHANISM

For a typical *driving mechanism*, see Fig. 3-2. This illustration is probably largely self-explanatory (the item annotated "power roll" is in fact only a segment of the power roll, as the actual power roll extends across the width of the machine; this particular roll, you will note, is the ridged type, as described earlier in this chapter).

SWITCH MECHANISM

A *switch mechanism* is shown in Fig. 3-3. In this case, the linkages between the switching lever and switch itself are quite

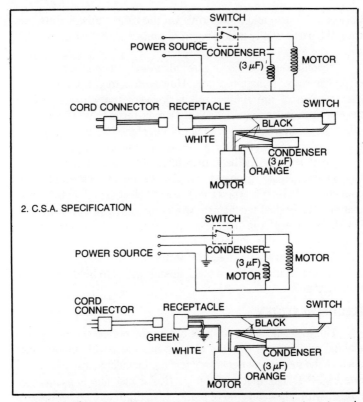

Fig. 3-1. While it is not considered necessary to be an electrical engineer to work on a typewriter, a rudimentary knowledge of basic electrical circuitry would be helpful. However, electrical problems are infrequent (courtesy of Brother International Corporation).

short. The electrical component of the switch is marked "micro switch." Note the stud extending from the bottom left end of this switch. In the *off* condition (Fig. 3-3A), this stud is pushed into the body of the switch to open the contacts of the switch. In the *on* condition (Fig. 3-3B) the switch has been caused to rock away from the switch lever link, allowing the spring-tensioned stud to extend from the switch, closing the contacts of the switch.

Another switching mechanism is shown in Fig. 3-4. In this particular mechanism, the switch and key lever stopper (EB-4) are interlocked so that when the switch is off, the key lever is locked to keep it out of operation. It works as follows. When the on side of the switch key (EO-1) is pushed down, the key lever (EO-63—not to be confused with "key lever") turns counterclockwise.

As the switch lever spring (EO-13) turns clockwise to the push knob of the switch (EO-20), the switch contacts are made (the switch is on). The key lever stopper (EB-4) is turned clockwise to release the key lever lock condition, through the pin riveted on EO-63. When the off side of the switch key is pushed down, the key lever (EO-63) turns clockwise to set the switch to the off position and the lock key lever (EO-63). Thus, the switch must stay in off position when the shift is locked.

Another switch mechanism is shown in Fig. 3-5. In this particular mechanism, the switch is remote from the lever that turns it on, connected by a linkage. When the switch lever (GK-18) is placed in on condition, the switch operating lever (GK-23) moves through the medium of the switch operating wire (GK-22), with the result that the A portion of GK-23 pushes down the B portion of the power switch (GK-25). Once the switch lever (GK-18) is placed in the on position, it remains there by the tension of the spring (GK-21).

TYPING MECHANISMS

The *typing mechanism* causes the typebar to swing up and strike the platen when keybuttons are depressed, the power for this action being transmitted through the power roll. Some

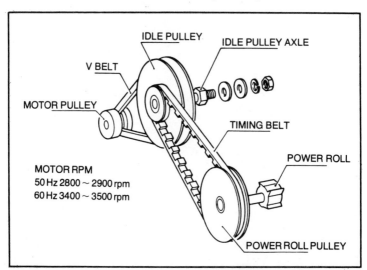

Fig. 3-2. There is nothing remarkable about the driving mechanism of an electric typewriter, at least from the viewpoint of the individual who is even slightly mechanically oriented (courtesy of Brother International Corporation).

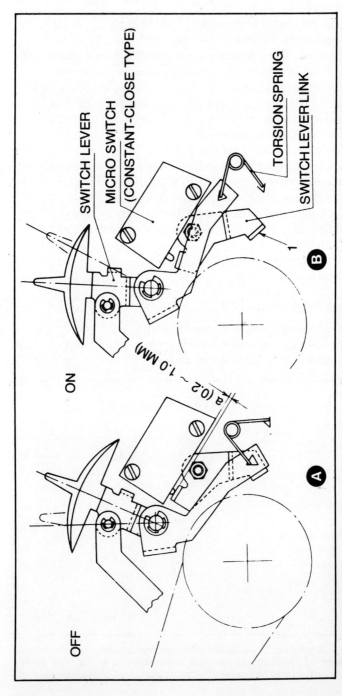

Fig. 3-3. This switch mechanism is from the Brother Model JP10. Read the text to understand fully how it works (courtesy of Brother International Corporation).

90

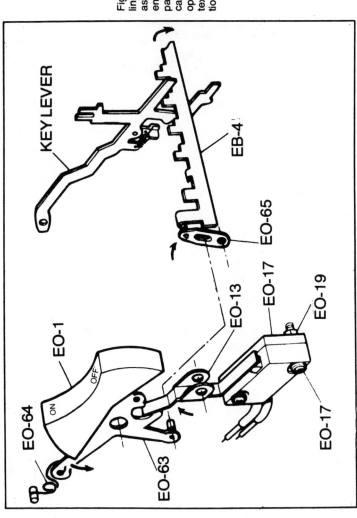

Fig. 3-4. The arrangement of the linkages in a switch mechanism are as varied as the ingenuity of the engineers who develop them. In this particular mechanism, the typewriter cannot be turned on until some other operation is performed--read the text (courtesy of Brother International Corporation).

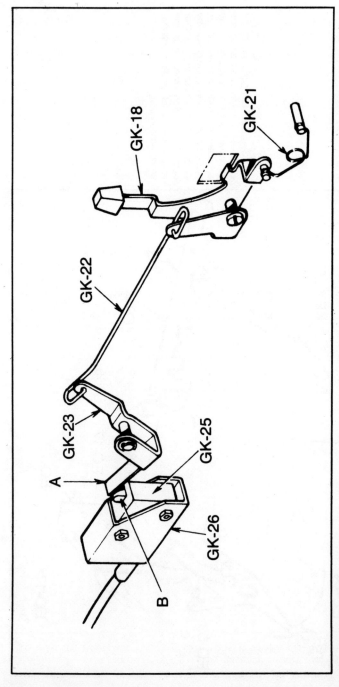

Fig. 3-5. Yet another way to arrange switching linkages is shown here. The switch is stabilized in the on position by the tension of the spring (GK-21) (courtesy of Brother International Corporation).

characters type only once per depression of the keybutton. Others repeat for as long as the keybutton is depressed (usually the repeat depression must be more than for single typing).

Non-Repeat Typing Mechanism in Fig. 3-6

See Fig. 3-6. When a key lever is depressed, the *dog shelf operating spring* is pushed downward. The dog shelf operating spring pushes the dog shelf down, engaging it with the power roll.

The power roll, rotating in the direction of the arrow, activates the dog shelf. This action is transmitted to the *bell crank*, which causes the typebar to swing up and strike the platen (the platen isn't shown).

The dog shelf operating spring maintains the position it took, for as long as the key is depressed. When the dog shelf returns, it forces the spring upward; thus, the mechanism operates only once.

Repeat Typing Mechanism in Fig. 3-7

Certain keybuttons are made to activate repeat mechanisms. Refer to Fig. 3-7.

When the repeat typing key lever is depressed, the repeat lever strikes the plate for repeat key lever and is stopped by the tension of the spring. At the same time, the *dog shelf driver (repeat)*

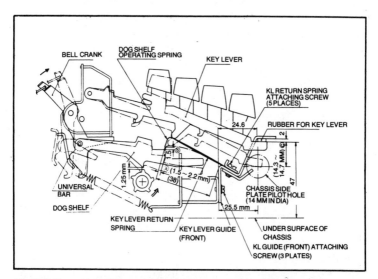

Fig. 3-6. If you study this non-repeat typing mechanism until you understand it, you will have a basic understanding of the power transmission principle of typebar typewriters (courtesy of Brother International Corporation).

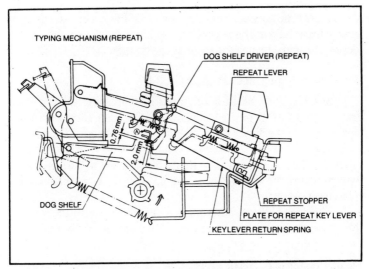

Fig. 3-7. A repeat operation repeats because of a difference in design between it and the non-repeat mechanism. Read the text to understand how (courtesy of Brother International Corporation).

pushes the dog shelf down, and the typebar swings up and strikes the platen.

When the dog shelf returns (after the typebar strikes the platen), the dog shelf driver (repeat) escapes due to the spring tension. It does not actuate the dog shelf again.

When the key lever is depressed still farther, the repeat lever spring (not labeled in the illustration) extends and acts until the key lever hits the *repeat stopper*. As the key lever is depressed, portion A of the dog shelf driver (repeat) again pushes the dog shelf down, and typing is repeated until the key lever is returned.

Non-Repeat Typing Mechanism in Fig. 3-8

When the key is depressed, the *latch actuator* on the key lever pushes the *dog shelf latch* down. As the dog shelf latch is pushed down, the dog shelf is pulled away from the latch by the spring (EC-63), in a clockwise direction, until it engages with the snatch roll (power roll—EO-68). Since the snatch roll always rotates counterclockwise, the dog shelf and dog shelf holder move in parallel, with the wires (EC-2 and EC-13) being the pivot points. This causes the bell crank to turn clockwise, swinging the typebar up to strike the platen (typebar is not shown in its entirety, and the platen is not shown at all).

When the dog shelf hits the adjusting screw (EC-5), the dog shelf is pushed out of engagement with the snatch roll. When the top part (B) of the dog shelf passes part A of the dog shelf latch, the spring (EC-63) pulls the dog shelf and dog shelf latch back to their original positions.

As the dog shelf disengages with the snatch roll, the dog shelf holder is pulled back to its normal position by the spring (EC-18). The bell crank, which is directly connected to the dog shelf holder, pulls the typebar wire to return the typebar to its resting position.

Repeat Typing Mechanism in Fig. 3-9

The repeat mechanism works as follows (refer to Fig. 3-9). When the key lever (EB-65, 66) for the repeat mechanism is depressed until the repeat stopper contacts the lower cushion

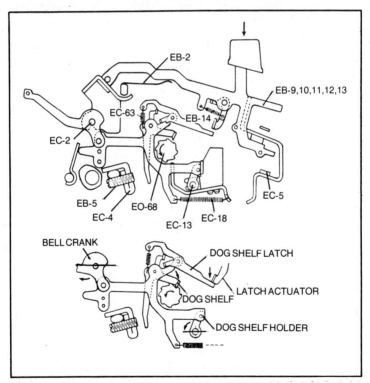

Fig. 3-8. While the principle of operation of this mechanism does not differ significantly from the one previously shown (for non-repeat action, that is), it is offered to further clarify the actions. EO-68, with the arrow pointing counterclockwise, is the end of the power roll (courtesy of Brother International Corporation).

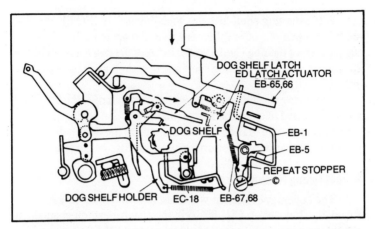

Fig. 3-9. This is the repeat mechanism of the same typewriter of Fig. 3-8. Study it in detail to note differences in the design of certain parts (courtesy of Brother International Corporation).

rubber (EB-5), the dog shelf latch and the dog shelf operate the same as in the foregoing non-repeat sequence.

When the key lever (EB-65, 66) is depressed more deeply, the repeat stopper contacts the cushion rubber (EB-5) and the key lever guide (EB-1). In this condition, when the dog shelf latch starts to restore, it comes into contact with the latch actuator.

The dog shelf latch contacts part D of the latch actuator first and pushes it counterclockwise. The edge of part E also contacts the dog shelf latch.

The dog shelf latch is pushed down by parts D and E of the latch actuator. The dog shelf meshes with the snatch roll, and operates repeatedly, to activate the typebar.

Non-Repeat Typing Mechanism in Fig. 3-10

When the *character key* is depressed, the key lever link attached to the key lever will push down the dog shelf (Fig. 3-10). Upon being pushed down, the dog shelf will engage with the *snatch roll*. Since the snatch roll rotates clockwise continuously, the dog shelf is moved in the direction of the arrow (1). The dog shelf, moving in the direction of the arrow, will disengage from the snatch roll when the A portion contacts the dog shelf stopper (see Fig. 3-10).

While the dog shelf is making this movement, the bell crank will be made to revolve counterclockwise, in the direction of arrow 2 (see Fig. 3-10). Through the revolution of the bell crank, the typebar will be made to move in the direction of arrow 3—that is, toward the platen (platen not shown). Finally, all the parts are returned to their home positions by the tensions of the various springs.

Repeat Typing Mechanism in Fig. 3-11

In the repeat mechanism, depressing of the character key will extend the action of the repeat lever, through the spring (GC-9, 10). See Fig. 3-11. When the repeat key lever is depressed until it contacts the repeat lever stopper, the dog shelf will make the same movement as in the non-repeat sequence.

After making one typing operation, the dog shelf will return to its original position and will again be lowered into contact with the snatch roll. This action will be repeated for as long as the character key is fully depressed.

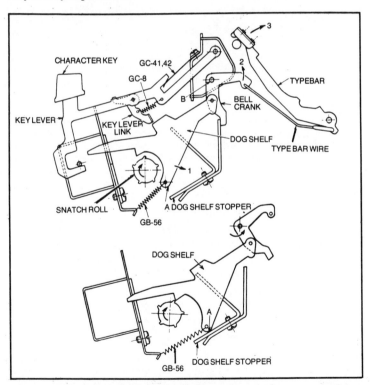

Fig. 3-10. This is an excellent illustration of the operation of a non-repeat typing mechanism. In later chapters you will learn how to adjust this mechanism (courtesy of Brother International Corporation).

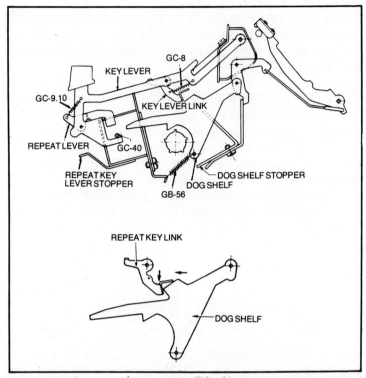

Fig. 3-11. This is the repeat mechanism for the typewriter of Fig. 3-10. Note in particular the difference in design of the part marked "key lever link," as well as the addition of a "repeat lever" (courtesy of Brother International Corporation).

ESCAPEMENT MECHANISM

The *escapement mechanism* moves the carriage leftward one pitch, each time a character is typed. See Fig. 3-12. When the typing key is pushed, the typebar (not shown) pushes the *escapement drive plate*, which pushes the escape crank A, escape crank B and the half space ratchet. Thus, the space ratchet is disengaged from the space ratchet wheel. (Note that the only function the power roll—not shown—would play in this sequence of movements is the movement of the typebar.)

Another escapement mechanism is shown in Fig. 3-13. When the typebar (not shown) is activated, it pushes the escapement drive plate (EA-58), causing the escapement crank (EJ-2) to turn clockwise.

The crank (EJ-2) pushes the half space ratchet (EJ-16) in a counterclockwise direction, turning the space ratchet (EJ-22) clockwise, until it disengages from the escapement rack (EK-102, 302). Simultaneously, the half space ratchet engages with the escapement rack, and the spring drum (not shown) moves the rack one-half pitch.

Springs (EJ-20, etc.) pull the half space ratchet (EJ-16) and space ratchet (EJ-22) back to their normal positions when the escapement drive plate (EA-58) returns. The half space ratchet disengages from the escapement rack, while simultaneously the space ratchet engages with the escapement rack. (Note again that the only function performed by the power roll is the activating of the typebar, with the escapement mechanism functioning similarly as it would in a manual machine, with the carriage being moved *leftward* by spring tension.)

Another escapement mechanism is shown in Fig. 3-14. When the type bar (not shown) pushes the *escapement drive plate unit* (GA-54) in the direction of the arrow, the *universal bar* (GA-57) is lowered, and the front escape crank (GF-26) will be rotated.

GF-26 will shift the half space ratchet (GF-37) to the place where GF-37 is engaged with the space ratchet wheel (GF-23).

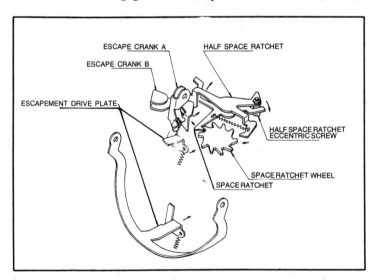

Fig. 3-12. The escapement mechanism of a typewriter is analagous to that of a clock, in that if the typist could type exactly one character each second, the length of a 60-character line of type could represent one minute on the "read-out." To become oriented to this illustration, mentally move the "escape-ment drive plate" into position by "welding" it at the break at the end of the shorter arrow. When a typebar swings up and hits this part, the escapement mechanism is put into action (courtesy of Brother International Corporation).

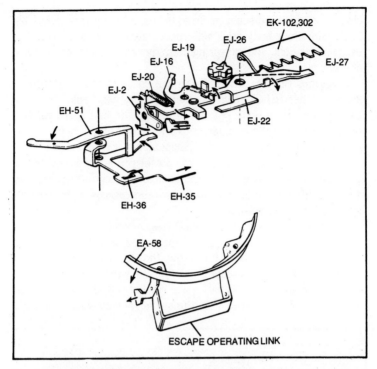

ESCAPE OPERATING LINK

Fig. 3-13. This escapement mechanism, like the one of Fig. 3-12, is from a Brother typewriter. Read the text to understand how it works (courtesy of Brother International Corporation).

The transmission of this action will be through the rear space crank (GF-30).

As GF-37 is engaged with the space ratchet wheel (GF-23), the space ratchet (GF-36) is disengaged from the space ratchet wheel (GF-23). This causes the carriage to be shifted a half space, by the tension of the spring drum (not shown).

GF-37 and GF-36 will return to their original positions through the tensions of the springs, while simultaneously GA-54 will return to its original position. The carriage will move leftward, by the tension of the spring drum, for another half pitch, and complete spacing will be accomplished.

SHIFT MECHANISM

The *shift mechanism* lowers the complete typebar assembly in such a manner that upper case characters will strike the platen. See Fig. 3-15. In this illustration, the solid lines indicate the lower case

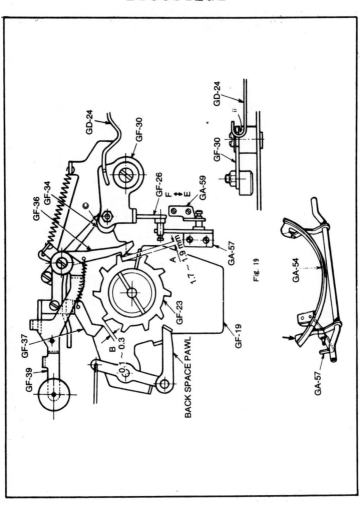

Fig. 3-14. Here is the escapement mechanism of yet another Brother electric typewriter. Don't misunderstand the space ratchet wheel (GF-23) to be the end of the power roll. The tolerances shown in this illustration will be explained more fully in a later chapter (courtesy of Brother International Corporation).

GD-24
GF-30
GF-36
GF-34
GF-37
GF-39
GF-26
F
E
GA-59
GA-57
GF-23
1.7 ~ 1.9 mm
A
B
0.1 ~ 0.3
BACK SPACE PAWL
GF-19

GD-24
GF-30
Fig. 19

GA-54
GA-57

101

position (that is, the sector is *up*), and dotted lines indicate the upper case condition (that is, the sector is *down*). When the shift keybutton (not shown) is depressed, the *shift wire* is pulled in the arrow direction. This movement is ultimately transmitted to the part that pivots at C, which is hooked to the end of the *shift balance spring*. This pulls the sector down (note the dotted line portion of Fig. 3-15).

Another shifting mechanism is shown in Fig. 3-16. When the shift key (EG-5, which happens to be on the left end of the keybutton panel) is depressed, the wire (EG-37) pushes the holder (EG-34) down (when the shift key on the right-hand end of the keybutton panel is depressed, the same action results, since the two shift keys are connected together through a connecting rod, the end of which is shown as EG-9).

As the holder (EG-34) is pushed down, the shift cam release pawl (lower) is disengaged from the shift clutch plate. As the spring (EG-22) pulls the shift cam operating pawl in the direction of the snatch roll (EO-68), the shift clutch plate turns slightly counterclockwise. The shift cam operating pawl engages the snatch roll (EO-68) to move the shift cam and shift clutch plate by one-half turn, and the shift clutch plate is stopped by the shift cam release pawl (upper).

Since the roller of the shift operating link (EG-25) is in contact with the shift cam, the operating link (EG-25) is pulled frontward by a spring (EG-39) by the same distance that the shift cam is moved by its one-half revolution. The SL rod (EG-29) turns counterclockwise to lower the sector plate holder (EA-65).

The holder (EA-65) comes down along the guide shaft (EG-65), until it contacts with the snap ring (EG-66). When the shift key is released, the holder (EG-34) is pulled back to normal position by the spring (EG-18), while the shift cam release pawl (upper) is disengaged from the shift clutch plate and the shift cam and clutch plate turn by one-half turn to mesh with the shift cam release pawl (lower).

When the shift cam turns backward, the operating link (EG-25) moves back and the SL shaft turns clockwise to push the holder (EA-65) upward against the spring (EG-39). When the shift lock key (EG-6) is depressed, the hook at the tip of the shift lock key lever slides over the shift lock plate (EG-11) and catches EG-11; the sector is now shifted and locked in place. When the shift key (EG-5) is depressed, the shift lock key lever is disengaged from the lock plate EG-11, through tension of the spring (EG-4).

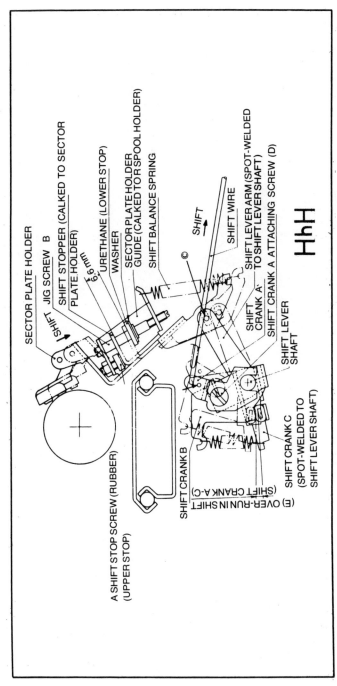

Fig. 3-15. This particular shift mechanism is activated manually, even though it is found in an electric machine. In certain other Brother electric models, shifting is powered through a transmission of the power of the power roll (courtesy of Brother International Corporation).

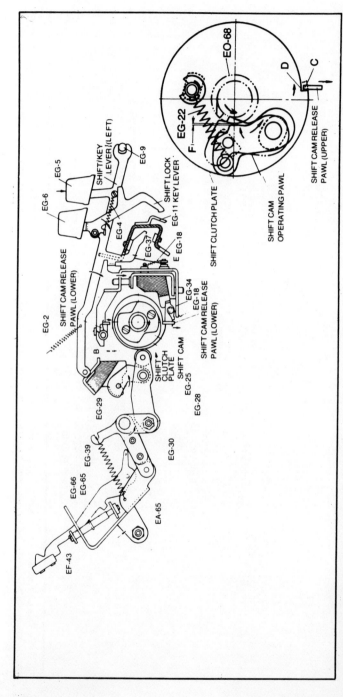

Fig. 3-16. In this Brother shifting mechanism, power from the power roll (called a "snatch roll"—EO-68—in Brother terminology) is transmitted to the mechanism (courtesy of Brother International Corporation).

Another shifting mechanism is shown in Fig. 3-17. When the shift lever unit (GD-1) is lowered, the shift crank (GF-7) is rotated counterclockwise. Through the rotation of GF-7, the shift wire (GF-14) will rotate the rear shift link (GF-15) counterclockwise. The rotation of GF-15 will lift GF-4 and GF-1 (GF-1, not shown, is the right end of the carriage frame), and thus the carriage is shifted.

When the shift lock key lever (GD-5) is pushed downward, the tip A of GD-5 will be lowered to contact the surface of the shift lock plate (GC-40), thus holding the carriage in the shift position. (Please note that the last steps of the described shift mechanism procedures explain how the shift lock operates.)

HALF SPACE MECHANISM

Some typewriters have a *half space mechanism*, which allows the typist to adjust spaces between words. The most common use of a half space function is to insert an extra character in a word that

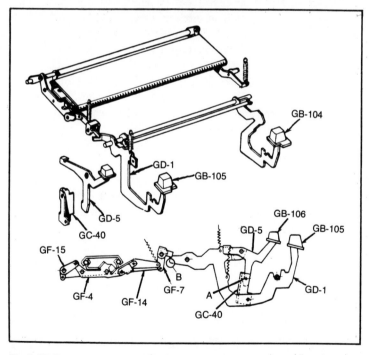

Fig. 3-17. Here, again, shifting is done manually on an electric machine, and this time, moreover, it is the carriage--not the typebar sector--that is shifted. To understand shift-locking, study the linkages of GB-106 (courtesy of Brother International Corporation).

was incorrectly typed, as in Fig. 3-18, with an end result that a half space is between the corrected word and adjacent words, rather than the normal space.

In the mechanism illustrated in Fig. 3-19, as in most half space mechanisms, the half space key must be held down while the characters are being typed. See Fig. 3-19.

When the half space key (EH-137) is depressed, the key lever (EH-138) pushes the half space rod (EH-162) backward, which in turn pushes the half space link (left-EH-146) counterclockwise and, simultaneously, the half space link (right—EH-151) clockwise. The operation link (EH-152), which is on the same shaft as the half space link (right—EH-151), is pushed by its bend counterclockwise to turn the escapement crank (EJ-2) clockwise.

The escapement crank (EJ-2) pushes the half space ratchet (EJ-16 of Fig. 3-13) so the carriage moves one-half pitch, until the space ratchet is disengaged from the space rack (EK-102, 302, Fig. 3-13), and the half space ratchet engages with the rack. The carriage remains at one-half pitch so long as the half space key (EH-137) is kept depressed. The typing keys can then be actuated.

When the half space key is released, the key lever (EH-138) is pulled by a spring (EH-139), and the rod (EH-162) is pulled by the spring (EH-145). The links (EH-146 and EH-151) are pulled by the spring (EH-150), and the escapement crank (EJ-2), half space ratchet (EJ-16), and space ratchet (EJ-22) are pulled to their normal positions by a spring (EJ-20—also Fig. 3-13).

SPACE MECHANISMS

The *space mechanism* moves the carriage leftward when the space bar is depressed. The mechanisms here illustrated are divided into single space and repeat space functions.

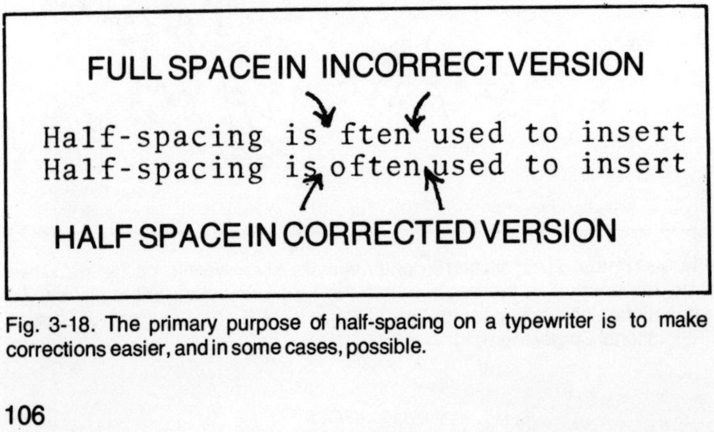

Fig. 3-18. The primary purpose of half-spacing on a typewriter is to make corrections easier, and in some cases, possible.

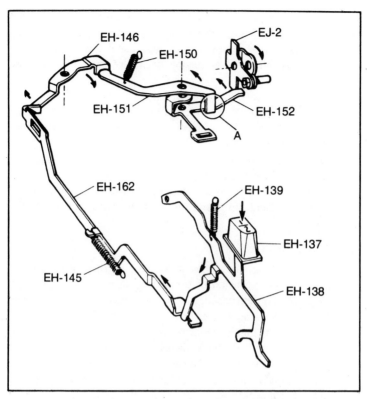

Fig. 3-19. Study this illustration, along with the text, to understand the half-space mechanism (courtesy of Brother International Corporation).

Single Space Mechanism

In the context of space mechanisms, single space means that when the space bar is depressed with moderate pressure, the carriage moves one pitch. See Fig. 3-20.

When the space bar is depressed, the space bar connector is pushed and operates escape crank B, and pushes the half space ratchet. The carriage moves one-half pitch.

When the space bar is released, it returns to home position. The half space ratchet disengages from the space ratchet wheel, and the full pitch of the carriage movement is completed.

Repeat Space Mechanism

Repeat space means that the carriage will continue to move leftward, engaging and disengaging with consecutive teeth of the escapement rack (thus, a pitch at a time), for as long as the repeat space key is held down. Refer again to Fig. 3-20.

When the space repeat key is depressed, the space repeat connector is pushed. The tension spring of the space repeat operating link is pulled.

The tension spring operates repeat balance and the pawl engages with the ratchet wheel. Simultaneously, the space ratchet comes off the space ratchet wheel, and a half space travel of the carriage is accomplished.

The ratchet wheel skips the pawl of the space repeat balance, and the space ratchet engages with the space ratchet wheel, again, to complete the full pitch of escapement. As long as the space repeat lever is held down and the tension spring operates, the action continues.

BACK SPACE MECHANISM

The *back space mechanism* moves the carriage rightward—that is, against the tension of the spring drum—when the back space keybutton is depressed. In the mechanism illustrated in Fig. 3-21, this action is transmitted through the power roll; moreover, in this particular mechanism, *repeat back spacing* can be accomplished by holding the back space key down. See Fig. 3-21.

When the back space key lever is pushed in, the repeat lever hits the repeat pad and stops. The back space key lever turns the back space operating crank.

The back space clutch spring, stopped by the back space operating crank (stop condition 1 in Fig. 3-21), comes off and transmits rotation of the power roll to the back space cam, and the back space cam turns. The back space clutch spring is stopped by the back space key lever stopper and, at the same time, the back space cam stops (see 2—"one step pushing in"—Fig. 3-21).

Through the rotation of the back space cam, the back space pawl (Fig. 3-21) turns the space ratchet inversely through the back space rod and completes the back space action.

When the back space key lever is returned, the back space operating crank returns to its original condition and the back space clutch spring, coming off the back space key lever stopper, is stopped by the back space operating crank. The stop condition is again in effect.

When the back space key lever is pushed in two steps, the tension spring of the repeat lever extends. The back space key lever hits the repeat stopper and stops.

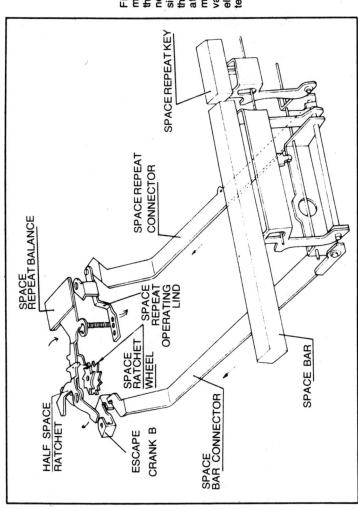

Fig. 3-20. This is the space mechanism of a Brother Model. Note that one connector (space bar connector, namely) operates into the single-space mechanism, whereas the space repeat connector operates into a repeat space mechanism. The mechanism is activated manually/mechanically, not electrically (courtesy of Brother International Corporation).

SPACE REPEAT KEY

SPACE REPEAT CONNECTOR

SPACE REPEAT BALANCE

SPACE REPEAT OPERATING LIND

SPACE RATCHET WHEEL

HALF SPACE RATCHET

ESCAPE CRANK B

SPACE BAR CONNECTOR

SPACE BAR

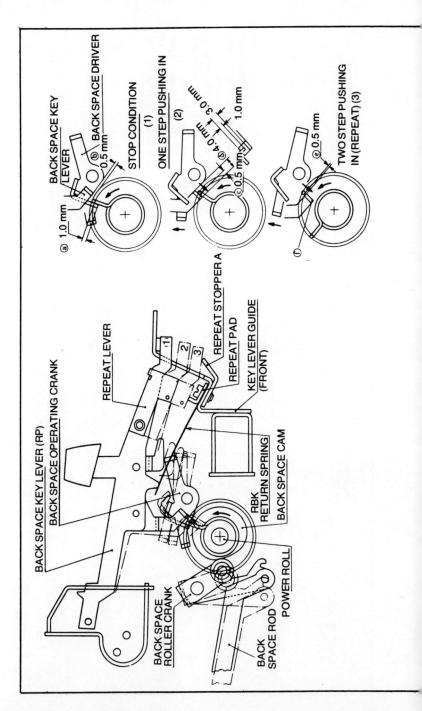

BACK SPACE KEY LEVER

BACK SPACE DRIVER

STOP CONDITION (1)

ⓑ 0.5 mm

ⓐ 1.0 mm

ONE STEP PUSHING IN (2)

ⓓ 4.0 mm

3.0 mm

1.0 mm

ⓒ 0.5 mm

TWO STEP PUSHING IN (REPEAT) (3)

ⓔ 0.5 mm

ⓕ

REPEAT LEVER

BACK SPACE KEY LEVER (RP)

BACK SPACE OPERATING CRANK

REPEAT STOPPER A

REPEAT PAD

KEY LEVER GUIDE (FRONT)

RBK RETURN SPRING

BACK SPACE CAM

BACK SPACE ROLLER CRANK

BACK SPACE ROD

POWER ROLL

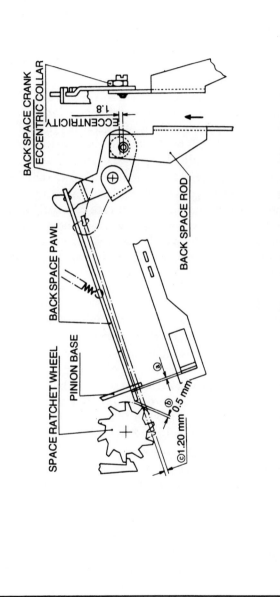

Fig. 3-21. As you study this back space mechanism, contrast it with those in the preceding chapter, in which manual effort was transmitted into linear motion of the mechanism; in this mechanism, power is transmitted through the power roll (shown in the illustration) (courtesy of Brother International Corporation).

When the back space key lever is pushed in two steps, the back space key lever stopper and back space operating crank come off the locus of the back space clutch spring. The back space clutch spring is turned by the power roll and continues to turn the back space cam, thus repeating the back space action for as long as the back space key lever is pushed down (notice 3—"two step pushing in"—Fig. 3-21).

Another back space mechanism is shown in Fig. 3-22. This mechanism does not take action from the power roll; nor does it have the repeat feature.

When the back space key (EH-154) is depressed, the back space cam spring (EH-159) is released from the back space key lever (EH-155), and it catches the back space collar (EH-157). The back space cam (EH-160) rotates and the back space crank unit (front—EH-140) is pushed backward by the cam (EH-160).

The movement of EH-140 pushes the backspace rod (EH-162) backward, which in turn pushes the two links. The back space pawl is guided into engagement with the space rack (EK-102) by the stud screw (EJ-34). Thus, the carriage is moved back one space.

The back space pawl and back space rod, after passing the top portion of the cam (EH-160), are returned to normal positions by the various springs. The back space cam spring (EH-159) is stopped by the key lever (EH-155), and the key lever is restored by the spring (EH-156).

Another back space mechanism is shown in Fig. 3-23. This mechanism is not powered through the power roll.

When the back space key (GB-102) is lowered, the back space lever (GC-12) pulls the back space wire (GC-14) in the direction of the arrow. The back space link (GC-15) is rotated by the foregoing action, pulling the connecting wire (GC-48) in the arrow direction. This shifts the back space pawl in the arrow direction, which rotates the space ratchet wheel (GF-23) clockwise.

The rotation of GF-23 is one pitch. This is transmitted into a linear motion through the engagement of the space pinion (GF-21) with the rack (GG-40). Thus, the carriage moves back (rightward) by one pitch.

CARRIAGE RETURN

The power of the *carriage return mechanism* is transmitted through the power roll on most electric machines, the carriage being pulled back by a belt. See Fig. 3-24.

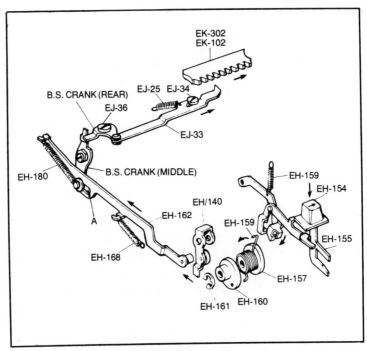

Fig. 3-22. The back space mechanism shown in this illustration is manually activated (courtesy of Brother International Corporation).

When the return key lever is depressed, the dog shelf driver pushes the return dog shelf into engagement with the power roll, which is rotating in the direction of the arrow (clockwise). This movement turns the return bell crank, which is part of the dog shelf.

The return bell crank turns the return operating link, and the return operating plate roller is held to the clutch spring through the tension of the spring. The return bell crank is held in this status by the return lock plate.

The return clutch spring winds itself around the return gear and transmits the rotation of the power roll to the return gear. The return gear turns the return drum, winds the return belt, and thus the carriage returns.

As the mechanism goes through the foregoing sequence, two other conditions have to be fulfilled. Line spacing must be accomplished; and the power against the carriage must be eliminated when the carriage hits the margin stop. These functions will be explained in the paragraphs immediately following.

To see another carriage return mechanism, refer to Fig. 3-25 (also included in this illustration are the line spacing mechanism and, in Fig. 3-26, the mechanism that disengages the return clutch so the power will cut off from the mechanism when the carriage hits the margin stop). When the carriage return key (JB-107) is depressed, the A portion on the return key lever unit (JJ-1) will depress the B portion of the return dog shelf (JJ-7).

JJ-7 rotates counterclockwise and engages with the snatch roll (JM-14), which rotates the link portion (C) of the clutch operating link unit (JJ-17) and spring (JJ-19). Simultaneously, JJ-7 comes into contact with the eccentric stud for the dog shelf stop (JJ-12), where it is operative until disengaged from the snatch roll, being held by the dog shelf lock crank (JJ-36).

Note a rubber installed on the C portion of JJ-17. This rubber depresses the return collar (JM-23) and operates the clutch. Then it transmits the rotation of the snatch roll (JM-14) to the return gear (JM-25). The return gear (JM-25) engages with the gear portion of the return drum (JJ-22), causing the return drum to rotate. As the return drum rotates, the return belt unit (JJ-34) starts to wind up. The tension of the return belt unit (JJ-34) pulls the line space operating lever (see the upper illustration of Fig. 3-25) downward, which accomplishes line spacing. The carriage is then moved rightward.

When the rightward-moving carriage reaches the left margin stop (JH-13—Fig. 3-26), it will push the carriage stopper (JF-62). The movement of JF-62 will be transmitted through the return release link (JJ-39), center return release link (JJ-42), the D portion of JJ-42 and the return release connector (JJ-43). Finally, the dog shelf lock crank (JJ-36) is rotated counterclockwise. JJ-36 and JJ-6 are disengaged, allowing JJ-7 (Fig. 3-25) to return to its original position. Meanwhile, the clutch is released, and the transmission of the rotation of the snatch roll to return gear (JM-25) is discontinued.

MARGIN STOPS

Margin stops per se are set manually on electric typewriters. However, as I pointed out in the previous section, the left margin stop mechanism must be interconnected to the carriage return mechanism in such a manner as to release the return mechanism when the carriage reaches the left margin stop. Moreover, when the carriage reaches the right margin stop (that is, the end of the line of typing), the typing key should lock; however, this is

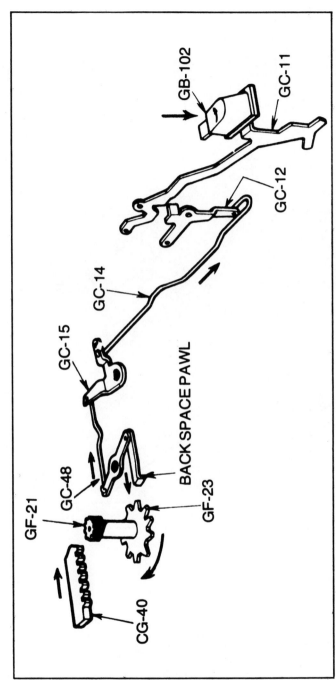

GB-102

GC-11

GC-12

GC-14

GC-15

GC-48

GF-21

GF-23

CG-40

BACK SPACE PAWL

Fig. 3-23. To further clarify the back space action, here is another manually activated system, from a Brother electric machine (courtesy of Brother International Corporation).

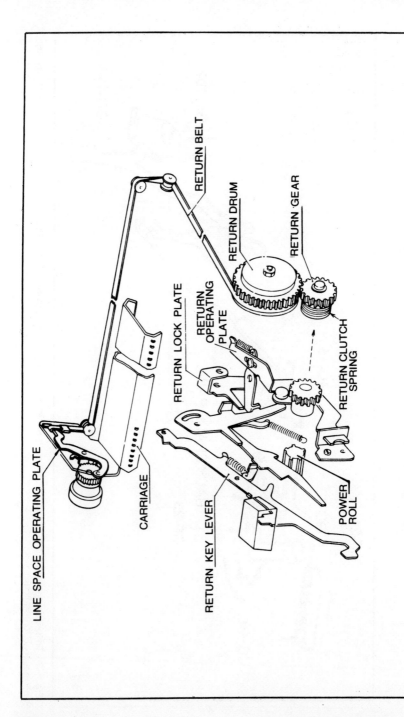

LINE SPACE OPERATING PLATE

CARRIAGE

RETURN BELT

RETURN DRUM

RETURN GEAR

RETURN LOCK PLATE

RETURN OPERATING PLATE

RETURN CLUTCH SPRING

RETURN KEY LEVER

POWER ROLL

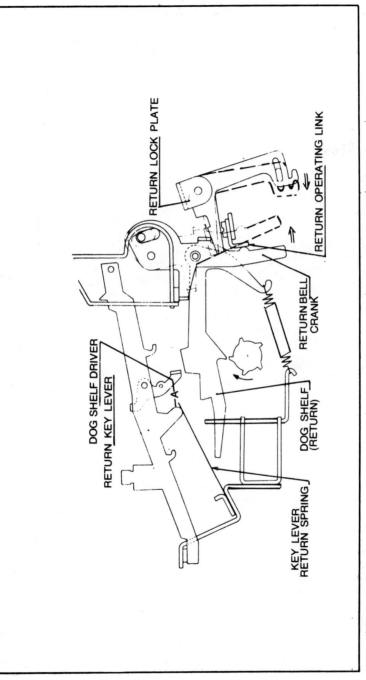

Fig. 3-24. The carriage return of this particular Brother Model is fairly typical of those found on electric typebar machines (courtesy of Brother International Corporation).

RETURN LOCK PLATE

RETURN OPERATING LINK

RETURN BELL CRANK

DOG SHELF DRIVER

RETURN KEY LEVER

DOG SHELF (RETURN)

KEY LEVER RETURN SPRING

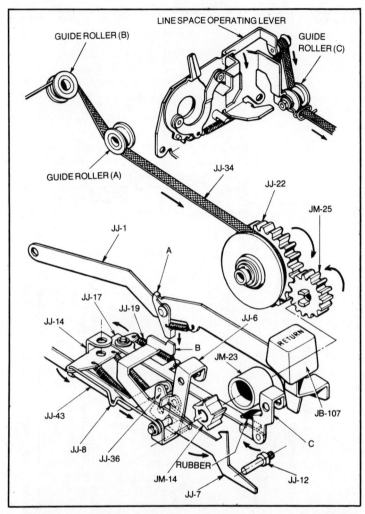

Fig. 3-25. In this illustration of a carriage return mechanism, the entire action of carriage return, its disengagement when the carriage hits the margin stop, and line spacing, is more clearly evident; however, read the text carefully (courtesy of Brother International Corporation).

accomplished much the same on manual typewriters (read the margin stop mechanism section of Chapter 2).

TABULATOR MECHANISMS

On most electric typewriters, the *tabulator mechanism* is essentially a manual operation and not powered through the rotation of the power roll. In other words, depressing the tab keybutton sets up a motion which is transmitted through various linkages and ultimately disengages a holding pawl (usually called a space ratchet) from the ratchet wheel. The tension of the spring drum pulls the carriage leftward until a tab stop pawl hits a preset tab stop. Some mechanisms incorporate a governor in this mechanism to keep the tab stop pawl from slamming the tab stop with too much force. See Fig. 3-27.

When the tap key is depressed, the motion is transmitted through the linkages and to the tab operating crank, which moves in

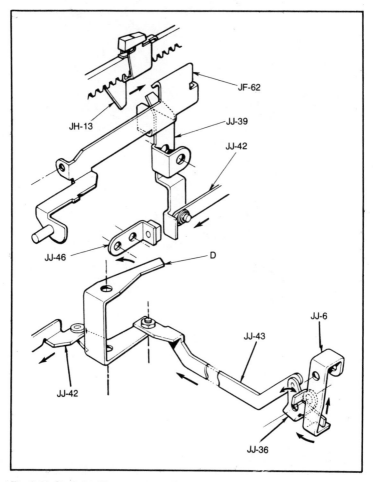

Fig. 3-26. Study this illustration in conjunction with Fig. 3-25 (courtesy of Brother International Corporation).

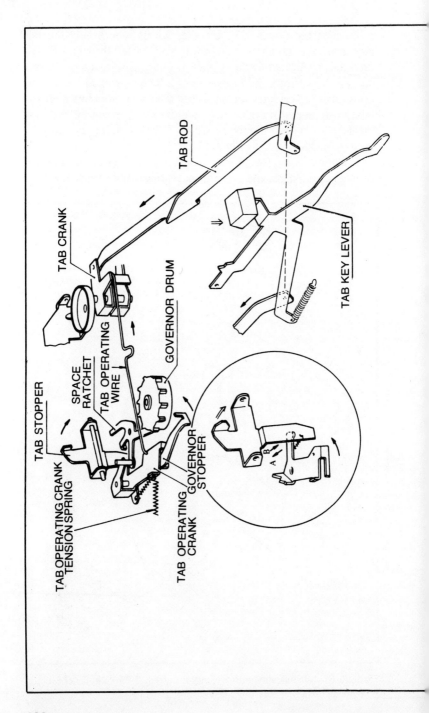

TAB ROD

TAB CRANK

TAB KEY LEVER

GOVERNOR DRUM

TAB STOPPER

SPACE RATCHET

TAB OPERATING WIRE

GOVERNOR STOPPER

TAB OPERATING CRANK TENSION SPRING

TAB OPERATING CRANK

A

B

120

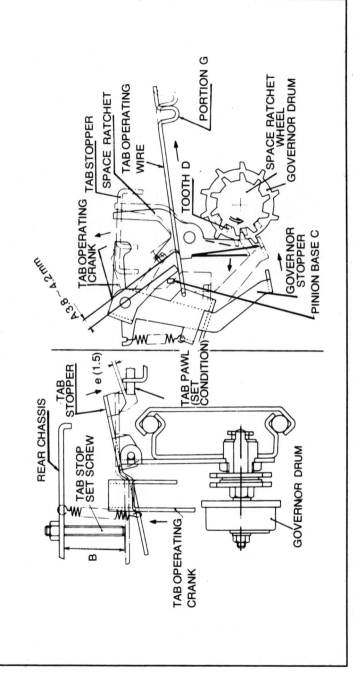

Fig. 3-27. Reading the text carefully will help you to understand this illustration—and vice versa (courtesy of Brother International Corporation).

the direction of A (see the encircled inset drawing). When the tab operating crank moves in the direction of A, against the tension of the tab operating crank tension spring, the tab stopper is freed to move to hit the tab stopper setscrew, and comes within the area of the tab pawl (see lower left illustration of Fig. 3-27).

The movement of the tab operating crank also releases the space ratchet from the ratchet wheel, allowing the carriage to run to the left. Simultaneously, the governor drum is stopped by the governor stopper (see lower right illustration of Fig. 3-27), which moves together through the tab operating crank and tension spring and produces a governor effect, due to the rotation of the governor weight following the movement of the carriage. This slows the speed of the carriage. If the tab key lever is held down, the tab stop pawl hits the tab stopper, and the carriage stops.

When the tab key lever is set back after the carriage is stopped by the tab pawl, the tab operating crank and tab key lever go back to their original positions by the tab operating crank tension spring and the tab key lever return spring. Due to the movement of the tab operating crank in the direction of B (encircled inset portion of upper illustration of Fig. 3-27), the tab stopper comes off the tab stop pawl. At this time, the space ratchet is within locus of the ratchet wheel teeth; therefore, the carriage moves about a half-pitch to the left, until it is stopped by the next tooth of the ratchet wheel, at which time the tab operation is completed.

The governor mechanism described in the foregoing section is shown in Fig. 3-28. It works as follows. The governor drum is fixed by the governor stopper (also see Fig. 3-27).

The space pinion shaft is turned by the movement of the carriage. The governor plate is attached to the space pinion shaft and turns with the shaft. Rotation of the space pinion shaft is accelerated by the large and small governor gears. The governor weight that is attached to the large governor gear is pushed to the inner wall of the governor drum, thus creating a braking effect on the space pinion shaft.

TAB SET AND CLEAR MECHANISMS

On most electric machines, the tab set and clear is a mechanical procedure, not powered through the power roll. For a representative mechanism, see Fig. 3-29.

As the tab set clear lever is moved forward and rearward, the movement is transmitted through the tab set clear rod, the tab set clear crank (front), the tab set clear wire and the tab set clear

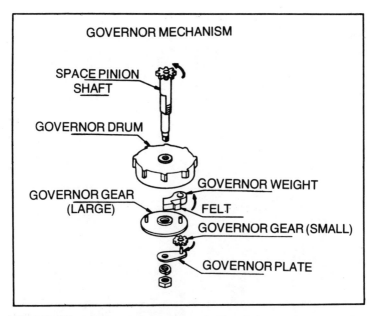

Fig. 3-28. This governor mechanism is a part of the tabulator mechanism of Fig. 3-27 (courtesy of Brother International Corporation).

crank. As a result, the tab set clear pawl is operated and the tab set clear stop pawl is either set or cleared, depending upon the direction of the original motion. When the tab set clear lever is released, it returns to an intermediate—or neutral—position through the tension of the tab set clear crank spring (not shown).

COLOR CHANGE AND RIBBON LIFT MECHANISM

On most electric machines, the up and down vibration of the ribbon is a function of and synchronized to the typebar action, and therefore it is only indirectly related to the rotation of the power roll. Likewise, the *color change mechanism*—that is, the placement of the ribbon to achieve upper half (black), lower half (red or correction) and no ribbon (stencil)—is a mechanical rather than an electrical procedure.

RIBBON FEED MECHANISM

On most electric machines, *ribbon feeding* is a mechanical rather than an electrical procedure, with the feeding action resulting from the action swings of the typebar. For a representative *ribbon cassette* system, see Fig. 3-30.

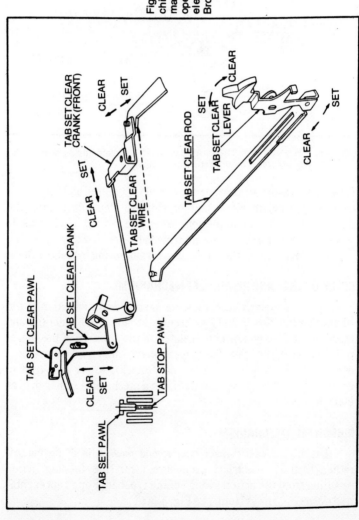

Fig. 3-29. Setting and clearing tab chips on this Brother electric machine is a manual/mechanical operation, as it is on most other electric machines (courtesy of Brother International Corporation).

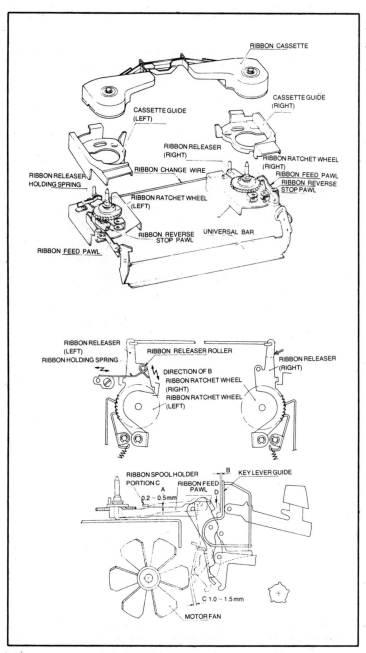

Fig. 3-30. This ribbon cassette system belongs to a Brother Model JP10 (courtesy of Brother International Corporation).

When a keybutton is depressed, the universal bar (Fig. 3-30) is moved, operating the left and right ribbon feed pawls. Only one pawl will be engaged with a ribbon ratchet wheel, determined as follows. The left and right ribbon releasers are connected through the ribbon change wire; therefore, either a left or right pawl will be engaged with its ribbon ratchet wheel, while the opposite one will be disengaged.

When the ribbon feed pawl returns to its original position after driving wheel teeth, the ribbon stop pawl prevents the wheel from going into reverse rotation.

RIBBON CARTRIDGE MECHANISM

The *ribbon cartridge mechanism* of the foregoing mechanism is shown in Fig. 3-31. Figure 3-31A shows the condition of the cartridge when it is out of the typewriter, in which the ribbon tightener pawl engages with the ribbon reel teeth. The reel cannot be turned in the direction from which the ribbon comes off, and portion G of the ribbon is pulled, so the slack of the ribbon is taken up.

Figure 3-31B shows the condition of the cartridge when it is in the typewriter, in which portion E of the cassette guide operates the tightener in such a manner that the pawl tooth of the tightener no longer engages with the teeth of the wheel, allowing the ribbon to be pulled off.

Figure 3-31C shows the ribbon eyelet operating the ribbon releaser at the end of the ribbon. The ribbon releaser is turned to reverse, and the ribbon is reeled back on to the reel.

LINE SPACE MECHANISM

On most electric typewriters, the *line space mechanism* is activated through the pulling force of the return belt—that is, the belt that returns the carriage. See Fig. 3-32.

When the carriage return mechanism is operated, the return belt (JJ-34) is under tension, causing the line space operating lever roller (JG-13) to be lowered. The line space operating lever is rotated clockwise.

The line space ratchet contacts the line space selector through the tension of the spring (JG)12). When the line space selector is set on the "1" position in the indicator (the indicator is not shown), the line space ratchet will engage with the line space ratchet wheel (JH-3), at the A portion, and shift JH-3 for a distance of two teeth. It stops by contacting the line space ratchet stop. At the same time,

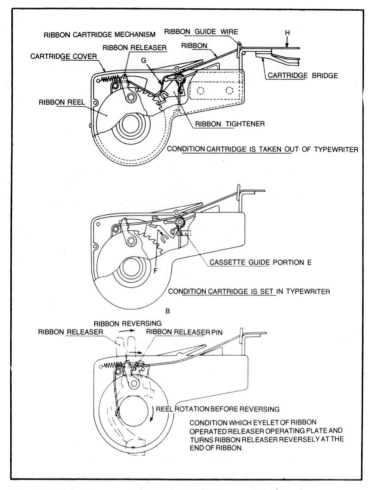

Fig. 3-31. The ribbon cassette itself of the ribbon mechanism of Fig. 3-30 is a mechanism within itself (courtesy of Brother International Corporation).

the line space operating lever will be slightly bent and stopped by contacting with the collar (JG-25). When the return mechanism is released, the line space operating lever will return to its original position through the tension of the spring (JG-15).

PAPER FEED AND RELEASE MECHANISM

The *paper feed* and *release mechanism* is practically the same on electric machines as on manual machines. You will remember that the paper feed system consists of a paper pan and set of feed

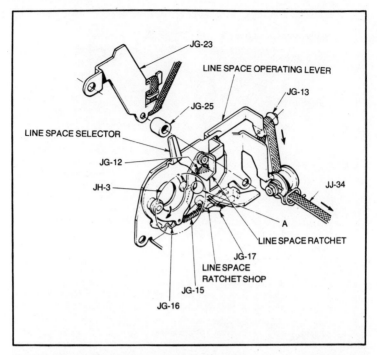

Fig. 3-32. This drawing was shown as an illustration in Fig. 3-25, since the line space mechanism action is a result of carriage returning (courtesy of Brother International Corporation).

rolls, with the latter working in conjunction with the platen to feed paper around the platen. Releasing of the paper is accomplished by moving the lever on top of the typewriter, which is connected to a mechanism that pushes the paper pan and feed rolls away from the platen. See Fig. 3-33.

CARRIAGE RELEASE MECHANISM

On most electric machines the carriage release mechanism is not powered through the power roll, but is a manual operation. See Fig. 3-34.

When the carriage release key (EK-169, 369) is depressed, the carriage release lever (EK-207, 407) turns counterclockwise to pull the bend of the space ratchet (EJ-22) in such a manner as to disengage it from the rack (EK-102, 302). When the key (EK-169, 369) is released, all the levers and the ratchet are returned to their normal positions through the various springs.

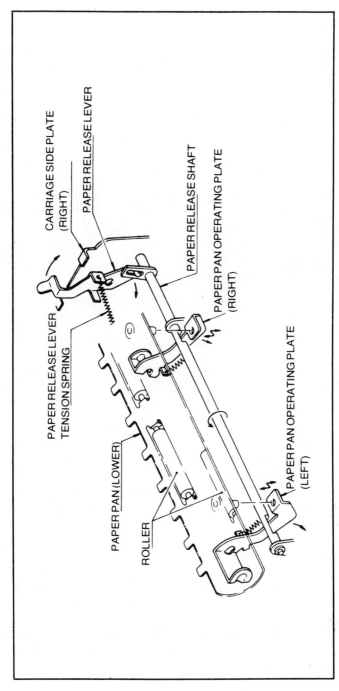

CARRIAGE SIDE PLATE (RIGHT)

PAPER RELEASE LEVER

PAPER RELEASE LEVER TENSION SPRING

PAPER RELEASE SHAFT

PAPER PAN OPERATING PLATE (RIGHT)

PAPER PAN (LOWER)

ROLLER

PAPER PAN OPERATING PLATE (LEFT)

Fig. 3-33. This illustration of the paper feed and paper release mechanism of the Brother JP 10 does not differ significantly from the mechanisms of an earlier discussed manual machine—it is simply offered as a refresher (courtesy of Brother International Corporation).

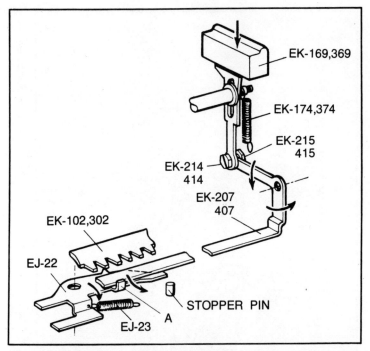

Fig. 3-34. The carriage release mechanism of most electric machines is manual—as is this Brother mechanism (courtesy of Brother International Corporation).

CORRECTION MECHANISM

It has been the trend in recent years that electric typewriters are equipped with a correction mechanism to make the correcting of typographical errors more easily done. A prerequisite of a correcting mechanism is that when the back space is made to correct the mistakenly typed character, the carriage does not move forward when the correcting typebar (i.e., the typebar that either covers up the incorrect character or lifts it off the paper) is activated. When the correct character is typed, the carriage moves forward the normal one pitch.

On some typewriters, the correcting medium is incorporated in the lower half of the normal typing ribbon, taking the place of the *red* half of the ribbon; on others, the correcting ribbon is completely separate from the typing ribbon. In either case, a preliminary step of putting the correcting ribbon (or lower half of the normal typing ribbon, as the case may be) into position to be struck by the typebar must be taken.

For an example of one correcting mechanism, see Fig. 3-35. In this mechanism, there is an extra typebar, used specifically for eliminating the mistakenly typed character. It is called the *correction font*. When the correction key is depressed, the typical process of making the dog shelf contact the power roll, to activate the correction font, is accomplished.

By the same depression of the correction key, the correction link wire rotates the A portion of the correction link, which moves the ribbon vibrator stopper out of the area of the ribbon vibrator movement. Simultaneously, the B portion of the correction link rotates the ribbon vibrator operating link. The ribbon vibrator is lifted up through the medium of the rear ribbon vibrator link wire, and the correction portion of the ribbon is set into position to be hit by the correction font. Since the correction font does not engage with the escapement mechanism, the carriage does not move when the correction font is activated.

PLATEN RELEASE

On most electric typewriters, the platen release (i.e., disengagement of the platen ratchet from the line space

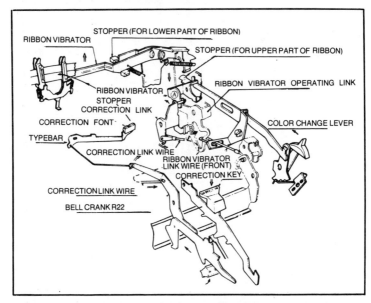

Fig. 3-35. This correction mechanism, which employs a "correction font," is quite an advanced one for a typebar typewriter. Read the text carefully to understand why (courtesy of Brother International Corporation).

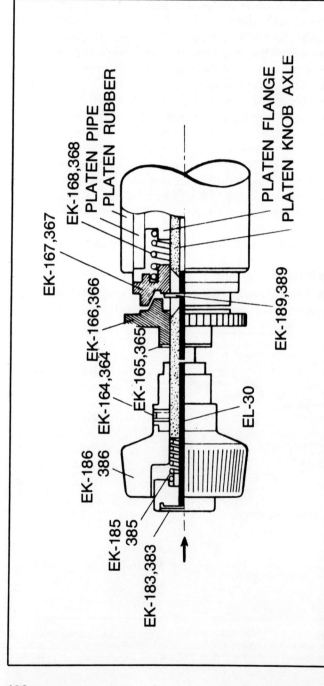

EK-167,367

EK-166,366

EK-164,364   EK-165,365

EK-186
386

EK-185
385

EK-183,383

EK-168,368
PLATEN PIPE
PLATEN RUBBER

PLATEN FLANGE
PLATEN KNOB AXLE

EK-189,389

EL-30

Fig. 3-36. This is an excellent illustration of the mechanism that allows the typist to disengage the platen ratchet, for platen freewheeling (courtesy of Brother International Corporation).

mechanism) is done manually. See Fig. 3-36. When the platen release push button (EK-183, 384) is depressed, the platen knob axle (EK-184, 383—not shown) is pushed in and the pin (EK-189, 389) pushes the coupler (EK-167, 367). Normally, the notched ends of the line space ratchet wheel (EK-166, 366) and coupler (EK-167, 367) are in mesh with each other so the platen is joined with the wheel (EK-166, 366); however, when the coupler (EK-167, 367) is pushed to disengage these notched ends, the platen is cleared from the ratchet wheel (EK-166, 366). when the push button is released, the coupler is pushed back to its normal position by the spring (EK-168, 368).

SUMMARY

Although all the mechanisms in this chapter are from actual electric typewriters, not all of them are unique to electric typewriters—in other words, the mechanisms of electric typewriters are a combination of mechanical and electrical. As you will remember, the power source of an electric typewriter is the continuously rotating power roll. This rotating movement is transmitted, as either rotating or linear movement, when certain parts are brought into contact with it. In almost all cases, the power for the carriage return is taken from the power roll (the carriage is returned by hand on a few electric machines, however). Some electric machines are shifted manually, while others are shifted under power from the power roll. Any action that is accomplished by help from the power roll requires much less manual effort from the typist, since the power roll is in effect supplying the force. Also, any action resulting from the power roll is much faster and more positive than the same action done manually. For these reasons, electric machines are the more popular, and therefore the more worthwhile to keep in repair. In subsequent chapters I will provide repair and adjustment information for specific brand/ models of typewriters, both manual and electric.

Chapter 4
Practical Tips for the Beginning Typewriter Repairman

If you have read the first three chapters of this book, it may be time for you to answer the question: *Just how involved do I want to get in repairing typewriters?* Speaking from the most practical viewpoint, you would need some quite special reasons to equip yourself for the sole purpose of doing the occasional repair job on your own typewriter. It is not inconceivable, however, that you might want to do the work yourself. You may depend heavily upon your typewriter in your own business but live in a remote area, where a call by a reliable serviceman is chancy in the first place, time-consuming in the second place and expensive in all cases, regardless of how difficult or easy the repair problem might happen to be.

Beyond repairing your own typewriter, you may wish to start a part-time business in typewriter repair. With that goal in mind, it is but one more step to visualizing that part-time business expanding into a full-time enterprise. No matter what your goals, there should be some information in this chapter that can help you.

STICKY, DIRTY TYPEWRITERS

Typewriters are thoroughly lubricated as they come from the factory. Because of the nature and thoroughness of this lubrication, the typewriter can be used for several years without the need for further lubrication. That is all quite well, but it does raise one serious problem. Because no ongoing program of lubrication is called for, and because consumer machines (home machines, as opposed to those used in offices) tend to be stored for long periods in areas where the air is dusty or grease-laden (as in spare rooms or near kitchen areas), the machine that was thoroughly lubricated in the beginning accumulates dust, lint and grease residue from the air. Moreover, through long periods of non-use, the original coating of lubrication gets gummy and sticky. The end result is a typewriter with no serious mechanical problems or misadjust- ments but one, nevertheless, that may have sticking typebars, erratic spacing, etc. This malfunctioning typewriter, which needs little more than a thorough cleaning and lubrication, is often seen by the professional repairman. In fact, even if the customer assumes that there is some mechanical problem, and the repairman can initially neither verify nor deny the problem, the repairman will routinely clean and lubricate a machine before attempting to repair it. Thus, cleaning and lubricating typewriters is an extremely important aspect of typewriter repair.

The professional repairman might argue that, because of the equipment requirements and amount of cleaning, rinsing and lubricating fluids necessary, a *thorough* cleaning, rinsing and lubrication is beyond the "handyman" repairman's capabiltiy. However, apart from the thorough, professional job of cleaning and lubing, there is an alternate method of cleaning and lubing, which might get a sticking machine back in operation. I'll explain both the thorough and the alternate—or less than thorough—ways of cleaning and lubing a typewriter.

THOROUGHLY CLEANING AND LUBING A TYPEWRITER

To thorougly clean a typewriter means to bring all the mechanical parts of the machine into contact with the cleaning agent. The simplest—but not quite the best—way to do this is to immerse the works of the machine in a vat (laundry tub, for example), containing the cleaning agent, where it is allowed to soak, usually for 12 to 24 hours. A more elaborate method is to steam-clean the machine. Professionally, this would be done in a steam-cleaning machine especially designed for cleaning typewrit- ers. Other, more elaborate methods employ hand spray guns, shower head machines, etc. However, one of the major suppliers of all kinds of typewriter cleaning equipment, tools, etc., the Ames Supply Company, recommends a complete immersion of the machine, with mechanical agitation. The machine suggested for this is the CLEAN-O-MATIC Model 500TA (Fig. 4-1). Whatever

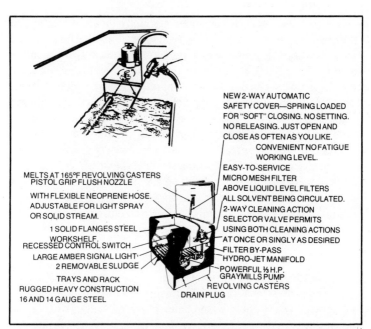

Fig. 4-1. The initial capital outlay for an agitating cleaning tank is relatively high, but it will cut down dramatically on in-tank cleaning time (courtesy of Ames Supply Company).

method is used, a thorough cleaning and lubing actually involves three steps: *cleaning, rinsing* and *lubricating*.

Equipment Requirements

The basic pieces of equipment necessary to thoroughly clean (and subsequently rinse and lubricate) a typewriter are an *air compressor* (Fig. 4-2), and a *vat* or cleaning machine. Since cleaning, rinsing and lubing requires three solutions, it would be helpful to have additional vats; however, one vat, equipped with a drain plug and a provision to save the solutions that are reusable, would do the job, although it would be highly inefficient. You should also have a basket in which to immerse the typewriter.

Cleaning, Rinsing and Lubrication Solutions

As a cleaning solution, Olympia recommends one consisting of 7 parts *Solvasol* #5 to 1 part *LIX* "12" Cleaner. Solvasol #5 is available from Socony Mobile Oil Distributors, in 55-gallon drums only. Lix "12" is a detergent-like product, especially to be added to spirits, available from Ames Supply Company, whose main office is

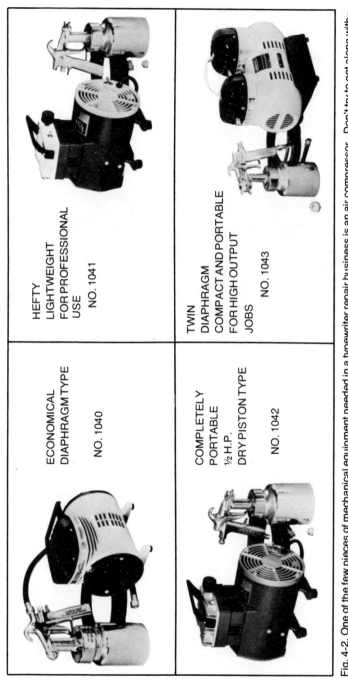

ECONOMICAL
DIAPHRAGM TYPE

NO. 1040

HEFTY
LIGHTWEIGHT
FOR PROFESSIONAL
USE

NO. 1041

COMPLETELY
PORTABLE
½ H.P.
DRY PISTON TYPE

NO. 1042

TWIN
DIAPHRAGM
COMPACT AND PORTABLE
FOR HIGH OUTPUT
JOBS

NO. 1043

Fig. 4-2. One of the few pieces of mechanical equipment needed in a typewriter repair business is an air compressor. Don't try to get along without one (courtesy of Ames Supply Company).

137

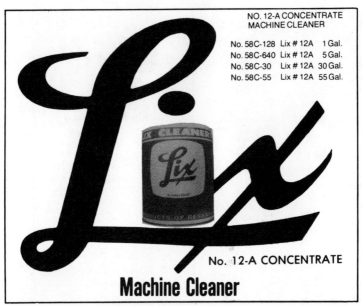

Fig. 4-3. Lix # 12A cleaner is to be used with and extends the use of cleaning fluid (courtesy of Ames Supply Company).

2537 Curtiss St., Downers Grove, Illinois 60515. Lix "12" Cleaner is available in either one-gallon, five-gallon, 30-gallon or 55-gallon amounts (Fig. 4-3).

The lubricating solution is an oil bath, which consists of 10 parts of mineral spirits to 1 part of Ames oil (No. 34L-32—quart—.946 liters, No. 34L-128—gallon—3.8 liters, No. 34L-640—5 gallons—18.9 liters), available in bulk. The oil may be mixed with a high-flash *naptha*, rather than the mineral spirits.

The Cleaning Process

Before immersing either a manual or electric typewriter in the various solutions, several steps should be taken to insure that certain parts of the machine don't come into contact with the solutions. On either a manual or electric machine remove all the outside covers, the platen, the bail rollers, the paper table and feed follers and any miscellaneous rubber parts.

On electric machines, also remove the power roll, if it is rubber, and all the electrical components. After removing all these items, blow out any loose, heavy dirt from the machine to avoid getting it in the solution.

If you use the soaking method, put the stripped machine in the dip basket and immerse it in the cleaning solution overnight. If you use the agitator cleaning machine, immerse the machine and agitate for 5 or 10 minutes. Whether you use the vat or agitating machine, when cleaning is complete, lift the machine up in the basket and let the excess fluid drip back into the tank so no fluid will be lost.

Rinsing and Lubricating the Thoroughly Cleaned Machine

After cleaning, the machine should be thoroughly rinsed to stop the cleaning action. Use any of the previously mentioned rinsing solutions or hot water. If you use water, the machine should be thoroughly dried in an oven, as any drops of moisture in the works can cause rust.

The last step is to place the machine in an oil bath, which consists of 10 parts of mineral spirits to 1 part Ames oil. As mentioned previously, high-flash naptha may be substituted for the mineral spirits. The spirits will evaporate, letting the oil adhere to the machine and providing a good, deep-down oiling. A lubrication tank called the "3-L Safety Lubrication Tank" (see Fig. 4-4) is available from Ames Supply Company for this purpose.

NO. 3-L SAFETY LUBRICATION TANK

NO. 2-R SAFETY RINSE TANK

Fig. 4-4. Separate tanks for the three steps of cleaning, rinsing and oiling save time and make the work easier (courtesy of Ames Supply Company).

GIVING A TYPEWRITER A
SUPERFICIAL CLEANING AND LUBING

Between thorough cleanings and oiling, minor sticking or binding troubles due to dirt and gum accumulation can occur. While it may be untimely or inconvenient to give the machine a thorough cleaning, you can clean and relubricate the machine with cleaners and lubricants—or combinations of both—supplied in pressurized containers (Fig. 4-5).

As with a thorough cleaning, it is not advisable to get the agent used for cleaning the metal parts in contact with rubber parts of the machine. Therefore, it is better to remove all the covers and parts mentioned previously including, in the case of the electric machine, the rubber power roll and electrical components.

Carefully remove dust and eraser residues from the interior of the machine. Clean the typefaces carefully, after putting a cloth under them, so that the soiled type cleaner doesn't drip on other

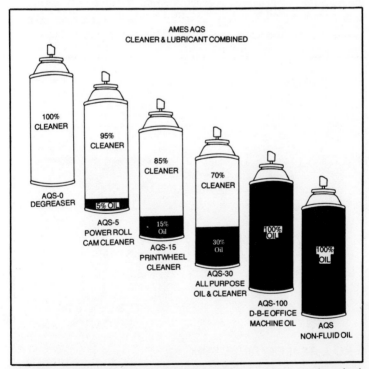

Fig. 4-5. In between thorough cleaning/oiling, sticking problems may be solved through the use of combination cleaners and oils in pressurized cans (courtesy of Ames Supply Company).

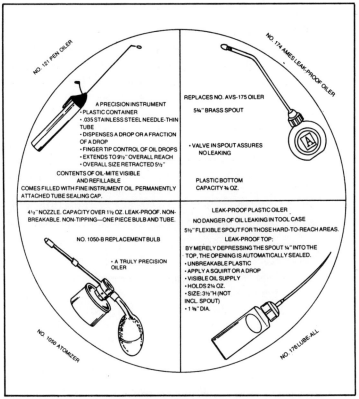

Fig. 4-6. When spot-oiling a typewriter, it's important to get the oil at the problem point, not on the platen, feed rolls or power roll; an oiler with a long spout will help in this task (courtesy of Ames Supply Company).

parts. If the typefaces are quite dirty, don't try to use the blotting paper or "dough" for cleaning. Instead, use a liquid cleaning agent.

Use the spray cleaner—or combination cleaner and oil—to do a job on the internal parts of the machine, following directions. Clean the keylever comb slots carefully with a dry brush. Do not lubricate them.

Don't use any of the all-purpose oils sold in hardware stores for oiling a typewriter. Do try to oil all the parts, without over-oiling.

In lieu of an overall lubrication as described, problem areas (such as the escapement pinion, etc.) can be oiled with the special oilers for machine lubrication, which have long, thin, flexible spouts (Fig. 4-6). Use typewriter oil, being sure no oil gets on the platen, power roll, feed rolls, bail rollers, etc.

COSMETIC CLEANING

Some professional repairmen seem to pay an inordinate amount of attention to the outward cleanliness of a typewriter. For this purpose, special cleaners and polishers are available (Fig. 4-7). Be sure to use the correct cleaner and polisher on painted surfaces, keybuttons, clear plastic card holders, etc., as the wrong solutions (such as denatured alcohol, for instance) can cause fogging. Don't clean the plastic keybuttons too enthusiastically, as it is possible to remove the characters. However, if this should happen, Ames Supply Company provides lacquer sticks (Fig. 4-8) in various colors, which can be rubbed into the engraved lines to restore the lost characters. Typewriters can be given the reconditioned look by painting the covers with special paints (Fig. 4-9). Paint ovens (Fig. 4-10) are used to give the paint job a professional look.

SELECTING TOOLS

Many of the tools which you have in your toolbox will be useful in working on typewriters. However, special tools, which anticipate the special needs of the professional typewriter repairman, are provided for the industry. The question of whether to get tools in standard or metric sizes is difficult, but it can be solved by getting both. Thin wrenches (Fig. 4-11) are especially useful, as are hex wrench and socket sets (Fig. 4-12).

A few special tools include the following:

☐ Spring hooks (Fig. 4-13).
☐ Typebar twisters (Fig. 4-14).

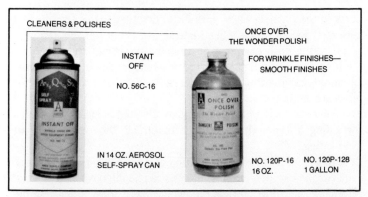

Fig. 4-7. For typewriter cosmetics, it's smart to use cleaners and polishes prepared for the industry, as some products around the home or shop may mar the finish or fog plastic parts (courtesy of Ames Supply Company).

ENGRAVER'S LACQUER STIK

BRIGHTEN UP CARRIAGE SCALES, TABULATOR RACKS AND KEYBOARDS.
RUB INTO ENGRAVED LINES. WIPE OFF EXCESS.

AVAILABLE IN THE FOLLOWING COLORS:

NO. 150-B BLACK	NO. 150-W WHITE
NO. 150-R RED	NO. 150-Y YELLOW

Fig. 4-8. Lacquer stick, which can be rubbed in engraved lines to restore lost characters, can save explanations and embarrassment when returning a typewriter to the customer (courtesy of Ames Supply Company).

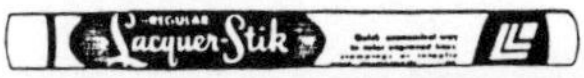

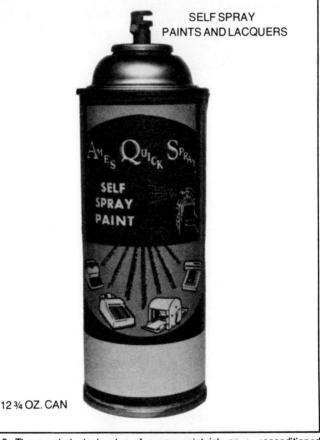

Fig. 4-9. The psychological value of a new paint job on a reconditioned typewriter is tremendous. Paints are available in a variety of "typewriter colors" (courtesy of Ames Supply Company).

SPECIFICATIONS FOR MODELS
1650-AMC & 1650-AM

ELECTRIC: 115V, 60 Cycle, Rating 2000 Watts, Temperature
  Ambient to 350°.

SIZE: 7.2 Cubic Ft. Inside dimensions: 26″W x 24″D x 20″H.
  Outside dimensions: 30″W x 26½″D x 24″H.

CONSTRUCTION: Fan forced air circulation. Sturdy welded steel
  construction inside and out.

EQUIPMENT: Comes equipped with 6′, 3-wire cord and adapter
  plug. Two removable sliding shelves and adjustable shelf sup-
  ports. Adjustable damper control plugs into any 115V outlet.
  Complete with operating instructions.

SHIPPING WEIGHT: 108 lbs.

MATERIAL AND WORKMANSHIP
GUARANTEED 1 YEAR

Prices do not apply where special fire department ordinances cover electrical appliances.

Fig. 4-10. Paint and drying ovens help turn out professional looking paint jobs
(courtesy of Ames Supply Company).

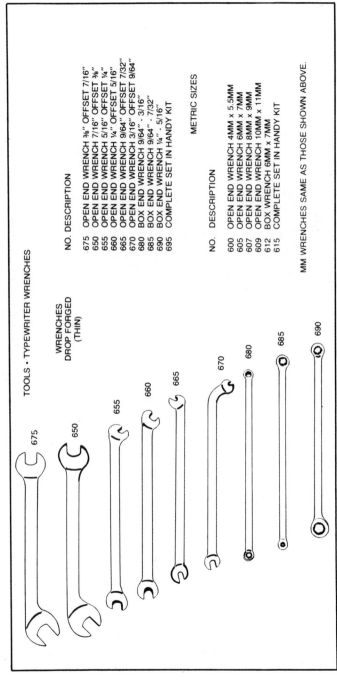

TOOLS · TYPEWRITER WRENCHES

WRENCHES
DROP FORGED
(THIN)

NO.	DESCRIPTION
675	OPEN END WRENCH 3/8" OFFSET 7/16"
650	OPEN END WRENCH 7/16" OFFSET 3/8"
655	OPEN END WRENCH 5/16" OFFSET 1/4"
660	OPEN END WRENCH 1/4" OFFSET 5/16"
665	OPEN END WRENCH 9/64" OFFSET 7/32"
670	OPEN END WRENCH 3/16" OFFSET 9/64"
680	BOX END WRENCH 9/64" - 3/16"
685	BOX END WRENCH 9/64" - 7/32"
690	BOX END WRENCH 1/4" - 5/16"
695	COMPLETE SET IN HANDY KIT

METRIC SIZES

NO.	DESCRIPTION
600	OPEN END WRENCH 4MM x 5.5MM
605	OPEN END WRENCH 6MM x 7MM
607	OPEN END WRENCH 8MM x 9MM
609	OPEN END WRENCH 10MM x 11MM
612	BOX WRENCH 6MM x 7MM
615	COMPLETE SET IN HANDY KIT

MM WRENCHES SAME AS THOSE SHOWN ABOVE.

Fig. 4-11. Just as auto manufacturers, typewriter manufacturers build the machine around the screws; thin wrenches help get into these kinds of places (courtesy of Ames Supply Company).

No. 865 SOCKET WRENCH SET
14-PIECE, 1/4" SQUARE DRIVE

NO 685
6 PT. SOCKETS
(Opening Size):
3/16" 7/32" 1/4"
9/32" 5/16" 11/32"
3/8" 7/16" 1/2"
10 PT. SOCKETS
(Opening Size):
1/4" 5/16"
REVERSIBLE RATCHET
4-3/4"
2" EXTENSION
SPINNER/EXTENSION
5-3/4" (1" x 3" handle, 2-3/4"
shaft)

No. 850 ALLEN HEX DRIVER UNIT

7 Piece Kit Consists of:
No. 850-C Amberyl handle with
clutch   No. 850-1
Hex bit 1/16" x 4 3/4"
No. 850-2 Hex bit 5/64" x 4 3/4"
No. 850-3 Hex bit 3/32" x 4 3/4"
No. 850-4 Hex bit 1/8" x 4 3/4"
No. 850-5 Hex bit 5/32" x 4 3/4"
No. 850-6 Hex bit 3/16" x 4 3/4"

IN HANDY PLASTIC CASE

Fig. 4-12. A variety of good quality tools will make your work a pleasure (courtesy of Ames Supply Company).

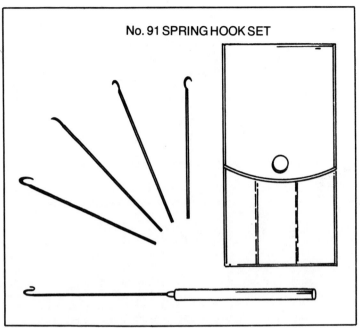

Fig. 4-13. A spring hook may be your most often used tool (courtesy of Ames Supply Company).

- ☐ Keylever benders (Fig. 4-15).
- ☐ Ribbon eyelet pliers (Fig. 4-16).
- ☐ Link benders (Fig. 4-17).
- ☐ Ribbon vibrator arm benders (Fig. 4-18).
- ☐ Segment pick (Fig. 4-19).
- ☐ Type cleaning brushes (Fig. 4-20).

Also see Table 4-1 for a suggested basic tool kit, as supplied by Ames Supply Company.

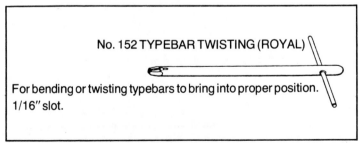

Fig. 4-14. If a typebar won't go through the guide correctly, the solution may simply be twisting it slightly (courtesy of Ames Supply Company).

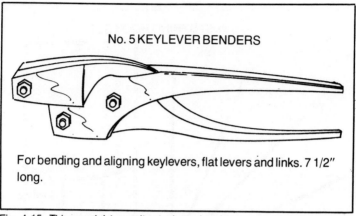

No. 5 KEYLEVER BENDERS

For bending and aligning keylevers, flat levers and links. 7 1/2" long.

Fig. 4-15. This special typewriter tool can bend levers and links back into alignment (courtesy of Ames Supply Company).

DESIGNING A WORKSHOP

If you begin thinking about a workshop, it follows almost logically that you'll also be thinking about some way to attract business. You'll also be wondering whether to stress service, i.e., machine repair, combine service with the sales of new or used machines or stress sales. Even if such an operation were conducted from your home (as in a garage), you would probably benefit from storefront frontage, even if at first the area was only a place to receive repair jobs.

Making the decision of whether to stress service or sales will be an important one in the long run, because it will determine how you plan to allocate your available capital between resale stock and equipment. If, for example, a repair business has a real potential for expansion, it would not be a viable long-range plan to set the repair shop in an area that is too small, or to invest money in equipment that would later prove inadequate. Moreover, most professionals advise against making up homemade equipment from random parts, since working the bugs out of such a system takes too much time from the more profitable activity of actual repair.

In the early stages of planning, it would be extremely helpful to receive advice from professionals and people in the industry. To that end, here is a quote from the current Ames Supply Company catalog: "Over the years, Ames Supply Company has helped thousands of dealers to set up shops or modernize their old ones. Ames would like to help you to select your equipment and to supply information on any problem you might have."

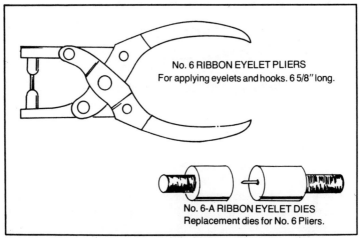

Fig. 4-16. With this tool you may avoid the task of ordering ribbons with eyelets (courtesy of Ames Supply Company).

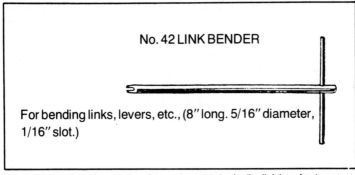

Fig. 4-17. A complete tool set can't be without this tool—the link bender (courtesy of Ames Supply Company).

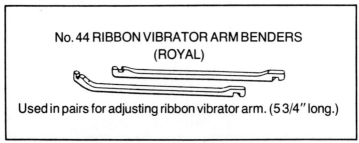

Fig. 4-18. Special tools for the typewriter repair industry can't be purchased in your local hardware store (courtesy of Ames Supply Company).

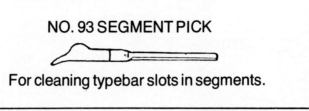

NO. 93 SEGMENT PICK

For cleaning typebar slots in segments.

Fig. 4-19. The segment pick is also an essential tool (courtesy of Ames Supply Company).

See Fig. 4-21 for a suggested floor plan, as provided by the Ames Supply Company, for a storefront and shop. Also, see Table 4-2 to understand what the numbered components of Fig. 4-21 represent and for a suggested list of shop and cleaning room accessories.

SECURING TECHNICAL INFORMATION ON TYPEWRITERS

In later chapters I will give step-by-step detailed instructions for repairing specific models of certain brand-name typewriters. While it is a temptation to say that this specific information is all you will need to work on other brand/models, it would be something of an overstatement to say it. The fact is that in all cases you should attempt to get the appropriate service manuals from the manufacturing or distributing firm. If you will need parts to complete the repair, you may get miscellaneous parts from Ames Supply Company and specific parts from either Ames or the manufacturer. To do this, you will need the appropriate parts catalog.

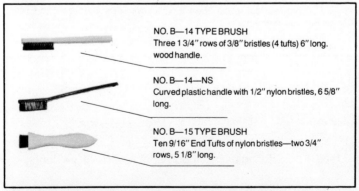

NO. B—14 TYPE BRUSH
Three 1 3/4" rows of 3/8" bristles (4 tufts) 6" long. wood handle.

NO. B—14—NS
Curved plastic handle with 1/2" nylon bristles, 6 5/8" long.

NO. B—15 TYPE BRUSH
Ten 9/16" End Tufts of nylon bristles—two 3/4" rows, 5 1/8" long.

Fig. 4-20. Don't criticize the typical user for not keeping typefaces clean—just be prepared to do it yourself (courtesy of Ames Supply Company).

Table 4-1. A Basic Typewriter Tool Kit (courtesy of Ames Supply Company).

	Ames Basic Tool Kit		
NO.	**DESCRIPTION**	**NO.**	**DESCRIPTION**
81-6	Screwdriver - 6" Blade, 3/16" Bit	509	Pilot Punch Kit - For Removal Of
81-8	Screwdriver - 8" Blade, 7/32" Bit		Spring or Roll Pins, Sizes: 1/16"
79-6	Screwdriver - 6" Blade, 9/64" Bit		5/64" 3/32" 1/8"
A-216-8	Screwdriver - 8" Blade, 5/32" Bit	1115	Special IBM Spring Hook - Spring
A-116-3	Pocket Clip Screwdriver - 3"		Loaded
	Blade, 3/32" Bit	910	Puller- 11 1/4"L, 3/16" Dia.
A-416-8	Screwdriver - 8" Blade, 1/4" Bit	92	Spring Hook & Scriber
881	Phillips Screwdriver - 6 1/2"L,	866	Boley Style Fine Tip Tweezers-
	3/16" Bit		5"L
883	Phillips Screwdriver - 7 5/8"L,	104-7	Extra Long Tweezers - Serrat-
	1/4" Bit		ed Tips, 6 3/4" L
16-5 1/2"	Parallel Flat Nose Cutting	103	Straight Nose Locking Forceps
	pliers - Open Throat, Comppound	74	Needle File Kit - 12 Sizes: No. 2
	Leverage, 5 1/2" L		Cut, 5 5/8"L
714	Tip Cutting Pliers - Jaw Size: 1/2"L	63	Handle For Files
	X7/32"W,4" Overall Leng	123	Wet Stone - Fine/Coarse
773	Short Needle Nose Pliers - Long	B-2	Cleaning Brush - For Inner
	Handle 8" L		Machine Parts, 1 3/8" Bristles,
704	Wiring Pliers - Serrated Duck		3/4"W
	Bill Jaws, 7 7/8"L	B-14-OS	Type Brush - (3) 1 1/4" Rows, 3/8"
713	Wiring & Pick-Up Pliers - Serrat-		Bristles, 6"L
	ed Jaws, Dowel Pin, Jaw Sizes	B-15	Type Brush - 9/16" End Tufts,
	Closed: 2 7/16" L X 1/2" W		5 1/8"L
350	Flat Double-End Spanner	HJJ-87-8	Set Screw Starter - 8"L
	Wrench Set - One End 5°, Other	174	Oiler
	End 75° Angle, Sizes: 1/8" - 1/4"	475	Small Magnetizer/Demagnetizer
351	Metric Double-End Spanner	1022	Keeper Setter - Small
	Wrench Set - 12 Sizes: 3MM - 10MM	77	Brass Hammer
354	Socket Wrench - 5MM	76	Mechanic's Hammer
356	Socket Wrench - 6MM	1380	Retractable Knife - Small
357	Socket Wrench - 7MM	734	Adjustable Wrench - 6"
1950	Socket Wrench - 1/4" Hex Opening	93	Segment Pick
1955	Socket Wrench - 5/16" Hex Opening	320MM	7 Piece Open End Metric Wrench
349	Olympia Adder Millimeter		Set-Sizes: 5.5MM - 11MM
	Wrench Kit	322	10 Piece Combination Offset Open
348	Hex Key Set - Millimeter Sizes:		End/Box End Wrench Set
	1.27MM - 5MM	323	8 Piece Open End Wrench Set
45	Standard Hex Key Set - Sizes:	83A	Parts Storage Box
	.050 - 5/32"	26A	Parts Storage Box
96	Centering Punch - 1/4" X 4"	789	Cleaning Cloths (5)
94	Pin Driving Punch - 1/4" X 4" With	1975	First Aid Kit Included
	1/16" PT.	916	Platt Tool Case Included
	Tool Kit No. 916 (TOOL CASE INCLUDED)		

Getting Service Manuals and Parts Catalogs From Companies Other Than IBM

Please understand that in giving the following information on typewriter firms, I have not personally been authorized to speak on behalf of these companies. You may correspond with any of them only to have your request denied or ignored. However, I do believe that an intelligently written, concise letter will draw the desired response. Your basic problem will be whether to request a service manual and parts catalog for one specific machine—in which case you would logically be planning to service your own machine—or a selection of manuals and parts catalogs for a variety of models manufactured by the firm. In the former case, you will have to provide the model number of your typewriter; in the latter case, your request may be up for some discussion, particularly if it is the policy of the company to establish franchised service dealers.

In no case is it advisable to try and order brand-name parts by simply providing the company with a visual or laymen's description

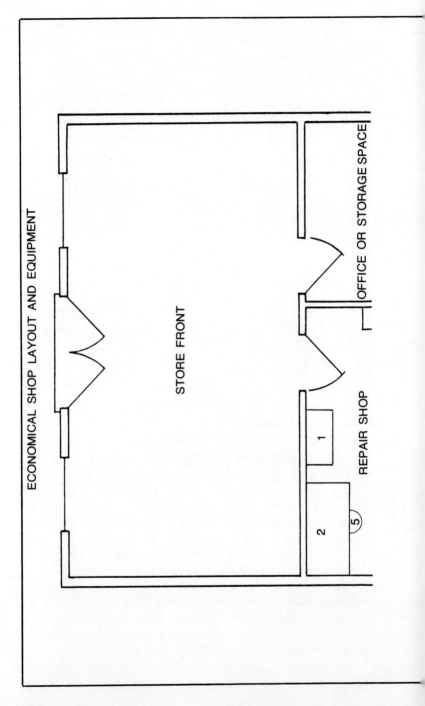

ECONOMICAL SHOP LAYOUT AND EQUIPMENT

STORE FRONT

OFFICE OR STORAGE SPACE

REPAIR SHOP

1

2

5

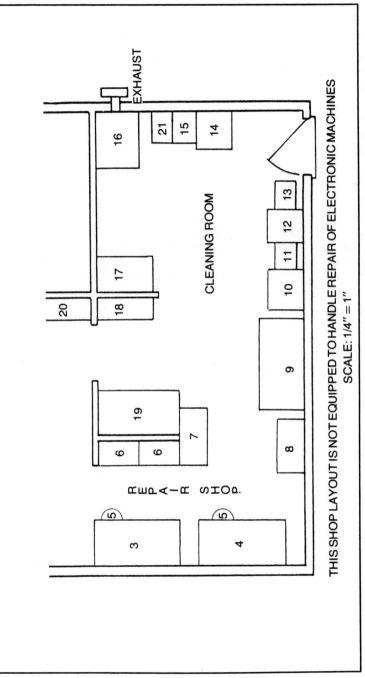

Fig. 4-21. Perhaps this shop plan and equipment layout can be modified to fit your garage, if you're planning a part-time business, or one that can grow (courtesy of Ames Supply Company).

of the part; you will always get a more favorable—and faster— response if you furnish the part number, as taken from an authorized parts catalog, together with the correct name of the part. Alternatively, you may order parts from, or through, Ames Supply Company. Here is an excerpt from the current Ames catalog, explaining its policy on parts ordering.

"The parts listed in the following section (the section mentioned is catalog pages of miscellaneous items, only a few of which are listed by manufacturers' numbers) are some of the miscellaneous items and assortment carried in stock. We stock and will continue to stock many thousands of available manufacturers' parts as well as many hundreds of parts that are now obsolete and no longer available from the manufacturer.

"Because our stock of parts is growing larger and more complex every day, it is becoming more difficult to publish a parts catalog of the items we stock as we have done in the past. Therefore, we do not publish a parts catalog.

"Since our stock numbers for parts are the same as each individual manufacturer's part number, we suggest that whenever possible you use their catalogs and parts number for ordering from Ames branches and agents. If you do not have a number send a sample or drawing of the part needed along with complete information as to the serial number of the machine, make, model, pitch, color, etc., and we will fill in the part numbers for you.

"If you cannot obtain the manufacturer's parts catalog you need, please let us know and we will try to supply what you want on special order. We do not keep a current list for parts catalogs in our offices due to their constant changing in availability and price. We will be glad to obtain this information for you upon your request if catalogs are needed."

The end of the foregoing paragraph is the end of the Ames catalog quotation.

Important Considerations

While I may have mentioned this before, it is important enough to bear repeating. When negotiating with manufacturers for service manuals and parts catalogs, you can assume that two considerations will be uppermost in the mind of the recipient of your request. Do you intend to reproduce (as through copying on a copy machine) these company publications? Do you intend to use these catalogs and manuals to falsely represent yourself as a factory-authorized service dealer of that company? The answers to

Table 4-2. The Numbered Components of Fig. 4-21 Are Explained Here (courtesy of Ames Supply Company).

Economical shop layout accessory description

Layout Number	Stock Number	Description	Layout Number	Stock Number	Description
1.	8045	6 Steel Shelves 3' x 2' x 7' for machines awaiting repair	8.	T-3000-3	Compressor
2.	2522	Work Bench 60" x 28" for checking machines to be repaired and estimating repairs	9.	2522	Steel Top Bench 60" x 28" for disassembling machines going into cleaning room
		Black and End Stops		2602	Black and End Stops
3.	2602	Black and End Stops	10.	2R	Rinse Tank
	2530	Wood Top Work Bench 60" x 28" for major and minor machine repairs — each should be equipped with lamp, turntable and minor tools	11.	4D	Drain Shelf
			12.	2R	Rinse Tank
			13.	4D	Drain Shelf
4.	2602	Black and End Stops	14.	3L	Lubrication Tank
	2503	Wood Top Work Bench 60" x 28" for major and minor machine repairs—each should be equipped with lamp, turntable and minor tools	15.	4D	Drain Shelf
			16.	1000A	Spray Booth
			17.	1650AM	Baking and Drying Oven
5.	2602	Back and End Stops	18.	8045	Steel Storage Shelves for machines drying and supplies for cleaning room
6.	1812	24" Stool	19.	2522	Steel Work Bench 60" x 28"
7.	1210	2 Flat Drawer Files for parts		2602	Back and End Stops
	8045	Steel Storage Shelves for excess shop equipment and machines going to cleaning room	20.	8045	6 Steel Shelves 3' x 2' x 7' for machines waiting to be checked out and picked up
			21.	5440	Flammable Liquid Storage Cabinet 30 gallon capacity

Additional repair shop accessories (not shown in diagram)

Quantity	No.	Description
3	871	Starter Sets of Tools
1	700	Soldering Iron
1	109C	Electric Drill
1	1024B	Drill Set
1	950	Dusting Nozzle
1	370	Moto-Tool Set
1	816	Gas Welding Kit
1	LB-1	Machine Carrier
3	102	Bench Lamps
3		Turntables

Additional cleaning room accessories (not shown in diagram)

Quantity	No.	Description
2	58C-640	Lix Cleaner
1	55 Gal.	Chlorinated Solvent
1	34L-640	Typewriter Oil - 5 Gal.

both these questions are, of course, *no*. I would suggest that you make a straightforward statement to this effect in your initial letter (not all companies are concerned about franchised service/dealers, however, and this question may not always arise). Finally, when corresponding with or trying to get publications or parts from manufacturers, allow plenty of time for a response. Which company executive do you address when making these special requests? Logic would seem to dictate that you correspond directly with the technical department; however, I usually have better luck if I contact the sales department (address the sales manager by name if possible—this information is generally available in the current *Standard and Poors Directory of Advertisers*, found in the reference section of libraries).

See the appendix for a list of typewriter manufacturers and/or distributors in the United States.

GETTING SERVICE MANUALS AND PARTS CATALOGS FROM IBM

The policy of IBM in furnishing service manuals and parts catalogs is that IBM is willing to sell these publications to anyone requesting them. IBM does not establish franchised service dealers, and in fact controls the sales of its products quite stringently, through field representatives called "marketing representatives." Accordingly, the only IBM-authorized repair service is through IBM field repairmen, called representatives in "customer engineering." What this means in effect is that no one in your town may advertise his own name, or firm name, as either an IBM sales or service representative; however, as a practical matter, repairmen can be and are trained, in independent training programs, to repair IBM typewriters. IBM phone numbers are listed in the yellow pages of regional or metropolitan phone books. The nationwide toll-free number for IBM is 800-631-5582, except in New Jersey, where it is 800-352-4960.

Identifying Old IBM Typewriters

Speaking of older IBM typewriters, IBM service manuals and parts catalogs combine information for standard and *Executive* machines. Both standards and Executives were manufactured in IBM Models A, B, C and D (all of these models were typebar machines, incidentally). The information on the nameplates of these older models does not always clearly state the model, in terms intelligible to the non-professional. Nameplates may be found in either (or both) of two places—on the bottom side of the machine and underneath the left-hand platen knob. There seems to be no clear-cut way to determine which of these nameplates will provide model information; however, one or the other of them will contain a serial number (don't confuse a serial number with patent numbers).

If you can't find any letter or number clearly designating the model of the IBM, provide the company with the serial number, together with the following facts:

☐ Whether it is a standard or Executive.
☐ The color of the machine.
☐ Whether it uses a carbon or a fabric ribbon.
☐ The length of the platen, and the length of the writing line.
☐ The pitch.
☐ The number of characters on the keyboard.
☐ Whether or not it has a decimal tab system. A decimal tab system differs from an ordinary tab system in that a series of tab set buttons can be preset to enable the typist to tab to a certain decimal digit in a column of dollars and cents figures.

With the foregoing information, together with the serial number, the IBM customer engineering people should be able to identify your machine model and tell you the appropriate service manual and parts catalog to use. They will either send it to you or refer you to the IBM person who will.

As a general rule, the model of the older IBM standard A, B, C and D models will be found on the nameplate underneath the left platen knob (you may have to move the carriage rightward to see this plate), although it will be stated as a *code number*, rather than by a letter. Generally, this code number will be to the left of and precede the serial number. It is a two-digit number, as follows:

—The code number "10" is the *black model*.
—The code number "11" is the Model A (usually grey).
—The code number "12" is the Model B.
—The code number "13" is the Model C.
—The code number "15" is the Model D.

On some Executives, the model will be found on a plastic nameplate, on the underside of the machine. In some instances, the model is clearly designated. The Model C Executive, which has an 86-character keyboard and a carbon ribbon, is the Model 41, for example. The same machine with a fabric ribbon is a Model 45. Most of these particular machines were tan in color. Executives were made with 1/32" and 1/36" unit escapements. The clue to the escapement pitch is supposed to be given in certain digits of the serial number. I won't attempt to tell you the code since I have not found it consistent. To figure out the escapement pitch yourself, you should understand that on the machine with the 1/32″ pitch, 10 three-unit characters will occupy 30/32″ on the paper.

One factor that may lead to some inconsistency in Executive identification is that if and when machines are factory-reconditioned, the plate beneath the left-hand platen knob may be removed, and a new number stamped into the metal. Sometimes this number is accompanied by the letter "R," to indicate *reconditioned*.

With Executives, as with standards, be sure to include as much information about platen length, kind of ribbon, etc., as possible.

Identifying Recent Model IBMs

In previous chapters of this book I have generally referred to all single element machines as "single element" machines; however, IBM designates this kind of machine as either the "Selectric" (code 21), "Selectric II" (code 26) or "Correcting Selectric" (code 26). IBM has quite recently marketed a machine comparable to the Selectric II, with additional features, which is called "Selectric III," for which I have no code number information.

The Selectric II and Selectric III may use either the carbon ribbon or fabric ribbon (the fabric ribbon machines are code number 84, which are the third and fourth digits of the serial number). Since the most notable feature of the coding system on IBM Selectrics is inconsistency, I can only suggest that you provide the following information when requesting service manuals and parts catalogs: platen length and writing line length, whether the machine is a single or dual pitch, the number of characters on the keyboard and whether it uses the film ribbon and Tech III ribbon interchangeably.

The older Selectrics had an 8½″ writing line with an 11.0″ platen. Other older Selectrics, as well as the newer correcting models, had 11″ and 13″ writing lines, with 13.5″ and 15.5″ platens, respectively.

RECONDITIONED PLATENS

Ames Supply Company, through its branch companies, offers the service of *reconditioning platens*. One way that a platen may be reconditioned is by grinding it; another is by recovering it.

Some professional repairmen recommend not grinding a platen because, they say, it decreases its diameter, causing the type head to travel an incremental distance farther before striking the platen, therefore changing the striking pressure. In some instances, decreasing the diameter of the platen may affect the way it contacts the feed rolls and cause paper feeding problems. However, I have never had any problems with platens that have been ground one time.

Obviously, the superior way to recondition a platen is to recover it. Here are some facts about platen recovering. The inner part of the platen is called its "core." Platen cores are designed through manufacture to take either a cushion rubber cover or a non-cushion rubber cover. Cushion platens have a rubber wall thickness of over 3/16″. Non-cushion platens have a wall thickness of under 3/16″ (Fig. 4-22). You cannot put a cushion rubber on a non-cushion core, or vice-versa.

Platens, and therefore platen covers, are coded by hardness, with the hardness selected by the following facts. *Code A* is generally used for one to four copies, most suitable on portables, or for only limited numbers of carbon copies—a soft platen. *Code M* is generally used for four to eight copies. This is standard hardness for machines that require harder platens than Code A—such as some IBMs, Underwood Rhythm Shift, certain Smith Coronas, and Royal MC. *Code E* is generally used for eight to 12 copies. Because of the hardness, it is only used on machines where needed. *Code S* is generally used for more than 12 copies, or for typing on extremely heavy paper or thin cardboard.

Generally, cushion platens have a rubber wall thickness over 3/16″ and non-cushion platens have a wall thickness under 3/16″.

Fig. 4-22. Recovering an old, pitted platen is a viable, relatively inexpensive "way out" for the customer. Ames Supply Company can provide you with more information on this service (courtesy of Ames Supply Company).

Stencil-Rite is generally used for cutting stencils, offset master and fluid masters. These are specially treated to resist the oils from the stencil. Stencil-Rite feed rolls should be used with Stencil-Rite platens. The cost of recovering a platen is determined by its length in inches.

For more information on reconditioning platens, contact Ames Supply Company, who will also provide you with information on shipping, etc.

ADJUSTING THE PRESSURE ON INDIVIDUAL TYPEBARS

Many electric typebar machines have a provision, in the form of separate adjusting screws, to adjust the typing pressures of individual typebars. On some machines there is a row of adjusting screws, accessible after removing the top cover of the machine (on the Olympia Model 35, for example). On other machines (notably IBMs) the screws are accessible at the underside of the machine (Fig. 4-23) after tipping the machine back.

At a given overall typing pressure, as determined by the calibrated setting of the typing pressure lever found on most machines, the pressure of individual typebars can change from time to time, with no apparent reason. Moreover, certain characters (seemingly the "a s" and "8s" on some older IBMs) seem to get out of adjustment more frequently than others.

To make individual adjustments, find the adjustment screws. Generally, the screws will be numbered (the numbers aren't on the screws themselves, but stamped into a metal bar in close proximity to the screws), with each number corresponding to a typebar. The number "1" corresponds to the typebar on the extreme left end of the assembly, number "2" next to "1," etc. After orienting yourself to the screws and corresponding typebars, do the following:

☐ Roll a sheet of paper into the machine. If you normally use a backup sheet, or multiple sheets for carbon copies, roll the normally used number of sheets into the machine so you'll end up with viable results.

☐ Set the pressure regulator at the normally used setting.

☐ Type every character—both upper and lower case—on the keyboard, to determine which needs adjustment.

☐ Remove the paper(s), which will be used as a reference when selecting screws to be adjusted, from the typewriter.

☐ Roll fresh papers into the typewriter. Gain access to the adjustment screws.

Fig. 4-23. You are looking at the underside of an IBM Model A typebar typewriter. Note the row of adjustment screws. Also note the bar above the screws, in which numbers, corresponding to typebars, are stamped. Turning the individual screws will change the pressure with which the corresponding typebar strikes the platen.

☐ Looking at your reference paper to see which screws need turning, tap the appropriate keybutton and note the results. If the impression is too light, turn the screw counterclockwise, in quarter-turn increments, while tapping the keybutton until the impression is dark enough. If the impression is too dark, or the typeface is cutting the paper, follow the procedure mentioned but turn the screw clockwise. There are no locking nuts on the adjustment screws, so you're all done when you complete this last step.

To judge your results accurately, be sure the typefaces are clean and the ribbon is fresh (in the case of a fabric ribbon, especially). In the case of a carbon ribbon, be sure it is of the right density, and that you are using the right kind of paper (also check such "idiot factors" as the position of the multiple copy lever, etc.). If all the impressions are consistently light, perhaps the machine needs cleaning and oiling.

REMOVING TYPEWRITER COVERS

There is no single set of instructions that can explain the removal of covers of all machines. Sometimes, removing the covers can be a major challenge. Covers almost always come off in

161

separate segments. Some are held on by screws with slotted heads, some with phillips heads, and some with hex heads. Some, such as the cover of the IBM Selectric II, are simply held on by two locking levers. If covers are held on by screws, it is helpful to have an assortment of good quality screwdrivers, and at least one that will hold a screw while removing or inserting it in a hard-to-get-to place (Fig. 4-24). Watch for springs, retaining washers, spacers, washers and rubber grommets. When removing cover segments, note how passage is made around and over external levers and keybuttons so you can replace them accordingly. Covers that can actually be replaced ever so slightly wrong can be the underlying cause of vibration noises when the machine is running.

STOCKING AN ASSORTMENT OF RIBBONS

For exacting customers, the kind and quality of ribbon impressions may be crucial to their satisfaction, as well as to their perception of the quality of the repair job you turn out. Apart from the kind and quality of the ribbon, you'll be faced with the problem of having to supply ribbon for the large variety of typewriters that you encounter. Here are a few facts about fabric ribbons.

Cotton Nylon and Silk Ribbons

Cotton ribbon is considered inferior to either *nylon* or *silk*, but does have the characteristic—which may be an advantage in some cases—of producing a blacker impression with a lighter blow from the typebar. It might be preferred for a manual typewriter, but the striking pressure of an electric machine would wear it out about twice as fast as it would a nylon or silk ribbon.

Nylon ribbon is considered an excellent ribbon, from the viewpoint of clarity, longevity and toughness. It gives an even impression throughout its life, and the impression is sharper and less feathery than that from a cotton ribbon. Nylon ribbon is available in three different grades, for specific applications.

Silk is also considered an excellent ribbon, which gives an even impression throughout its life. The impression is sharp and clear, but not as black as that of cotton.

If you must stock ribbons conservatively, most customers would be satisfied with cotton and nylon. It would probably be helpful if you were to explain the characteristics of each.

Fabric ribbons are available on spools and cartridges to fit specific machines. The spool or cartridge must fit the machine. The ribbon itself must be of the correct width to feed through the

POSITIONING SCREWDRIVER

No. HJJ-87 POSITIONING SCREWDRIVER

Heat treated expanding steel bits engage firmly in screw plot by simple pushing motion. After use, bits are restored by pushing release rod that extends beyond knurled handle.

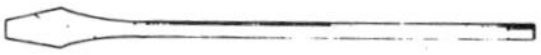

No.	Bit Width	Overall Length
HJJ-87-8	9/64″	8″
HJJ-87-10	3/16″	10″

Fig. 4-24. It's essential to have a positioning screwdriver when working on a typewriter (courtesy of Ames Supply Company).

ribbon guide and not so narrow as to lose part of the impression. In some cases the ribbon must be fitted with a hook for attaching to the take-up spool, as well as an eyelet to work in conjunction with the ribbon-reversing mechanism. The commonly encountered ribbon widths for conventional typewriters are ½″ and 9/16″.

Fabric Ribbon Numbering System

One fabric ribbon numbering system, on ribbons supplied by Ames Supply Company, is coded from TW1 through TW37 (with some omissions), which includes ribbons to fit most fabric ribbon typewriters. You wouldn't need all of these ribbons since part of them fit special purpose machines. Here is a list of ribbon that would be most sought-after.

☐ **TW1.** A ½″ ribbon with eyelets 6″ from each end; fits *Brother* Standard; *Hermes* Standard Electric and Portable; and *Underwood* O/S and Portable.

☐ **TW2.** A ½″ ribbon with eyelet ½″ from the end; fits *Noiseless* Standard and Portable; *Remington* Standard, Electric, 17 and Portable N/S; and Underwood No. 150 Core and Electric O/S.

☐ **TW3.** A ½″ ribbon with a 1″ loop on outside end; fits Royal Standard and Electric.

☐ **TW4.** A ½″ ribbon; fits *L. C. Smith* Standard; Smith Corona Standard and Electric O/S.

☐ **TW5.** A ½″ ribbon; fits Underwood No. 150 Flange and Electric, N/S.

☐ **TW6.** A ½″ ribbon; fits *R. C. Allen* Standard and Electric.

☐ **TW7.** A ½″ ribbon; fits Remington Visible.

☐ **TW8.** A 9/16″ ribbon on a toothed metal spool; fits IBM Models A and B.

☐ **TW9.** A 9/16″ ribbon on a plastic spool; fits IBM Models C and D.

☐ **TW10.** Not listed.

☐ **TW11.** A 9/16″ ribbon with eyelets 6″ from each end and a hook on the outside end only; fits Royal Electric Portable 9/16″ and Royal Ultronic 9/16″.

☐ **TW12.** A ½″ ribbon with eyelets 3″ from each end; fits Olivetti Standard Electric and Portable.

☐ **TW13.** A 9/16″ ribbon, is the same as TW11 but without hook and eyelets; fits *Adler* 9/16″ and Royal 590, 690, 970 and 971.

☐ **TW14.** A ½″ ribbon with eyelets 6″ from each end; fits Corona Portable No. 3 Auto.

☐ **TW15.** A ½″ ribbon; fits Corona Corsair and Corona Portable Skywriter.

☐ **TW16.** A 9/16″ plastic cartridge ribbon; fits IBM Selectric Model 072.

☐ **TW17.** A ½″ ribbon with eyelets 6″ from each end; fits a Corona Portable, No. 4, Jr. and Prof.

☐ **TW18.** A ½″ ribbon with eyelets 5″ from each end; fits a Smith Corona Portable, Portable Electric and Compact; and the Smith Corona Standard and Electric N/S.

☐ **TW19.** Not listed.

☐ **TW20.** A ½″ ribbon; fits Remington Portable O/S (to 1953).

☐ **TW21.** A ½″ ribbon, same as TW1 with eyelets, but shorter; fits Royal Portable.

☐ **TW22.** A ½″ ribbon, same as TW1, but without eyelets; fits *Adler* Standard, Electric N/S and Portable; *Facit* Standard, Electric, and Portable N/S; and Olympia Standard, Electric and Portable.

☐ **TW23.** A ½″ ribbon; fits Adler Standard and Electric O/S; and Facit Standard, Electric and Portable O/S.

☐ **TW24.** A ½″ ribbon; fits Corona Portable No. 3 O/S.

☐ **TW25, TW26, TW27, TW28, TW29, TW30, TW31.** These fit special purpose machines.

☐ **TW32.** A ½″ ribbon; fits *Royalite* Portable.

☐ **TW33, TW34, TW35, TW36, TW37.** These fit special purpose machines.

Ribbons listed above without eyelets work in the designated machines because those machines don't require an eyelet for ribbon reversing.

Mylar and Polyethylene Ribbons

If a carbon ribbon is listed as polyethylene, it gives off all its coating in one strike of the type head. It must be used on a machine that advances the ribbon one full character each time a character is typed.

If a ribbon is listed as *Mylar* (or reusable Mylar), it is to be used on a machine that advances the ribbon only an increment of a space.

Polyethylene ribbons make thinner, sharper characters than do Mylar ribbons. Some typists establish preferences for either polyethylene or Mylar.

Certain polyethylene ribbons produce an impression that can be lifted off the paper with either a sticky or dry correction tape or lift-off tab. Correction tapes are used on machines designed for them. Lift-off tabs are available in the case the machine will not accept the tape.

Mylar impressions cannot be lifted off the paper, but they can be covered up. Cover-up correction tapes are available for certain typewriters. Cover-up tabs are available in case the machine will not accept the correction tape.

Carbon Ribbon Numbering System

One carbon ribbon numbering system codes carbon ribbons from CR3 through CR44 (with some omissions), as follows:

☐ **CR3.** A 5/16″ × 4″ (the latter number is the diameter of the spool of ribbon when brand new) that fits IBM Models A, B, C and D, and all machines listed under CR4. Mylar ribbon.

☐ **CR4.** A 5/16″ × 4″ polyethylene ribbon for Adler N/S (after 1969); Facit; Hermes 705; IBM Models A, B, C and D; Olivetti Editor 4, 5 and S14; Olympia, except Model 35 (it won't fit the Model 35 because the diameter when new is too large to fit the machine; however, in a pinch part of the ribbon can be taken off and discarded, to decrease the diameter of the spool); Remington, after 1961; Royal, most models; Smith Corona and Underwood.

☐ **CR5.** Not listed.

☐ **CR6.** A 9/16″ × 235′ polyethylene ribbon; fits IBM Model 071, including Nos. 711, 713 and 715.

☐ **CR7.** A 9/16″ polyethylene plastic cartridge ribbon; fits IBM Selectric 072.

☐ **CR8.** 5/16″ × 4″ polyethylene ribbon, same as CR4 but with optional cartridge; fits IBM Models C (late) and D; Remington Model No. 26; Royal 441; and Royal 660 and 662.

☐ **CR8A.** Same spool as CR4, but with optional cartridge and reverse wound; fits Hermes 705L and 799, Olympia Electric 65 and Remington 100E.

☐ **CR9.** 5/16″ × 4″ polyethylene ribbon, same as CR4, but without plastic center core; fits Remington O/S.

☐ **CR10.** 1/2″ × 440′ polyethylene ribbon fits Olivetti Editor 2 and 3.

☐ **CR11.** 9/16″ Mylar ribbon in a plastic cartridge, is the same as TW16, except TW16 is fabric; fits IBM Selectric 072.

☐ **CR12.** 5/16″ × 3½″ polyethylene ribbon; fits Adler O/S, Hermes and Olympia Model 35.

☐ **CR13.** 9/16″ × 350′ polyethylene ribbon; fits IBM Composer, a special "cold typesetting" machine.

☐ **CR14.** 5/16″ × 3½″ polyethylene ribbon with twin reels; fits Royal Electric Model 565, Royal twin reels.

☐ **CR15.** 5/8″ × 406′ polyethylene cartridge ribbon; fits IBM Selectric II and Selectric III. It is identified by the pink portion of ribbon at the end, called the "pink leader."

☐ **CR16.** 5/8″ × 290′ reusable Mylar ribbon (it is reusable in the sense that it is transported through the machine in increments small enough to allow overlapping of the characters; however, it is never reversed and reused); fits IBM Selectric II and Selectric III. It is identified by the blue leader, which means it can be corrected with the cover-up correction tape or tab.

☐ **CR17.** A 5/16″ nylon cartridge ribbon; fits the SCM Coronamatic.

☐ **CR18.** 5/16″ polyethylene cartridge ribbon; fits the SCM Coronamatic.

☐ **CR19.** 5/16″ Re-Rite, cartridge ribbon; fits the SCM Coronamatic.

☐ **CR20.** 5/8″ × 405′ correctable polyethylene cartridge ribbon, with a yellow leader indicating that it can be corrected with the lift-off correction tape CR21; fits Adler SE 1000-C/CD; Facit 1850 NS; Hermes 808 NS; IBM Selectric II and Selectric III; Olympia SGE 77; and Royal 5000-C/CD.

☐ **CR20A.** Similar to CR20 but with 505′ of ribbon. Orange leader indicates that it can be corrected with CR21-B lift-off tape.

☐ **CR20B.** Similar to and fits the same machines as CR20A, with minor, non-functional differences in the construction of the cartridge. Can be corrected with CR21B lift-off tape.

☐ **CR21.** Sticky lift-off correction tape, used with CR20 ribbon; fits Adler SE 1000-C/CD; Facit 1850 NS; IBM Selectric II and Selectric III; Olympia SGE 77; and Royal 5000-C/CD.

☐ **CR21A.** Dry lift-off correction tape; fits Adler SE 1000-C/CD; Facit 1850 NS; IBM Selectric II and Selectric III; and Royal

5000-C/CD. To be used with CR20 correctable film ribbon, when used on a foreign made machine, except Hermes 808 and Olympia 77.

☐ **CR21B.** Sticky lift-off correction tape, to be used on Adler SE 1000-C/CD; Facit 1850 NS; IBM Selectric II and Selectric III; Royal 5000-C/CD. It is to be used with the CR20A correctable film ribbon.

☐ **CR21C.** Dry lift-off correction tape; fits Adler SE 1000-C/CD; Facit 1850 NS; IBM Selectric II and Selectric III; Royal 5000-C/ CD. To be used with the CR20A and CR20B ribbons when used on a foreign machine except Hermes 808 or Olympia 77.

☐ **CR22.** 9/16" × 235' correctable polyethylene ribbon; fits IBM Selectric Model 071, including 711, 713 and 715. Lift-off tabs included.

☐ **CR23.** 5/16" by 4" correctable polyethylene ribbon for IBM Models A, B, C and D, and other machines listed under CR4. Same as CR4 except that it can be corrected with lift-off tabs included.

☐ **CR24.** Not listed.

☐ **CR25.** Cover-up correction tape, for blue leader Mylar ribbons. It can be used on IBM Selectric II and Selectric III.

☐ **CR26.** Not listed.

☐ **CR27.** Cover-up correction tape, for use with CR15 ribbon; fits IBM Selectric II and Selectric III.

☐ **CR28.** 5/8" × 405' correctable polyethylene ribbon to be used on IBM Selectric II and Selectric III, and Remington SR101. Corrects with lift-off tape or tabs, tabs included.

☐ **CR28A.** ⅝" x 505' correctable polyethylene cartridge ribbon; fits Facit 1850; Hermes 808 OS; IBM Selectric II and Selectric III; and Remington SR 101 and MT 200. Lift-off tabs included.

☐ **CR28B.** 5/8" × 505' correctable polyethylene cartridge ribbon; fits Facit 1850; Hermes 808 OS; IBM Selectric II and Selectric III; and Remington SR 101 and MT 200.

☐ **CR29.** 9/16" × 150' correctable polyethylene cartridge ribbon, identifiable by yellow leader, corrects with lift-off tabs, included; fits IBM Selectric 072 (this is the same cartridge as TW16, but with different kind of ribbon).

☐ **CR30.** 9/16" × 264' polyethylene cartridge ribbon; fits Adler SE 1000 and Royal 5000 OS.

☐ **CR31.** 9/16" × 48' nylon cartridge ribbon; fits Adler SE 1000 and Royal 5000 OS.

☐ **CR32.** 9/16" × 264' correctable polyethylene cartridge ribbon; fits Adler SE 1000 and Royal 5000 OS. Lift-off tabs included.

☐ **CR33.** 9/16″ × 264′ Mylar cartridge ribbon; fits Adler SE 1000 and Royal 5000 OS.

☐ **CR34.** 5/8″ × 405′ polyethylene cartridge ribbon; fits IBM Selectric II Electronic Composer.

☐ **CR35.** 5/16″ × 4″ correctable polyethylene ribbon—is the same as CR23, but with optional cartridge, and will fit the machines listed under CR8.

☐ **CR35A.** 5/16″ × 4″ correctable polyethylene ribbon; fits Hermes 705L and 799; Olympia Electric 65; and Remington 100E.

☐ **CR36.** *Qume* cartridge ribbon; this is a 1/4″ by 300′ multistrike ribbon with blue leader.

☐ **CR37.** Dry lift-off tape to fit Hermes 808 and Olympia SGE 77.

☐ **CR37A.** Dry lift-off correction tape to fit Hermes 808 and Olympia SGE 77.

☐ **CR38.** 9/16″ × 30′ nylon cartridge ribbon; fits Olivetti Audicart 5 and 6.

☐ **CR39.** 5/8″ × 394′ polyethylene cartridge ribbon; fits Olivetti Lexikon 90.

☐ **CR40.** A cartridge nylon ribbon; fits Olivetti Lexikon 90.

☐ **CR41.** Dry lift-off correction tape; fits Olivetti Lexikon and Olivetti Lexikon 90C.

☐ **CR42.** 5/8″ × 394′ correctable polyethylene ribbon; fits Olivetti Lexikon 90C; and Olivetti Lexikon 92C.

☐ **CR43.** 5/16″ × 5½-yard nylon cartridge ribbon; fits Olivetti Lexicart 80 and Olivetti Lexikon 82/83.

☐ **CR44.** 5/16″ × 16.4-yard Mylar ribbon that fits Olivetti Lexicart 80 and Olivetti Lexicart 82/83.

GIVING A CUSTOMER AN ESTIMATE

The hourly rate of typewriter repairmen is higher than that of auto mechanics. At a time when auto mechanic rates were about $19 an hour, typewriter repairmen charged around $30 and IBM "customer engineers" charged around $40 to $45. Most repairmen also inform potential customers that traveling to and from the repair job requires an extra mileage fee. Some repairman avoid this extra charge by making routine weekly trips to outlying areas, with the understanding that a machine repaired at the repairman's shop will not be returned until the first subsequent routine trip after parts have arrived and the machine has been repaired. Most repairmen do not provide a loaner machine while the customer is waiting for the repair to be completed; however, this practice does vary somewhat with how urgently the machine is needed, and with the good will the repairman hopes to establish.

In most cases, if the repairman is seeing the machine for the first time, and it is obviously dirty, the original estimate will include the cost of a thorough cleaning and oiling, at a flat rate. This rate is from $30 to $40 but will, obviously, vary with location and inflation.

After taking on the commitment of keeping a machine in repair, and knowing that the machine has been recently cleaned and oiled, most repairmen will try to make minor repairs at the customer's location—especially in the case of office machines. Generally, the repairman will ask the occasional user of a small typewriter to bring it into the shop and save the expense of pickup and delivery.

In most cases, the cost of a clean/oil and "general overhaul" (the general overhaul may not amount to much, however, since a thorough cleaning and oiling generally solves a lot of problems) will also include the cost of a new ribbon, in the case of a fabric ribbon. However, installing a new carbon ribbon (on a carbon ribbon machine, that is) will not improve the quality of typing from the machine, unless the ribbon was actually past its shelf life. They do this because the quality of the ribbon is so intimately connected with what the customer perceives as good performance from a typewriter.

"Marking up" the wholesale cost of parts and supplies, to arrive at a retail figure, is an important aspect of business. Throughout business in general, markup percentage figures range from 30% to around 50%, with the cost of transportation of the item passed on to the customer, one way or other. Working with percentage figures can be tricky, and many merchants use a "handy-dandy" computer chart for this purpose. I prefer to understand the formula, and then use an electronic calculator to make the process quick and easy.

Here is an example. Suppose you have decided that 40% is a fair markup on a certain item. This item costs you $15, plus $1.50 UPS charge to have the item sent to your shop, from Seattle, Washington. The customer cost of the item is arrived at by *subtracting* 40% from 100%, and dividing the remainder (60%) into the wholesale price. Finally, add the transportation cost; thus, $\frac{\$15}{.60} = \$25.00 + \$1.50 = \$26.50$. The retail price of all parts and supplies should be established in this manner, in accordance with the markup you decide on, and included in the repair bill. Whether these charges are actually expressed or not depends upon various factors. For example, if you quote a flat rate for a clean/oil, which includes a ribbon as a matter of routine, the cost of the ribbon may not be shown on the bill. Markup figures on various items may vary, depending upon such factors as how long an item is likely to be held before selling it, and whether or not it has a shelf life. The general rule being that the more perishable an item is, the higher its markup to recover possible losses.

If you charge going prices for repair work, including the normal markup on parts, you will be expected to warranty your work. Some repair warranties are for 30 days; some are for 45 days.

In order to attract business, some repairmen offer service contracts under which, for a stated annual fee, they provide service for certain, listed machines. Currently, IBM is charging about $90 a year to provide service for the IBM Selectric II. Some repairmen model their service contracts on the IBM contract. If you decide to write up service contracts, you will be selective about which brands and models—and the age of the machine—they apply to. You should probably consult with an attorney to check legal ramifications and the wording of the contract. In any case, the serial number of the covered machine should be shown on the service contract.

SUMMARY

In this chapter I have attempted to describe the most commonly seen complaints by professional repairmen. These are sticky, gummy machines, pitted or aged platens, and erratic pressures on electric typebar mechanisms. Sometimes, ribbon or paper or a combination of the two, can cause problems which the customer might perceive as mechanical. For example, if a faded ribbon or hard paper produces a dim impression, the user might think the striking pressure isn't adequate.

Just as with any other activity in life, you don't repair typewriters in a void. Somewhere along the way you'll have to contact someone to get parts, supplies, tools or just information. If the machine isn't one that is included in the chapters of this book that follow, I would highly recommend that you get the appropriate service manuals and parts catalogs. The former are necessary for an intelligent evaluation of any mechanical problems. The latter will give a name and number which you can relate to your parts distributor—rather than a visual description and made-up name— thereby establishing a viable relationship with this unseen person, upon whom you will depend for fast, dependable service.

The business aspects of starting up a typewriter repair business might be tough, because competition is ever-present. Most professional repairman rely heavily upon "commercial" accounts—that is, accounts with businesses which use typewriters—rather than on consumer accounts. If you don't see many commercial accounts in the offing, you might do well to rethink your start-up strategy and perhaps look for another location. In any case, set up your shop to be as well-equipped and to operate as efficiently as possible. You'll find, even at $30 to $45 per hour, that you'll have to work efficiently to make up for time taken in other aspects of the business—including talking to customers.

Chapter 5
Making Repairs and Adjustments on the Olympia Model B-12

All of the information on the Olympia Model B-12 contained in this chapter has been provided through the courtesy of OLYMPIA USA INC., Box 22, Somerville, NJ 08876. Olympias of all models—including electrics as well as manuals—have been in use in the United States for many years. Olympia has recently marketed the Model SGE 77, which incorporates such advanced features as the single element—or, speaking more precisely, the changeable spherical element—and self-correction mechanism.

The Olympia Model B-12 (Fig. 5-1) has an 88-character keyboard. It takes a paper of 32.0 cm (approximately 12½") in width and types a line 29.7 cm (approximately 11.7") long. It is available with a choice of either pica style type of 10 characters to the inch, or either of two elite styles of 12 characters to the inch in a choice of either Spanish or American language (Fig. 5-2). As purchased, the machine is equipped with a black-and-red ribbon, touch controller, full set tabulator, automatic repeat spacer and push variable.

PARTS OF THE OLYMPIA MODEL B-12

For a more detailed description of the Olympia Model B-12, see Fig. 5-3. Item #1 is the *space bar*.

Item #2 is the "automatic repeat spacer". Depressing and holding this keybutton will cause the carriage to move and continue to move leftward, remaining in pitch, until the keybutton is released.

Fig. 5-1. In this chapter, complete instructions will be given for making adjustments and repairs on this machine, the Olympia portable manual Model B-12 typewriter (courtesy of OLYMPIA USA INC.).

```
OLYMPIA Typewriters, with their perfect type alignment
Fractions and Numerals:  ¼ ½ 1 2 3 4 5 6 7 8 9 0

OLYMPIA Typewriters, with their perfect type alignment and
Fractions and Numerals: ¼ ½ 1 2 3 4 5 6 7 8 9 0

OLYMPIA Typewriters, with their perfect type alignment and
Fractions and Numerals:  ¼ ½ 1 2 3 4 5 6 7 8 9 0
```

Fig. 5-2. The Olympia Model B-12 is available with these type styles. When buying a typewriter, the choice of type style is important, and should be based upon specific requirements: Pica is large and easy for editors to read; elite takes up less space if space is at a premium (courtesy of OLYMPIA USA INC.).

Item #3 is the *shift keybutton*; depressing and holding this keybutton shifts (lowers) the type segment so upper case characters can be typed. Releasing the keybutton returns the segment to normal position, where lower case characters can be typed.

Item #4 is the *shift -lock keybutton*. Depressing the shift-lock keybutton shifts-and-locks the segment into position, so that both hands are freed to type upper case characters.

Item #5 is the *margin release keybutton*. Just momentarily depressing this keybutton allows the typist to begin a line of type ahead of the preset left-hand margin or to type beyond the preset right-hand margin (a warning bell sounds approximately six spaces ahead of the right-hand margin-locking position).

Item #6 is the *touch control lever*. Setting this lever at "L" (light) decreases the amount of manual pressure needed to activate the typebar; and setting it at "H" (heavy) increases the amount of manual pressure needed. In effect, this compensates for the inherent difference in manual typing pressures exerted by different people.

Item #7 is the *tabulator keybutton*. Touching this keybutton will tab the carriage to a preset tabulator stop.

Item #8 is the *ribbon color selector*, which allows the typist to select either the black or red portion of the ribbon on which to type. If an all-black ribbon is used, either position of the ribbon selector will produce a black impression. If a correcting ribbon is substituted for a black-red ribbon, a change of "color" will put the ribbon in position to make corrections.

Item #9 is the *back space keybutton*. Momentarily depressing this keybutton will move the carriage back (rightward) one space.

Item #10 is the *tabulator set-clear lever*. This works exactly as the traditional tab set-clear systems described in previous chapters. All the tabs can be cleared simultaneously by moving the carriage to the extreme left and, while pulling the lever to the clear position, returning the carriage to the left-hand margin stop.

Item #11 is the *left-hand platen knob*, in which is incorporated the *spacing ratchet gear*. By depressing and holding the button in the center of the knob, the platen will be disengaged from the ratchet gear and will roll freely. Releasing the button returns the mechanism to normal operating mode.

Item #12 is the *line space lever* (also called the "return handle"), which serves the dual purpose of line space lever and handle by which the carriage is returned rightward to the left-hand margin stop. When this lever is pushed, it contacts the internal

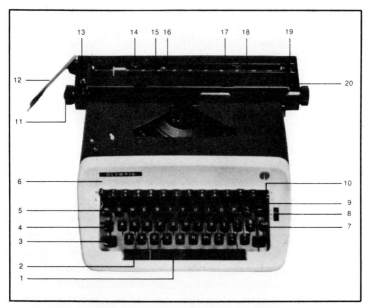

Fig. 5-3. This illustration shows the positions and functions of the various operator controls of the Model B-12 (courtesy of OLYMPIA USA INC.).

mechanism which turns the platen the appropriate distance for 1, 1½, or 2 line spaces—thereby moving the paper a corresponding distance.

Item #13 is the *line space selector lever*. Setting this lever at the numbers "1," "1½," or "2" causes the platen to roll a corresponding number of line spaces when the line space lever (Item #12) is pushed. Setting the line space selector lever at "R" produces the same result as depressing the central button of the left-hand platen knob—that is, it allows the platen to be rolled freely by hand.

Item #14, of which there are two, are the *margin stop sets*, by which both the left-hand and right-hand margins are set. Item #15 is the *erasure table*, providing a convenient place to erase errors.

Item #16 is the *paper support arm* (see this item extended for use in Fig. 5-1).

Item #17 is the *paper bail* and *alignment guide*. It provides an indicator for alignment of paper and holds the paper firmly against the platen.

Item #18 is the *paper pan*. The paper should be inserted between this pan and the platen. The paper pan has a paper alignment scale that serves as a guide for setting equal margins.

175

Item #19 is the *carriage release button*. Depressing and holding this button allows the carriage to be moved either rightward or leftward to any desired position. Releasing the button returns the carriage to normal operating mode.

Item #20 is the *paper release lever*. Moving this lever releases the grip that is exerted between the platen and feed rolls, allowing the typist to make adjustments in the positioning of the paper in the machine, or to remove the paper quickly.

DEVELOPING THE RIGHT MENTAL ATTITUDE TO REPAIR AND ADJUST TYPEWRITERS

Before attempting to correct problems on the Model B-12, think about the possible causes of these problems. Check for loose, missing or broken screws, nuts, retainers, springs, studs or rivets. Connecting levers, links, etc., should move freely and not bind. Binding may indicate a need of lubrication, or it may indicate the need for adjustment. The interrelationship of the many different mechanisms makes it necessary for each adjustment to be performed in the proper sequence, always keeping in mind what other function or functions may be affected.

CLEANING AND OILING THE OLYMPIA MODEL B-12

Always consider the possibility that the machine needs cleaning and oiling, even though it may not have been used frequently or over long periods. As I said in the previous chapter, long periods of non-use may result in the original oiling of the machine to become sticky, but with no mechanical problems having developed.

If you are not yet equipped to clean and oil a typewriter, be sure you have read Chapter 4, describing the various methods of thorough cleaning and oiling. If your judgment tells you that oiling may be needed, but that a thorough cleaning and oiling is not needed, consider the possibility of a more superficial job, using the pressurized combination cleaners and oilers, or the long-spouted oil cans for spot-oiling. For a thorough cleaning and oiling, the Olympia company recommends essentially the same equipment for cleaning-oiling as that discussed in Chapter 4—that is, an agitating cleaning tank, lubrication dip tank, air compressor, drain rack, etc.

Before immersing the Model B-12 be sure to remove all the cover plates, the platen and bail rollers, and the lower paper table and feed rollers. More information will be given later in this chapter on the actual removal of these components.

For the rest of the cleaning and oiling procedure, proceed as described in Chapter 4, being absolutely sure to include all three steps of cleaning, rinsing and oiling. If you elect to use the hot water rinse (not recommended by Olympia, however), immediately dry the machine in an oven to prevent rust from developing. Then proceed to the oil bath.

If you decide on a superficial oiling, proceed as described in Chapter 4. Olympia recommends lubricating the escapement pinion, bearing surfaces of shoulder screws, the seats of the levers and links of the moving parts, and the various flexible couplings, but only if absolutely necessary. If you oil these points, use Ames—or comparable—typewriter oil; oil lightly and don't let oil drip on any of the components you would have removed for an immersion of the machine. Polish the chrome-plated parts with a soft dry cloth, and clean the covers carefully with a polishing liquid. Do not use water.

Remember that a typewriter cannot be considered clean unless the typefaces are also cleaned. No typewriter will give good results with a faded ribbon.

If a thorough cleaning and oiling, checking of loose or broken screws, etc., does not solve a problem, you may assume that the problem is mechanical. Proceed as follows.

THE BACK SPACE DOESN'T WORK

The back space mechanism of the Model B-12 is shown in Fig. 5-4. Note that the mechanism consists of linkages, levers, springs and the escapement wheel (item 6 in Fig. 5-4), consisting of a toothed wheel and small pinion.

If the back space arm spring (7) is unhooked, the back space may fail. Hook the spring.

If the engagement of (5a) with the escapement wheel (6) is too shallow, the back space may fail. Examine and adjust the engagement.

If any *E-Ring* is loose, the back space may fail. E-rings are the C-shaped retainers (Fig. 5-5).

THE CARRIAGE BINDS

Symptoms of carriage binding may be type-piling, erratic tabulation or poor movement of the carriage during the return.

If the roller and rail are out of adjustment, the carriage may be too tight. To correct this, align the rail.

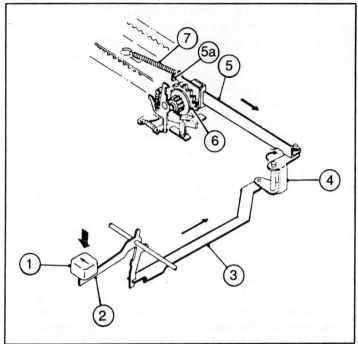

Fig. 5-4. This is the back space mechanism of the Model B-12 (courtesy of OLYMPIA USA INC.).

If the spring drum binds or is too tight, the movement of the carriage may be erratic. To correct this, free up or replace the spring drum. The procedure for adjusting the spring drum will be shown later in this chapter in the adjustments section.

If the carriage rack and escapement wheel pinion gear mesh too tightly, the carriage may bind. To correct this, adjust the carriage. This adjustment will be shown later in this chapter in the adjustments section.

If the escapement wheel binds, the carriage movement will be affected. To correct this, adjust or lubricate the escapement wheel.

THE SHIFT BINDS

The segment shift mechanism of the Model B-12 is shown in Fig. 5-6. If the mechanism binds on the torsion bar (item 4 in Fig. 5-6), you may experience shifting problems. The torsion bar is held in the left and right side frames by the shift center screws (6), one on each end, and locking nuts (7). Adjust the tightness of these screws.

If the shift balance spring (item 8 in Fig. 5-6) is unhooked or binds, you may experience shifting problems. Check this spring.

If the segment base (item 9 in Fig. 5-6) binds, you may experience shifting problems. Check the segment base and adjust; a detailed drawing of the segment will be shown later in this chapter.

THE SHIFT-LOCK FAILS TO LOCK

The shift-lock of the Model B-12 is shown in Fig. 5-7. The complete procedure for adjusting the shift-lock will be given later in this chapter in the adjustments section.

THE ESCAPEMENT MALFUNCTIONS

An improperly operating escapement may be indicated by the piling up of letters, in which case the carriage is not moving each time a typebar is activated; or by skipping, in which case the carriage is moving more than one pitch when a typebar is activated.

First, make sure the carriage isn't binding, which could be caused by all reasons listed in the carriage binds section.

The escapement mechanism of the Model B-12 is shown in Fig. 5-8. If the escapement trip is out of adjustment, the letters may pile or skip. This adjustment will be described later in this chapter in the adjustments section.

If the margin stop is out of adjustment, the escapement may be affected. This adjustment will be explained later in this chapter in the adjustments section.

Note that the movement of the segment universal bar (item 4 of Fig. 5-8), as it is pushed by the typebar, is involved in the movement of the escapement. Thus, if the universal segment bar

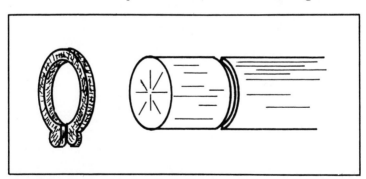

Fig. 5-5. The C-shaped washers that hold parts on shafts are called E-rings in this chapter.

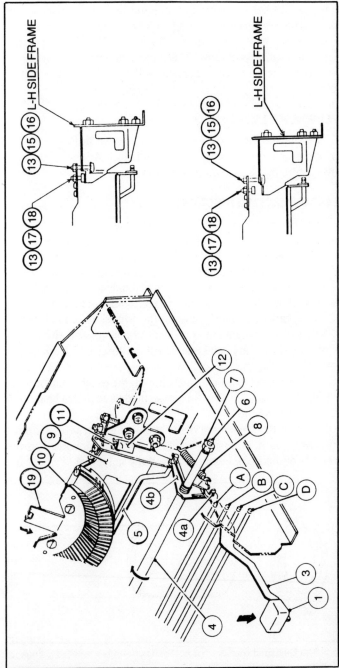

Fig. 5-6. This illustration shows the shift segment and right hand side frame of the Model B-12. The segment lowers when the shift keybutton is pushed down. It should move freely and precisely (courtesy of OLYMPIA USA INC.).

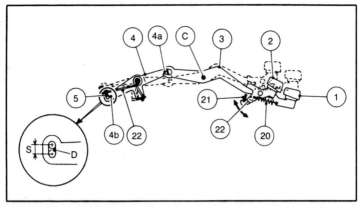

Fig. 5-7. This is the shift-lock mechanism of the Model B-12. Note especially the items marked (21) and (22). If the latter doesn't hook under the former, the shift-lock won't function properly. The adjustment for correcting such a condition will be shown later in this chapter (courtesy of OLYMPIA USA INC.).

binds, the escapement will not move properly and the letters will pile. Check and adjust the movement of the universal segment bar.

Some crowding of the letters may be indirectly caused because the spacing mechanism does not work properly. The spacing mechanism is shown in Fig. 5-9. If the space links (items 3 and 3a of Fig. 5-9) are binding or don't fit properly, spacing may be erratic. Check this point and adjust if necessary.

If the carriage rack and pinion mesh is too deep, the escapement will not work properly. Adjusting this mesh will be described later in this chapter in the adjustments section.

THE CARRIAGE FAILS TO LINE LOCK

The carriage should stop at the preset margins under the following conditions. When the carriage is returned by hand, it should lock at the left-hand margin. When the extreme end of the typing line—about six characters past the sound of the warning bell—is reached, the carriage should lock at the right-hand margin.

The margin stop mechanism of the Model B-12 is shown in Fig. 5-10. You are viewing this mechanism as if looking from the back of the machine; thus, item 10 is the left-hand margin stop, and item 12 is the right-hand margin stop. When the carriage is moved rightward by the handle, the left margin stop (10a) contacts the carriage stopper (5a) and locks the carriage at the left-hand margin stop. The margin stop (12) is set where the right-hand typing line should maximally end. When the carriage is moved leftward by

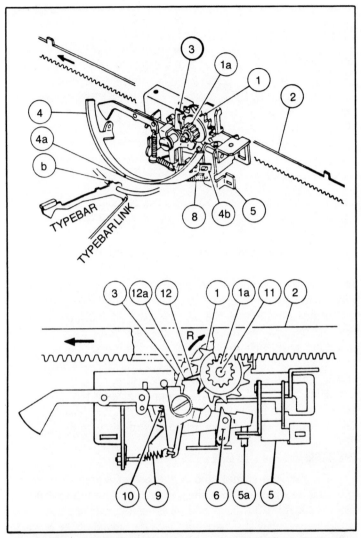

Fig. 5-8. This is the escapement mechanism of the Model B-12. The typebar strikes the universal bar, which activates the escapement trip and the carriage is moved. There are several adjustments that can be made in this mechanism, all of which will be discussed later in this chapter (courtesy of OLYMPIA USA INC.).

typing, the right margin stop (12a) contacts the carriage stopper (5a), while at the same time carriage stopper (5c) touches the back frame (20a). Thus, the slide of the carriage stopper (5) is stopped, and the movement of the carriage is stopped.

An erratic movement of the carriage can cause a failure of the margin to lock. Check the roller and rail.

Binding of the margin lock plate (item 8 of Fig. 5-10) can cause failure of the margin to lock. The procedure for correcting this will be given later in this chapter in the adjustments section.

Binding of the carriage stopper (items 5, 5a, etc. of Fig. 5-10) can cause failure of the margin to lock. Adjustment of the carriage stopper will be given later in this chapter in the adjustments section.

Failure of the carriage stopper to lock can cause failure of the margin to lock. The procedure for correcting this will be given later in this chapter in the adjustments section.

THE LINE SPACE FAILS TO SPACE OR IS IRREGULAR

"Line space" means the vertical spacing between lines. The line spacing mechanism is shown in Fig. 5-11.

If the line space feed pawl (item 4a of Fig. 5-11) is defective, it may not engage the tooth of the line space ratchet (item 5 of Fig.

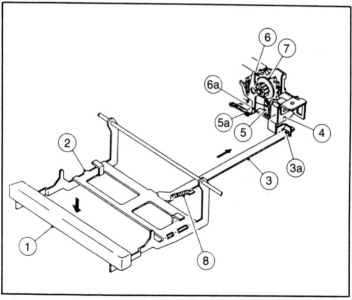

Fig. 5-9. The spacing mechanism of the Model B-12 is simple and straightforward. Remember this is essentially a release mechanism and that the actual motion of the carriage is caused by the main spring. When reading the text, make the distinction between the spacing mechanism, which means horizontal spacing between words; and vertical line spacing, which means the vertical spacing between lines (courtesy of OLYMPIA USA INC.).

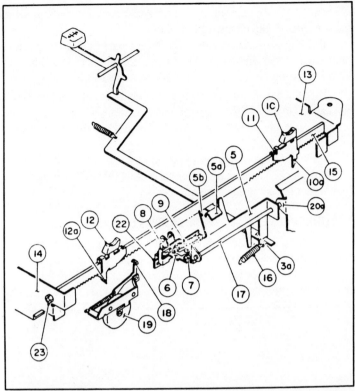

Fig. 5-10. This is the margin stop mechanism of the Model B-12. Items 10 and 12 are the margin stops, which can be moved by the operator; and the keybutton marked with the double arrow is the margin release button, which makes it possible to bypass these stops for special reasons. You're looking at this mechanism from the rear, so that (14) is actually the right hand side frame, as viewed from the front of the machine (courtesy of OLYMPIA USA INC.).

5-11), and line spacing cannot be accomplished. To correct this, replace the line space feed pawl. The complete removal procedure for this mechanism will be given later in this chapter in the removing the line space mechanism section.

If the platen binds, line spacing may be affected. Check and adjust the alignment of the platen, making sure it is installed correctly.

If the detent heel (item 9 in Fig. 5-11) is not properly formed (the *form* of a part is its shape, which may be changed by bending—or "forming"), line spacing may be affected. Form the detent heel so that the spring (item 10 of Fig. 5-11) pushes the detent heel between the teeth of the line space ratchet.

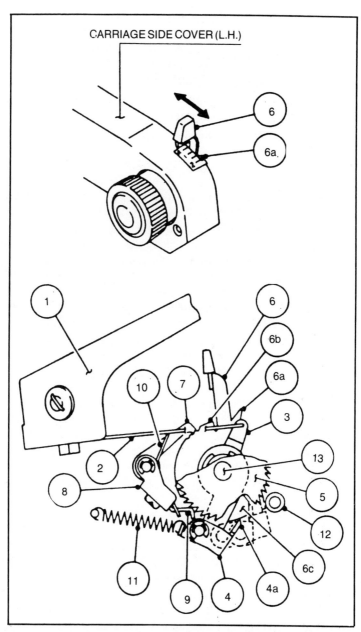

Fig. 5-11. This is the line space mechanism of the Model B-12. It looks complicated on paper, but simple in the machine itself. Later in this chapter you will be shown how to completely disassemble this mechanism (courtesy of OLYMPIA USA INC.).

185

If the line space dog spring (item 11, Fig. 5-11) is unhooked broken or slack line spacing may be affected. Replace the spring (parts numbers will be given at the end of this chapter).

THE PAPER FEED DOESN'T FEED OR FEEDS ERRATICALLY

The paper should roll into the machine moderately straight and, once adjusted, should remain straight during vertical spacing while typing. As you will remember, paper feeding is accomplished as the platen rolls, due to the grip of the paper between the platen and the feed rolls. As the paper is thus fed, its leading edge must also slide along over the paper pan. The feed rolls are incorporated into but a part separate from the paper pan. For a perspective view and end view of the Model B-12 paper feed system, see Fig. 5-12. The large circle of the end view represents the end of the platen, item 7 is the paper pan, and the feed rolls are shown by the two small circles to the right and left, directly under the paper pan (two other sets of similar feed rolls would be out of view on the other end of the assembly).

Remember that the feed rolls turn only by the action of the platen; therefore, if the feed rolls do not contact the platen quite positively, paper feeding will be affected. Check the tension of the paper release spring (item 3 in Fig. 5-12).

If any feed rolls sticks or binds while the other feed rolls turn properly, there is the possibility that the paper will twist slightly as it is fed. All the feed rolls should turn freely.

If any foreign matter, such as sticky tape, gets stuck to the surface of the paper pan, it can catch the leading edge of the paper and affect feeding. Likewise, gummy residue left when foreign matter is removed can possibly cause problems. Clean the paper pan with denatured alcohol. Finish by polishing the paper pan with a dry, soft cloth.

If the clearance between the front and rear edges of the paper pan and platen are not correct, the paper will not be fed properly. Assuming the entire assembly is correctly installed and everything is in alignment, this situation can only be corrected by reforming the paper pan. Look at the end view of Fig. 5-12 to see where clearance is needed.

If the paper bail tension is uneven, or the bail rolls are displaced or stuck, paper feeding may be affected during typing. This could be caused by a disconnected spring, loose misalignment at the ends of the bail, etc. This is a highly visible part and problems should be easy to diagnose.

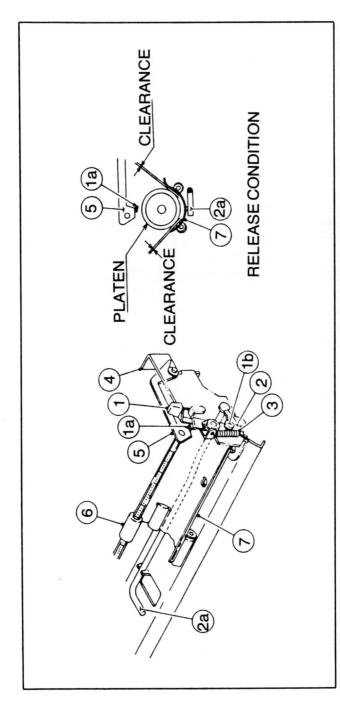

Fig. 5-12. The perspective view of this illustration should give you a clear idea of how the paper release works. The end view shows the path the paper must take from the time it is inserted behind the platen, until it appears behind the ribbon. Remember that the paper release works on the paper pan, not on the platen (courtesy of OLYMPIA USA INC.).

THE PAPER RELEASE WILL NOT RELEASE
THE PAPER WHEN THE PAPER RELEASE LEVER IS PULLED

When the paper release lever is moved to the release position, the paper pan and feed rolls are moved well away from the platen. The paper can be moved around freely. The perspective view of Fig. 5-12 shows the paper release mechanism. Item 1 is the paper release lever. When it is moved, the release pin (1b) pushes the L-shaft (2a). The paper pan (7) is released or pushed away from the platen.

If the paper release lever is misadjusted or defective, it may not accomplish sufficient clearance between the platen and paper pan when it is moved. Check this part. If necessary, replace (the part number of the paper release lever will be given at the end of this chapter).

THE MARGIN FAILS TO RELEASE
WHEN THE MARGIN RELEASE BUTTON IS DEPRESSED

The margin release mechanism of the Model B-12 is shown in Fig. 5-13. If the carriage stopper spring (item 16 of Fig. 5-13) is unhooked, the margin release will not release. If the carriage stopper (item 5 of Fig. 5-13) binds, the margin release will not release.

If the release stroke of the carriage stopper is insufficient, the margin release will not release. The procedure for adjusting the carriage stopper will be given later in this chapter in the adjustments section.

THE TAB SET-CLEAR FAILS TO CLEAR

The tab set-clear is shown in Fig. 5-14. If the tab chip (item 6 of Fig. 5-14—which is one of several) is worn, the tab set-clear may fail to clear that chip. Replace the chip or chip rack. The procedure for removing the tab-rack—together with exploded parts and numbers—will be given later in this chapter.

If the tab chip binds, the tab-clear may fail to clear. Adjust the tab chip.

If the tab rack (the tab rack contains all the chips) is bent or misformed, the tab clear may fail to clear. Reform the rack.

If the linkages of the tab set-clear mechanism bind, the tab clear may not clear. Examine the cause of binding and correct it.

THE TABULATOR FAILS TO TAB

The tabulator mechanism of the Model B-12 is shown in Fig. 5-15. When the tab keybutton (1) is depressed, the motion is

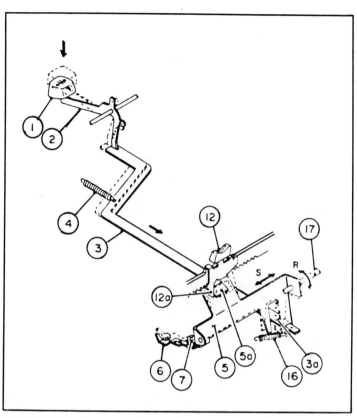

Fig. 5-13. This is the margin release mechanism of the Model B-12. It is helpful to study this illustration in conjunction with Fig. 5-10, which shows the complete margin stop mechanism. Its purpose is to momentarily undo what was done by setting the margin stops. The dotted lines are the positions of the levers when the keybutton is at home position (courtesy of OLYMPIA USA INC.).

ultimately transmitted to the crank (6), which rotates, raising the tab stopper (7) and simultaneously releasing the fixed dog (9) from the escapement wheel. Thus, the carriage moves, stopping when the tab stopper touches the tab chip (14). When the tab keybutton is released, the tab stopper lowers through the tension of the spring (4). Simultaneously, the fixed dog returns to engage in the escapement wheel and the mechanism returns to normal operating mode.

If the fixed dog (9) fails to release from the escapement wheel, the tabulator will not tab. This may require some adjustment of the tabulator main bar (item 5 of Fig. 5-15; however, the entire mechanism should be considered).

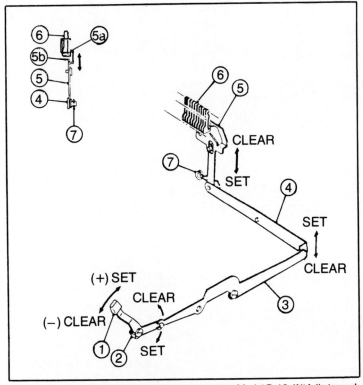

Fig. 5-14. This is the tab set-clear mechanism of the Model B-12. If it fails to work properly, there are some adjustments that can be made on it, which will be shown later in this chapter.

If the tabulator brake exerts too much braking action on the movement of the carriage, the tabulator may not tab. The procedure for adjusting the tabulator brake will be given later in this chapter in the adjustments section.

THE CARRIAGE MOVES WHEN TABBING BUT FAILS TO STOP AT A PRESET STOP

Failure of the carriage to stop at a preset tab stop may indicate a problem with the tabulator stopper (item 7 of Fig. 5-15) or with the tabulator chip rack. See a removal procedure for, and exploded view of, the tabulator mechanism later in this chapter.

THE TYPEBAR FAILS TO PRINT WHEN ACTIVATED

For a view of the typing mechanism, see Fig. 5-16. Note that the point marked "3" is the center of revolution when the key lever

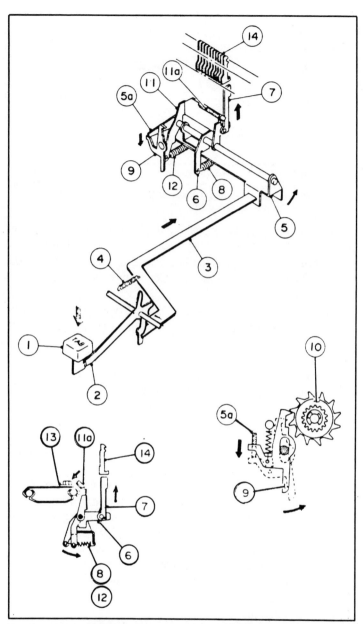

Fig. 5-15. This is the tabulator mechanism of the Model B-12. When studying the text, make the distinction between this mechanism, which causes the carriage to move to a tab stop; and the tab set-clear mechanism of Fig. 5-14, which programs the tab chip positions, which are chosen according to the needs of the typing format (courtesy of OLYMPIA USA INC.).

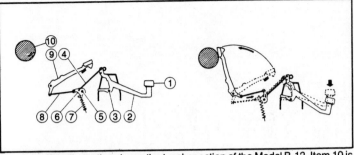

Fig. 5-16. This illustration shows the typebar action of the Model B-12. Item 10 is the end of the platen. Later on you will see a perspective view of this action, and it will become more clear for you (courtesy of OLYMPIA USA INC.).

(2) is pushed (as a result of pushing the keybutton). Thus, the key lever link (4) is pulled, rotating the key lever sub lever (6) around its fulcrum point (5), which pulls the typebar link (8), causing the typebar (9) to swing around on its fulcrum point and strike the platen (10).

If any of the links or levers bind, the typebar action will be affected. Removal of the key levers and links will be explained in this chapter.

If any of the levers or links are unhooked, the corresponding typebar will not be activated. After examining and correcting the cause of unhooking, reconnect these parts.

If the segment universal binds, the typebar will be impeded in its upward stroke toward the platen (the segment universal bar is item 4 in Fig. 5-8).

If the margin lock plate (item 8 in Fig. 5-10) blocks the connection plate (item 22 in Fig. 5-10), the operation of the connections will be discontinued. The key lever will be locked (as it would normally be in the case of right margin locking). If this occurs when the carriage is not in position to lock the right margin, the margin lock plate should be adjusted. This adjustment will be shown later in this chapter in the adjustments section.

If the gap between the typeface and platen is too wide, the typeface will not strike the platen. This can be corrected by a ring and cylinder adjustment, described later in this chapter in the adjustments section.

If the typebar binds during its action, it may not strike the platen. This may be corrected by adjustment (as a slight twisting or bending of the typebar) or, in extreme cases, by removing and replacing the typebar. Also, check the sub lever and connecting links. The procedure for removing a typebar will be shown later in this chapter.

If the typebar fails to return, the cause may be a misalignment of the typebar in the typebar guide, or a disconnected sub lever link (sub levers will be shown in perspective later in the chapter).

THE MACHINE FAILS TO SPACE WHEN THE SPACE BAR IS TAPPED

To see the spacing mechanism of the Model B-12, see Fig. 5-17. If the space bar stroke is too short, the machine will not space. Adjusting the space bar stroke will be described later in this chapter in the adjustments section.

If the carriage binds, spacing may not be effected when the space bar is tapped. Read again the information earlier in this chapter on carriage movement problems.

If the escapement mechanism binds, spacing may not be accomplished when the space bar is tapped. This may be corrected by adjusting the mesh of the escapement wheel pinion with the carriage rack; the procedure for this adjustment will be shown later in this chapter in the adjustments section.

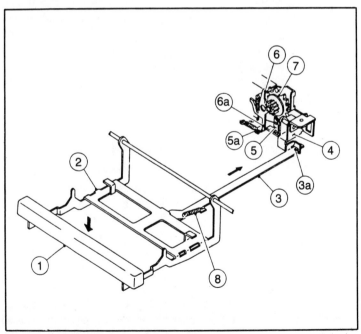

Fig. 5-17. Here again is the spacing mechanism illustration, repeated to save you trouble of leafing back through the pages (courtesy of OLYMPIA USA INC.).

THE REPEAT-SPACE FAILS TO REPEAT

When the automatic keybutton is depressed and held, the Model B-12 should continue to space—that is, repeat space—until the margin lock is reached or the keybutton is released. The repeat space mechanism is shown in Fig. 5-18. When the keybutton (1) is depressed, the repeat link (3a) pushes the swing controller (4a—lower illustration). This releases the swing dog (5) from the swing controller (4b—lower illustration), through the tension of spring (8). Thus, (5a) pushes fixed dog (9a), causing the fixed dog (9) to be released from the escapement wheel, allowing the carriage to move leftward. So long as the keybutton (1) is held down, the swing dog (5) will continue the swing operation, resulting in a continuous movement of the carriage leftward.

If the swing dog spring is defective or unhooked, the repeat space may not function. The part number of this spring will be given at the end of this chapter.

If the repeat space key lever has an insufficient stroke, the repeat space will not repeat. This can be corrected by an adjustment which will be described later in this chapter in the adjustments section.

If the spring drum is weak, the repeat space may not repeat. Decreasing or increasing the tension (power) of the spring drum will be discussed later in this chapter in the adjustments section.

If the swing dog fails to release from the escapement wheel, the repeat space will not repeat. If this is caused by a burr on the swing dog, remove the burr; otherwise, oil the dog and escapement wheel.

THE RIBBON LIFT WILL NOT PLACE THE RIBBON
FULLY BETWEEN THE TYPEFACE AND PLATEN DURING TYPING

If the ribbon lift is not sufficient, part of the character will be lost. This can be corrected by adjusting the ribbon lift. This procedure will be shown later in this chapter in the adjustments section.

THE RIBBON IS NOT FED

The ribbon feed mechanism of the Model B-12 is shown in Fig. 5-19. It works as follows. When the key lever (1) is operated, the ribbon universal bar (2) pulls the ribbon feed link (4) and the ribbon feed lever (3). This causes the gear feed pawl (5) to mesh into the teeth of the ribbon ratchet gear (6) and rotate that gear the distance

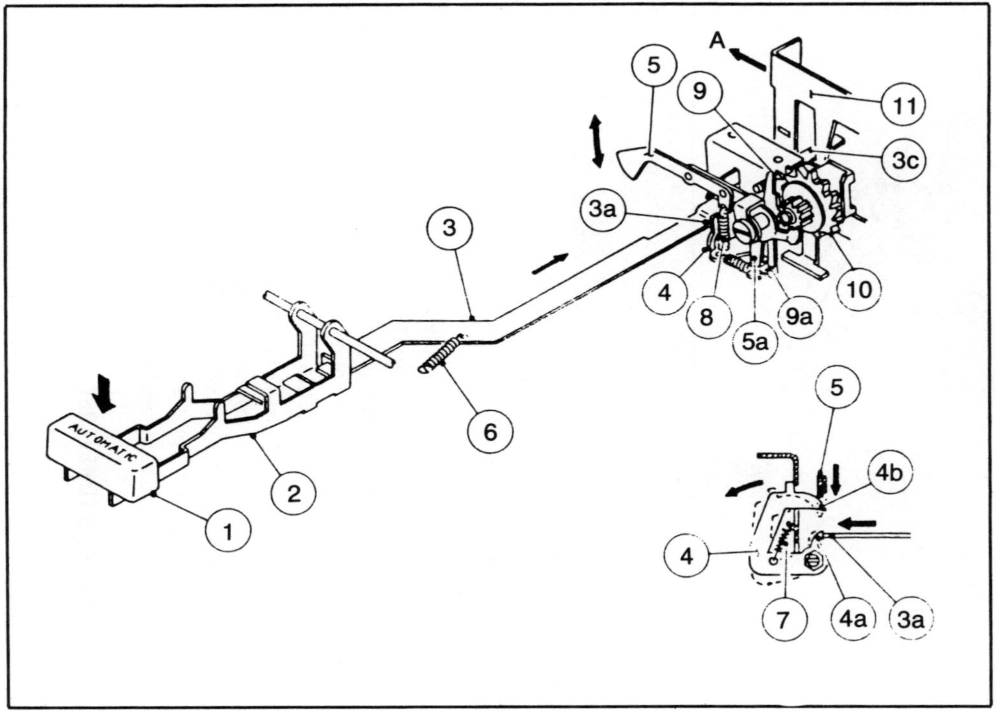

Fig. 5-18. A miracle of engineering, the repeat space mechanism creates an illusion of electric power in a non-electric machine. Study the text to understand how it works (courtesy of OLYMPIA USA INC.).

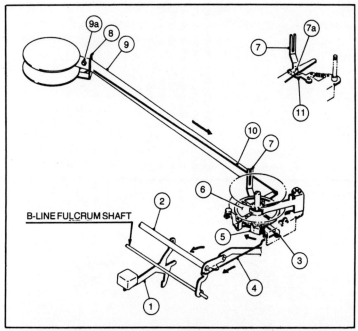

Fig. 5-19. This illustration shows the ribbon feed mechanism, as well as the reverse mechanism. If you're not quite sure what the key lever (1) represents, it represents any one of the key levers that can be activated by a keybutton, and that motion can be made to turn the ribbon ratchet gear (6) an incremental distance. The ribbon must have an eyelet (9a) for the reverse mechanism to work (courtesy of OLYMPIA USA INC.).

of a tooth, thus pulling the ribbon from the opposite spool and winding it onto the driven spool.

If the ribbon spool binds on the ribbon spool cups, the ribbon will not feed. This can be corrected by forming the spool cups.

If the ribbon ratchet gear (item 6 of Fig. 5-19) is defective, the ribbon will not feed. The parts numbers for the left and right ribbon ratchet gears will be given at the end of this chapter.

If the ribbon feed pawl is not meshing into the teeth of the ribbon ratchet gear, it may need forming or oiling. If the feed pawl needs replacing, you should understand that it is integral to the part called the "feed lever (right or left) complete," the parts numbers of which will be given at the end of this chapter.

THE RIBBON FAILS TO REVERSE

When the ribbon is becoming fully wound onto one spool, the eyelet on the opposite end of the ribbon will be pulled to the slot of the ribbon reverse trip lever. Since the eyelet will not allow the ribbon to pass through this slot, the pull of the ribbon will swing the ribbon reverse trip lever, causing the feed pawl of that spool to engage in the teeth of the ribbon ratchet gear. Simultaneously, because the mechanism is connected through the reverse link (10), the feed pawl of the opposite spool disengages from the teeth of its ribbon ratchet gear.

If there is no eyelet in the ribbon, the ribbon will not be reversed. Use the eyelet pliers to install an eyelet, or install a ribbon with eyelets. Use ribbon TW 1, with eyelets, or TW 22 without eyelets and install the eyelets.

If the eyelet passes through the slot of the ribbon reverse trip lever (item 8 of Fig. 5-19) slot, the ribbon will not reverse. This can be corrected by closing the slot slightly.

If the ribbon reverse trip lever binds, the ribbon will not reverse. Free the bind, oil the pivot points, etc. The adjustment of various other parts of the ribbon reversing mechanism will be shown later in this chapter in the adjustments section.

THE VARIABLE LINE SPACER FAILS TO OPERATE

The variable line spacing mechanism is shown in Fig. 5-20. The platen knob (7), variable ratchet (7-1) and platen shaft (8) are connected, and the push rod (5) is inserted into the push button (6).

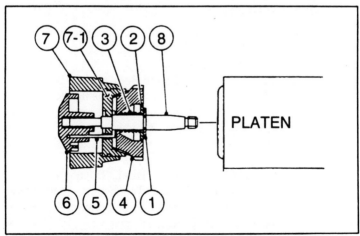

Fig. 5-20. This is a cutaway view of the variable line spacer of the Model B-12. In this context, "variable" means that the platen can be made to "freewheel", and thus vary the distance between the lines for special purposes. The disassembly procedure for this mechanism will be shown later in this chapter (courtesy of OLYMPIA USA INC.).

The variable ratchet wheel (4) is engaged with the variable ratchet (7-1) by the spring (3). The assembly is held together with the E-ring (1) and spring pat (2). When the push button (6) is pushed, the push rod (5) pushes the variable ratchet wheel (4), releasing it from the variable ratchet (7-1). This frees the platen. If it should remain in this condition when the push button is released, line spacing cannot be accomplished when the return handle is pushed.

If the spring pat (item 2—washer—of Fig. 5-20) binds, and the platen does not return to normal operating mode, the variable line spacing will not operate. The condition of the spring pat can be determined by removing the E-ring (1). Deburr the spring pat if necessary, or oil it. The part number of the spring pat will be given at the end of this chapter.

If the meshing of the detent heel (item 9 of Fig. 5-11) and platen gear (item 5 of Fig. 5-11) is too shallow, line spacing will not be accomplished when the return handle is pushed. To correct this, lubricate the detent heel or replace it (the part number of the detent heel will be given at the end of this chapter).

ADJUSTMENTS

After troubleshooting, the various mechanisms in the Olympia Model B-12 can be adjusted, if deemed necessary.

Adjustment of the Line Space

When the return handle is pushed, the line spacing should be accurate on all settings of the line space selector. Make the adjustment in three steps, as follows.

Adjustment Of The Line Space Feed Quantity. Refer to Fig. 5-21. The line space feed pawl (6) should be moved up to the stopper pawl (7) by operating the return handle. The gap between the return handle bracket (2) and the stopper pin (3) must be 0.2-0.5 mm in this operating position. To make the adjustment, bend part (a) of the line space link (4).

Adjustment Of The Detent Heel. Do not make this adjustment until after the foregoing adjustment has been made. The detent heel (8) should be adjusted to be between the teeth of the ratchet wheel (12) when the line space feed pawl (6) is pushed up to the stopper pawl (7). To make this adjustment, loosen the screw (9). Tighten the screw when the adjustment is complete. (Note that this adjustment solves the two earlier-mentioned problems: that of irregular spacing and failure to line space.)

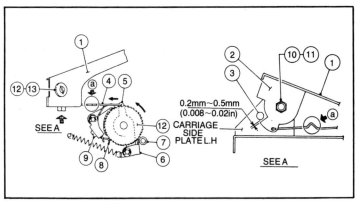

Fig. 5-21. Here is another view of the line spacing mechanism of the Model B-12, showing how to adjust it (courtesy of OLYMPIA USA INC.).

Adjustment Of The Return Handle For Smooth Operation. To adjust the return handle (1) for smooth operation, adjust setscrews (12 and 13) and nuts (10 and 11).

Adjustment Before Typing

See Fig. 5-22. For best results in typing, the gap between the left margin stop (2) and carriage stop (1a) should be as follows. On a pica machine the gap should be 1.27 mm (0.05″). On the elite machine the gap should be 0.91 mm (0.035″).

To make the adjustment, the two screws (3) should be loosened, and the stopper bracket (item 5—mounted on the back frame) adjusted right or left. Tighten the screws.

Adjustment of the Margin Stop

During typing the carriage should stop at the right margin stop five to seven characters after the warning bell has sounded. Refer to Fig. 5-23.

The gap between the margin lock plate (item 5 of Fig. 5-23A) and connection (item 6 of Fig. 5-23A) should be 0.8-1.3 mm in *normal status* (Fig. 5-23B). The margin lock plate (5) should be extruded from connection (6) by a minimum of 0.5 mm in *lock status* (Fig. 5-23C).

To make this adjustment, move the carriage to the extreme end of the left side and loosen screw (4 of Fig. 5-23A); then move the margin lock g (4 of Fig. 5-23A); then move the margin lock setter (3) left or right. If a full adjustment cannot be made with this procedure, the adjustment before typing should be made again.

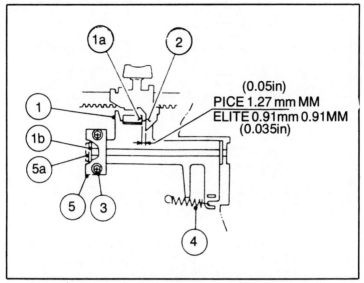

Fig. 5-22. To adjust the machine before typing, read the text and refer to this illustration (courtesy of OLYMPIA USA INC.).

After the foregoing adjustment has been made, do the following. Check that the gap between the margin lock plate (6) and margin lock setter (3) is a minimum of 0.1 mm when the margin lock plate is pushed to the extreme right (Fig. 5-23D).

Adjustment of the Depth of Engagement Between the Carriage Rack and Pinion Gear

The pinion gear of the escapement wheel should not mesh too tightly or too loosely with the carriage rack. See Fig. 5-24.

The gap of engagement between the carriage rack (1) and pinion gear (2) should be checked at left side, center and right side to be 0.3 mm. To make this adjustment, the screws (3) should be loosened and the rack adjusted upward or downward. (Note that this adjustment may solve the problems of carriage binding, faulty escapement and failure to space.)

Adjustment of the Tension of the Main Spring

The tension of the main spring causes the carriage to move leftward during typing, during spacing, or when the carriage is released. See Fig. 5-25.

To adjust the pulling force of the main spring, find the hole (6a) in the back frame (6). While holding the nut (4) with a nut driver,

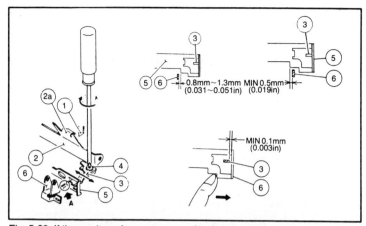

Fig. 5-23. If the carriage does not stop and lock at the right margin about five to seven characters after the warning bell has sounded, adjust it according to the instructions in the text, referring to this illustration (courtesy of OLYMPIA USA INC.).

insert a screwdriver through the hole (6a). Turn the screwdriver in the direction of "R" to increase the pulling force of the spring. Turn the screwdriver in the direction of "L" to decrease the pulling force of the spring. (Note that this adjustment will solve the problems of carriage movement, providing there are no other underlying causes for faulty movement of the carriage.)

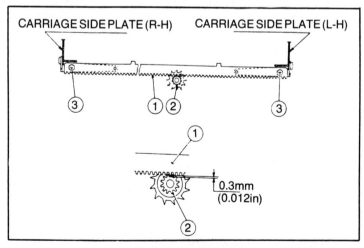

Fig. 5-24. Just as with any rack and pinion engagement, there should be just a slight clearance between the pinion gear teeth and the rack teeth—in this case, 0.3 mm. This is an easy adjustment to make (courtesy of OLYMPIA USA INC.).

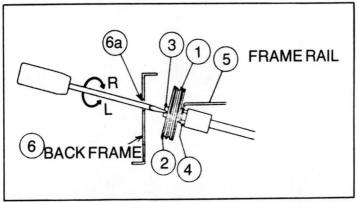

Fig. 5-25. The main spring is the power source for the movement of the carriage leftward; arm power returns it rightward and retensions the spring, within the limits of its adjustment. This illustration shows, and the text explains, how to make that adjustment (courtesy of OLYMPIA USA INC.).

Adjustment of the Tab Rack

If the tab set-clear mechanism fails to set or clear tabs, the tab rack may need adjusting. See Fig. 5-26.

The adjustment should be made so that the shank of the tab set-clear finger (1a—Fig. 5-26B) and tab chip (2) match each other. To do this, loosen screws (3—Fig. 5-26A) and adjust the tab rack. The length of hooking between the tab set-clear finger (1a) and tab chip (2) should be 1.5-2.0 mm (see Fig. 5-26C). If the tab set-clear finger (1a) does not set the tab chip (2) when the tab set-clear lever is moved to set, the part (F—Fig. 5-26D) can be formed with a pair of pinchers, until the necessary hooking is achieved.

Adjustment of the Carriage Stopper

If the margin fails to lock or release, the carriage stopper may need adjustment. See Fig. 5-27 (for a perspective view of the carriage stopper, see item 5 of Fig. 5-13).

Referring to Fig. 5-27, the length of carriage stopper (2) should be 2.5-3.0 mm from the margin stop. Regarding the movement of the carriage stopper (2), the margin lock setter (3) is stopped by the escapement base (4). Make the adjustment by forming the part "A" of the margin lock setter (3).

Adjustment of the Space Key Lever

If the machine fails to space when the space key is pushed, the space key lever may need adjustment. See Fig. 5-28.

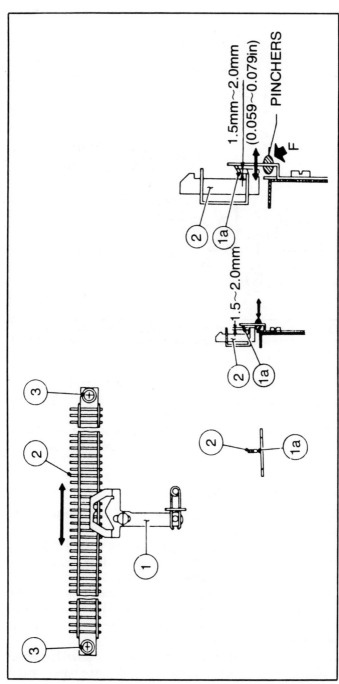

Fig. 5-26. In effect the tab rack is a mechanical programming which tells the carriage where to stop when a tab button is pushed. This illustration shows how it works and what adjustment clearances are needed to keep it working (courtesy of OLYMPIA USA INC.).

PINCHERS

1.5mm~2.0mm
(0.059~0.079in)

1.5~2.0mm

F

203

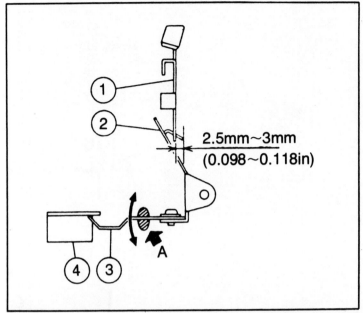

Fig. 5-27. This illustration, together with the text, shows and tells how to adjust the carriage stopper so the margin will lock where you want it to lock (courtesy of OLYMPIA USA INC.).

The space key lever (1) is released when it is pushed against the rubber stopper (2) by 1.0-1.5 mm (see gap B). Adjust this clearance by forming the stopper (1b).

The gap between connection (4) and space bar link (3a) should be 0.1-0.3 mm (see gap A). Adjust this by forming the space key lever push part (1a).

Adjustment of the Repeat Space

If the repeat spacer fails to repeat, it may be corrected by an adjustment. See Fig. 5-29.

The repeat space key lever (1) is released when it is pushed against the stopper rubber (2) by 1.5-2.0 mm (see gap B). This adjustment is made by forming the stopper (1a).

The gap between the swing controller (4) and shank (3a) of the repeat space link must be 0.3-0.5 mm (see gap A). This adjustment is made by forming the position marked with the arrow (F), in the lower illustration of Fig. 5-29.

The adjustment of margin lock in repeat space should be made by forming the part marked with the arrow (E) of the repeat space

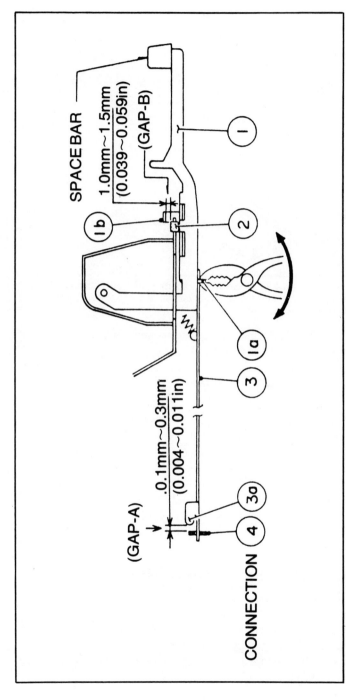

Fig. 5-28. This illustration graphically shows the adjustments necessary to make the spacing mechanism function properly; the text further clarifies the procedure (courtesy of OLYMPIA USA INC.).

205

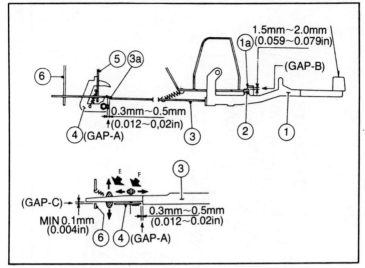

Fig. 5-29. Adjustments of the repeat spacing mechanism involve forming certain parts to maintain the right clearances. Read the text also (courtesy of OLYMPIA USA INC.).

link. However, the gap between the carriage stopper (6) and repeat space link (3) must be a minimum of 0.1 mm (see gap C).

Adjustment of the Tabulator Brake

If the machine fails to tabulate because the tabulator brake is too strong—or if, conversely, the brake is too weak, causing slamming of the carriage against the stop—the problem may be corrected by adjustment. See Fig. 5-30.

The gap between the tab link (5) and tabulator main bar (4a) should be 0.1-0.3 mm. Make the adjustment by forming part (B).

The gap between the tabulator brake (1) and carriage rail (2) should be 0.5 mm. Make this adjustment by forming part (A). (The cross-hatched lines in the illustration represent the end of the pliers.)

Adjustment of Segment Position and Segment Shift Operation

By now you know that the segment is the unit containing the typebars, which can be shifted down and up to type upper and lower case characters. If the segment fails to shift, or the typebar guide (the typebar guide is a part of the segment) is out of alignment because of misalignment of the segment, the segment position can be adjusted. See Fig. 5-31.

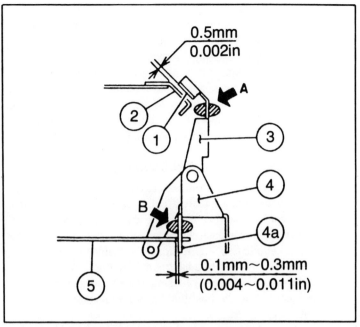

Fig. 5-30. This is a profile view of the tabulator braking system, which keeps the carriage from slamming against the tab stops. Adjustment of the braking power is made by forming parts (courtesy of OLYMPIA USA INC.).

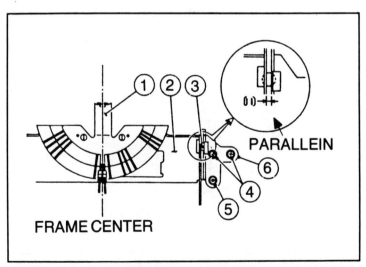

Fig. 5-31. If any component could be considered the "nerve center" of a typewriter, it would be the segment. This illustration shows and the text explains how to align it for best performance (courtesy of OLYMPIA USA INC.).

The typebar guide (1) must be positioned at the center of the frame or body of the equipment. This adjustment can be made by moving slide guides (6-right and 7-left) leftward or rightward, as needed. Do this after loosening the screw (4) and nut (5).

The segment should shift smoothly when the shift keybutton is pushed. If the motion is not smooth, or if there is too much laxity in the movement, the slide bases (6 and 7) should be adjusted accordingly. To do this, loosen the screw (4) and nut (5). The slide guides (6 and 7) must be parallel with the segment base (2).

Adjustment of Upper and Lower Case Characters

When a typeface strikes the platen, it must hit the platen on an arc of the curvature of the platen that is essentially in the same plane as the typeface, so that part of the character will not be lost. For both upper and lower case characters, this is determined by the height of the segment. If impressions are faulty because of this height, it may be corrected by adjustment. See Fig. 5-32.

Adjust the capital letter by loosening the lower stopper screw (2). Lock the screw in position with the locknut when the adjustment is completed.

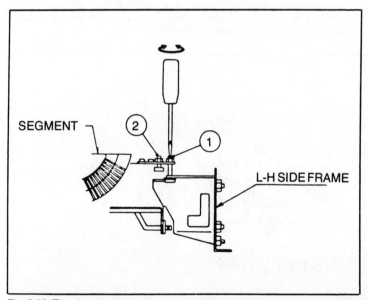

Fig. 5-32. The elevation of the segment in relation to an approximate centerline of the platen has a lot to do with the quality of the impressions made when the typebar strikes the platen. Adjusting this elevation is accomplished through adjusting screws, secured by locknuts (courtesy of OLYMPIA USA INC.).

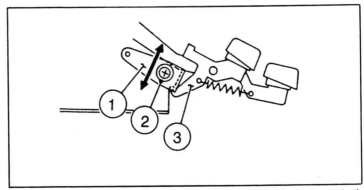

Fig. 5-33. The shift lock is the mechanism which enables the typist to use both hands for typing upper case characters. The critical point of this mechanism is where (2) and (3) meet; read the text (courtesy of OLYMPIA USA INC.).

Adjust the small letter by loosening the upper stopper screw (1). Lock the screw in position with the locknut when the adjustment is complete.

These screws have their counterparts on the other end of the segment. When the adjustment is completed, both sets of screws should be adjusted the same to maintain symmetry across the segment.

Adjustment of the Shift Lock

Failure of the shift lock to lock may be corrected by adjustment. See Fig. 5-33.

The shift lock lever (3) should be correctly located in respect to the shift lock plate (1), so that hooking will occur when the keybutton is depressed. Adjust by loosening the screw (2) and moving the shift lock plate (1) up or down, as needed for locking. Tighten the screw.

Adjustment of the Escapement Trip

If letters are piling or gapping because of skips in the carriage escapement during typing, the escapement trip may need adjustment. See Fig. 5-34.

When a typebar approaches the platen, just when it is 3.0-5.0 mm from the surface of the platen, the carriage should move one-half space. This is possible because the universal (6) pushes the connection (1), causing the adjuster screw (2) to push the loose dog (4), and causing the escapement wheel to be rotated one-half pitch. Adjust by rotating the adjustment screw (2), which is

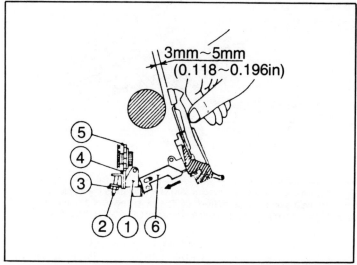

Fig. 5-34. This illustration shows how to adjust the escapement trip. Also, read the text (courtesy of OLYMPIA USA INC.).

mounted on the connection (1). The nut (3) is to prevent the disconnection of the adjuster screw (2).

Adjustment of the Warning Bell

The warning bell should sound five to seven characters before the carriage locks at the right margin. If it doesn't, it needs adjustment. See Fig. 5-35.

The distance between the tip of the bell hammer (2) and the shank (1a) of the margin stop (1) should be 1 mm (see the circled portion of the illustration). Adjust by forming the bell base (3b). The bell spring (5) should be twisted by 1½ revolutions before it is hooked at the bell base (3a).

Adjustment of the Ring (Typebar Guide) and Cylinder (Platen).

If the model B-12 is not printing because the typeface is not hitting the platen or is hitting the platen too lightly, the problem may be corrected by adjustment. See Fig. 5-36.

The clearance between the typeface and platen should be 0.05-0.15 mm, so that the typebar is tight against the ring. To make this adjustment, loosen two screws (1) mounted on the frame rail (5). Move the slide base (4) in one direction or the other, as shown by the double-pointed arrow. Part (2) is the tapping plate of the screw (1).

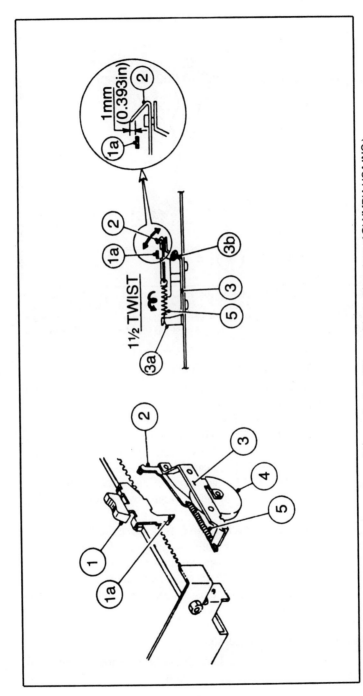

Fig. 5-35. This illustration shows the adjustment of the warning bell. Also, read the text (courtesy of OLYMPIA USA INC.).

211

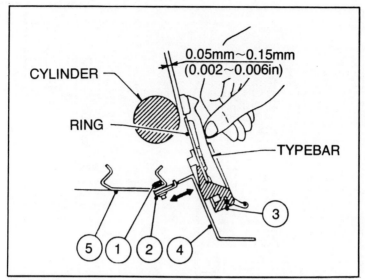

Fig. 5-36. This profile view of the typebar mechanism and segment should make it obvious that the position of the segment in relation to the surface of the platen determines the force with which the typebar strikes the platen. Don't confuse this adjustment with that of the escapement trip (courtesy of OLYMPIA USA INC.).

Adjustment of Ribbon Select and Ribbon Lift

If the upper and lower portions of the ribbon are not positioning properly between the typeface and platen, this problem may be corrected through adjustment. See Fig. 5-37.

Adjustment Of The Ribbon Select. The color detent spring (2) must press the cam lever (5). The amount of pressure should be adjusted so that the cam lever (5) does not move when the ribbon is lifted, and the color select operation of the ribbon selector (1) can be made smoothly. Adjust by forming the spring pad (3).

Adjustment Of The Ribbon Lift. Loosen the screw (4) and adjust the detent spring (2) as follows. Adjust the detent spring (2) in the direction of A to increase the ribbon lift. Adjust the detent spring in the direction of B to decrease the ribbon lift. Note: The color select detent spring (2) must be parallel with the side frame (see lower illustrations).

Adjustment of the Ribbon Vibrator

For smooth operation, the ribbon vibrator should be adjusted as follows (Fig. 5-38). The gap between the ribbon vibrator (7) and

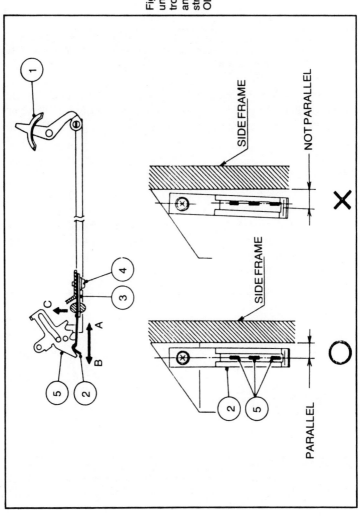

Fig. 5-37. Read the text carefully to understand the mechanism that controls both the amount of ribbon lift and which half of the ribbon will be struck by the typebar (courtesy of OLYMPIA USA INC.).

213

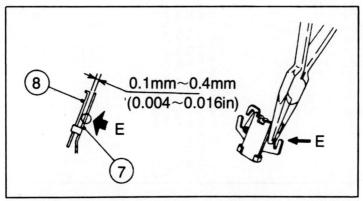

Fig. 5-38. The ribbon vibrator should be far enough from the typebar guide that it moves up and down freely, yet not so far as to cause the ribbon to rub against the paper. Read the text (courtesy of OLYMPIA USA INC.).

the typebar guide (8) should be 0.1-0.4 mm. If there is no gap, the vibrator will not operate smoothly; if the gap is too large, the paper will get smudged from the ribbon. Adjust by forming part (E) of the vibrator.

Adjustment of Automatic Ribbon Reverse

Ribbon reversing should be accomplished, as explained previously, through the pull of the ribbon eyelet exerting a motion on the ribbon reverse lever, with that motion working into the reverse link (item 3 in Fig. 5-39). If the reverse link (3) is too long or too short, the reverse lever (1 and 2) should be formed to make the necessary adjustment.

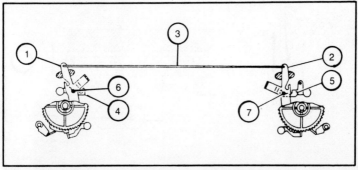

Fig. 5-39. The ribbon reversing mechanism looks more complicated on paper than it does in the machine. The absolute length of the reverse link (3) is fixed, but its effective length can be changed by forming certain parts, as explained in the text (courtesy of OLYMPIA USA INC.).

The ribbon reverse lever pins (6 and 7) are locked at the center of the ribbon reverse cam (4 and 5). When reverse levers (1 and 2) are pushed by the eyelet of the ribbon, the reverse lever should shift smoothly.

REMOVAL OF COVERS, COMPONENTS AND MECHANISMS OF THE OLYMPIA MODEL B-12

Before immersing the Model B-12 in a cleaning tank, or before making any major adjustments or repairs, the covers should be removed; further, before immersing, the bail and bail rolls and the platen, lower paper table and feed rollers should be removed. If it should become necessary to remove any mechanisms of the Model B-12, they should be removed in a certain sequence.

Removing the Covers of the Olympia Model B-12

The covers should be removed in three steps. First, remove the ribbon spool cover (Fig. 5-40). Secondly, remove the front cover, as follows. Remove the front cover binding screw and nut from each side (Fig. 5-41). Then remove the front cover binding screw, one on each side of bottom (Fig. 5-42). Remove the front

Fig. 5-40. A basic truth of machine repair and adjustment is that you can't do anything effective until the outer covers are removed, and on some machines this can be a formidable job in itself. On the Olympia Model B-12, the procedure is made simple by following the steps outlined in this illustration through Fig. 5-45. Here, remove the ribbon spool cover (courtesy of OLYMPIA USA INC.).

Fig. 5-41. Remove the front cover binding screw and nut from each side (courtesy of OLYMPIA USA INC.).

cover (Fig. 5-43). Thirdly, remove the machine from the main cover, as follows. Remove the main cover binding screws (Fig. 5-44). Slide the machine out of the main cover (Fig. 5-45).

Removing the Carriage Unit

To remove the carriage unit, proceed as follows. Move the carriage rightward. Use a hooked wire to remove the draw band from the hook (Figs. 5-46A and 5-46B). Hook the other end of the wire on the frame, as shown in Fig. 5-46A.

Move the carriage to the extreme right by pushing the carriage stopper (item 2 of Fig. 5-46B) to the escape hole of the left side plate (item 3 of Fig. 5-46B) with the tip of a screwdriver. Remove the carriage from the left side plate (3 of Fig. 5-46B).

Set the tab set-clear lever at the set position, and move the carriage to the right. Remove the carriage. Remove the ball bearing, retainer and ratchet (item 5 of Fig. 5-46B).

Removing/Disassembling the Carriage

Removal and disassembly of the carriage is done as follows. To remove the paper bail scale, refer to Fig. 5-47. Remove springs

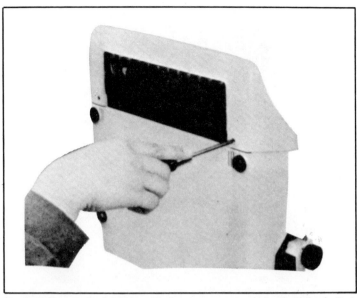

Fig. 5-42. Remove the front cover binding screw, one on each side of the bottom (courtesy of OLYMPIA USA INC.).

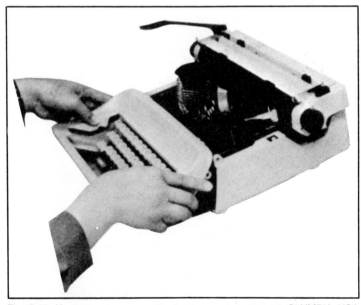

Fig. 5-43. Now you can remove the front cover (courtesy of OLYMPIA USA INC.).

Fig. 5-44. Remove the main cover binding screw (courtesy of OLYMPIA USA INC.).

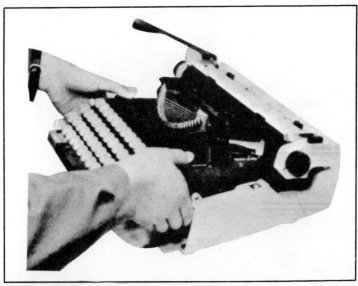

Fig. 5-45. Finally, slide the machine chassis out of the cover (courtesy of OLYMPIA USA INC.).

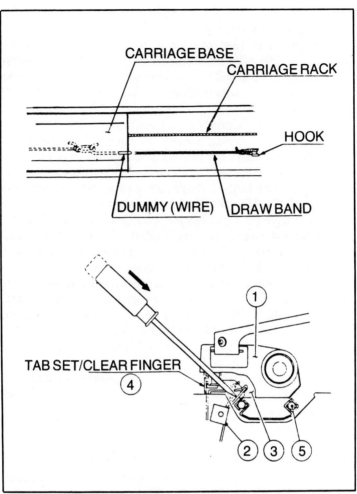

Fig. 5-46. The carriage can be removed as a unit. To understand how, study this illustration and read the text (courtesy of OLYMPIA USA INC.).

(21—two in all) and E-rings (20—two in all) mounted on the left and right sides. With these parts removed, the paper bail scale (22) can be removed from the left and right side plates.

To remove the erasure table, refer to Fig. 5-47. Remove the table shaft (27) and spring (28) from the left and right side plates. Now the erasure table (26) can be removed.

To remove the platen and paper pan, refer to Fig. 5-47 and 5-48. Release the line space selector (39 of Fig. 5-48) and the paper release lever (12 of Fig. 5-47). Remove both platen knobs, and remove the platen from the carriage. Now the paper pan (4 of Fig. 5-47) can easily be removed.

To remove the feed rollers, refer to Fig. 5-47. After removing the paper pan, remove the E-ring (57 of Fig. 5-47). Then remove the feed roller metal and the left-hand part (56 of Fig. 5-47) from the paper pan, along with the front and rear feed rollers (53 and 54 of Fig. 5-47).

To remove the carriage rack, refer to Fig. 5-47. Margin stop the carriage at the central position. Remove the setscrews (5 of Fig. 5-47) and remove the carriage release lever (6 of Fig. 5-47) and spring (10 of Fig. 5-47). Remove the rack setscrews (7 and 8 of Fig. 5-47). Now take the carriage rack out from between the upper carriage rail (30 of Fig. 5-47) and the carriage base.

To remove the paper release lever, see Fig. 5-47. After the right-hand platen knob (1) is removed, the E-ring (11) and spring (13) should be removed. Now the paper release lever (12) can be removed; thus, the L-shaft arm (14) can also be removed.

To remove the margin rack and paper support plate, refer to Fig. 5-47 and 5-48. Remove the screws (item 17 of Fig. 5-47, two in all), and washers (item 18 of Fig. 5-47, for two screws), and remove the tabstop rack (item 19 of Fig. 5-47). Next, remove the margin rack set nuts (item 23 of Fig. 5-47, two in all). Then remove the mounting screw (item 16 of Fig. 5-47) and extract the right side plate (item 29 of Fig. 5-47) from the paper support plate (item 25 of Fig. 5-47) and the margin rack (item 24 of Fig. 5-47) from the left side plate (item 52 of Fig. 5-48).

Removing/Disassembling the Line Space Mechanism

To remove and disassemble the line space mechanism, proceed as follows (see Fig. 5-48). To remove the return handle, remove the nut (49) and then remove the steel ball (47). Next, remove the lever setscrew (44) and the handle plate spring (48). Now remove the return handle (45). Next, remove the setscrew (41) and the nut (42), after which the handle bracket (46) and spacer (43) can be removed.

To begin removing the line space, first remove the left-hand platen knob (51). Then remove the E-ring (31), spring (34) and line space feed arm (32). Now the line space link (33) can be removed.

To remove the line space detent arm, remove the E-ring (35). Then the detent arm (36), detent spring (37) and detent arm (38) can be removed.

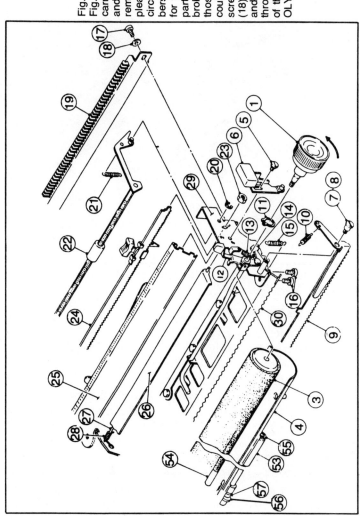

Fig. 5-47. This illustration, along with Fig. 5-48, shows the parts of the carriage. To get the most out of this and other blow-up illustrations in the removal section of this chapter, please understand two facts. The circled numbers are not parts numbers, but simply reference numbers for the textual explanations. When parts are exploded on paper, the broken connecting lines show where those parts would join if the parts could be reassembled; for example, screw (17) passes through washer (18), through the hole in the tab rack, and—following the broken line—through a not-visible hole in the back of the side frame (29) (courtesy of OLYMPIA USA INC.).

221

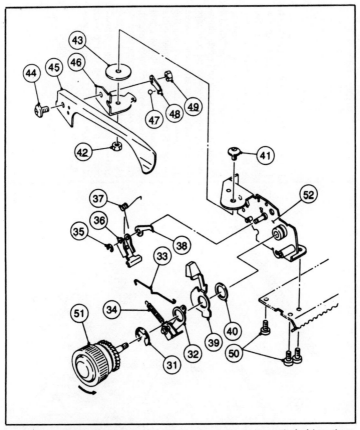

Fig. 5-48. Here are the parts of the line space mechanism, exploded (courtesy of OLYMPIA USA INC.).

Removing the Key Lever Sub Lever

The key lever sub lever is item 3 in Fig. 5-49 (each key lever has its corresponding sub lever). The sub lever should be removed first. Then the key lever can be removed.

Still referring to Fig. 5-49, to remove a sub lever, first remove the fulcrum shaft stopper (2—two in all). Use a dummy to push out the sub lever fulcrum shaft (1). Remove the sub lever (3) and the sub lever spring (4). When reinstalling the sub lever (3), the proper mounting must be used.

Still referring to Fig. 5-49, to remove a key lever, first remove the key lever link (5). Then remove the setscrews (6 and 13), and then remove the tab set-clear lever (7), fulcrum wire stoppers (8-right and 11-left) and touch control lever (12). Push out

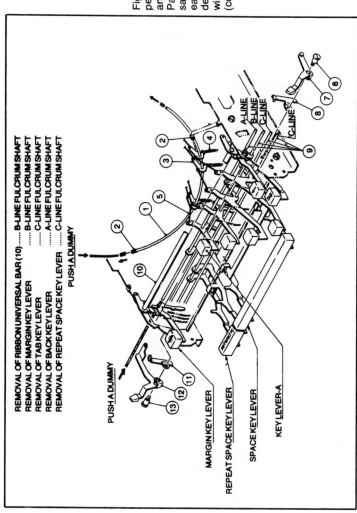

REMOVAL OF RIBBON UNIVERSAL BAR (10) ...... B-LINE FULCRUM SHAFT
REMOVAL OF MARGIN KEY LEVER ...... B-LINE FULCRUM SHAFT
REMOVAL OF TAB KEY LEVER ...... C-LINE FULCRUM SHAFT
REMOVAL OF BACK KEY LEVER ...... A-LINE FULCRUM SHAFT
REMOVAL OF REPEAT SPACE KEY LEVER ...... C-LINE FULCRUM SHAFT

PUSH A DUMMY

PUSH A DUMMY

MARGIN KEY LEVER
REPEAT SPACE KEY LEVER
SPACE KEY LEVER
KEY LEVER-A

A-LINE
B-LINE
C-LINE
C-LINE

Fig. 5-49. As promised, here is a perspective view of key levers, links and sub levers of the Model B-12. Parts that look alike are not necessarily interchangeable; therefore, each individual part should be ordered by its own part number, which will be given later on in this chapter (courtesy of OLYMPIA USA INC.).

223

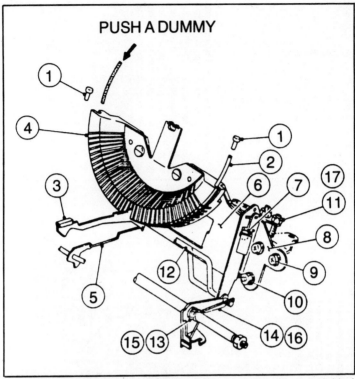

Fig. 5-50. Read the text and study this drawing to learn how an individual typebar, or complete segment, can be removed. To order a typebar, just name the symbol it prints (courtesy of OLYMPIA USA INC.).

the key lever fulcrum shaft (9) with a dummy, and the key lever can be removed.

Removing a Typebar

To remove a typebar, refer to Fig. 5-50. Remove the fulcrum shaft stoppers (1—two in all). Then use a dummy to push the typebar fulcrum shaft out. Now the typebar (3) can be extracted from the segment (4). Finally, remove the typebar link (5).

Removing the Complete Segment

To remove the complete segment, refer to Fig. 5-50. Remove both shift arm springs (13-right, and 15-left) from the segment base hanger shaft (12). Now slide the segment base hanger shaft leftward/rightward to remove it from the shift arm (14-right and 16-left) and the segment base (6). Next, remove the shift upper stoppers (11-left and 17-right). Then remove the screws (9—two in all) and nut (10), and move the slide guide (8) to the right. Then the steel balls (7, right and left) can be removed. Now the complete segment can be removed.

Removing the Segment Universal Bar

After the complete segment has been removed, it can be disassembled into the segment universal, and the universal crank. See Fig. 5-51.

To remove the segment (1), first remove the spring (2) and screw (3—four pieces). After removing the segment, to remove the segment universal bar, first remove setscrews (5—two pieces) and corresponding nuts (6—two pieces). Remove the segment universal (4).

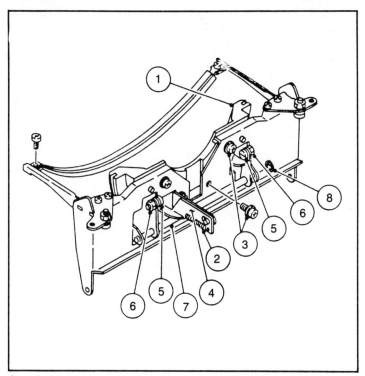

Fig. 5-51. With the complete segment taken out of the machine, the segment, segment universal bar and various other parts can be removed. Just remember that when you go this far in dismantling your typewriter, your only friends in reassembling it are your patience, mechanical skils, and illustrations and instructions in this book (courtesy of OLYMPIA USA INC.).

To remove the universal crank, first remove the E-ring (8). Then remove the complete universal crank.

Removing the Shift

To remove the shift, refer to Fig. 5-52. To remove the touch control, first remove the setscrew (15). Remove the touch control lever (14) and wire stopper (15).

After removing the touch control lever (14) and wire stopper (15), remove the setscrews (1 and 15) and then remove the tab set-clear lever (2) and wire stopper (3). Use a dummy to extract the C-line fulcrum shaft (4). Finally, remove the two shift key levers (5 and 6).

To remove the shift torsion bar (10), begin by removing the segment lift springs (8—left and right) and then remove the shift arm springs (7—left and right) from the segment base hanger shaft (9). Next, remove the locknuts (11—left and right) from the center screws at the ends of the torsion bar (10). Now the torsion bar (10) can be removed by sliding the hanger shaft (9) leftward/rightward.

Removing the Color Change Mechanism

To remove and disassemble the color change mechanism, first remove the ribbon vibrator and then the color change. See Fig. 5-53. Shift lock before beginning to remove the ribbon vibrator (5). Remove the ribbon from the ribbon vibrator (5). Then remove the E-ring (2) and the ribbon lift bar (1). Then remove another E-ring (3), after which the crank (4) can be removed. Now remove the E-ring (7) and set point (8). Then remove the ribbon vibrator (5) from the typebar guide and extract it from the machine.

To remove the color change, first remove the setscrew (9). Then remove the ribbon selector (10) and the select link (11). Then remove the E-ring (13) and lift link (12). Then remove the screw (14), spring pad (15) and detent spring (16). Then remove the E-ring (17) and cam lever (18).

Removing the Tab Set-Clear

To remove the tab set-clear mechanism, see Fig. 5-54. Assuming that the covers have not been removed, the back cover (1) must be removed. The mounting screws (3—left and right) of the tab rack should be removed.

To remove the tab set-clear finger (4), remove the E-ring (6) and lever setscrew (5). To remove the tab set-clear lever (9) and connecting linkages (12 and 14), remove the lever setscrews (10, 11 and 13).

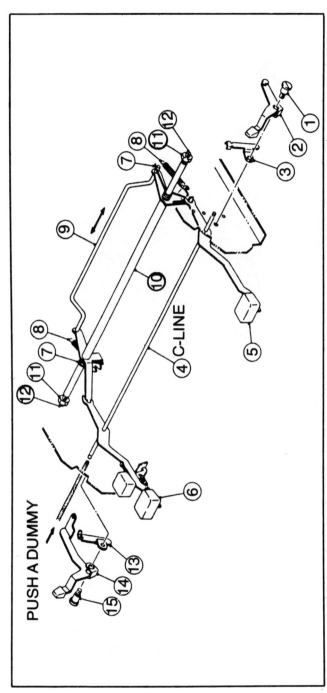

Fig. 5-52. Here is the mechanism that shifts the segment (without the segment), with some parts exploded. For better orientation to this illustration, consider that the ends of the torsion bar (10) pivot in the two side frames, with the pressure at these points being adjusted through the center screws (12), held in adjustment with the locknuts (11) (courtesy of OLYMPIA USA INC.).

227

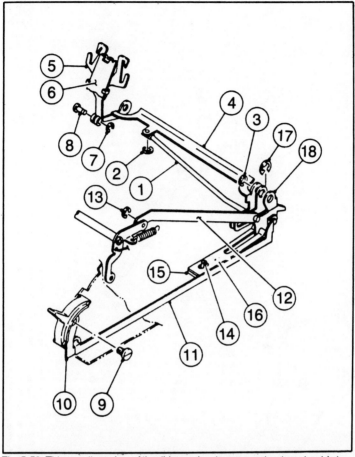

Fig. 5-53. This excellent view of the ribbon color change mechanism should give you a clear understanding of how it works, when studied in conjunction with the adjustment procedure earlier described; however, the purpose of the illustration is to show you how the mechanism is disassembled (courtesy of OLYMPIA USA INC.).

Removing the Escapement

To remove the escapement, refer to Fig. 5-55. Remove the carriage unit. Read the description of how to do this in the removing the carriage unit section earlier in this chapter.

Remove the E-ring (1), spring (3) and the back space pawl (2). Extract the space bar link (5) in the direction of (C). Extract the repeat space link (6) by moving it first in the arrow direction (a), then in the arrow direction (b). Remove the escapement from the carriage base (8) by first removing screws (7—three in all).

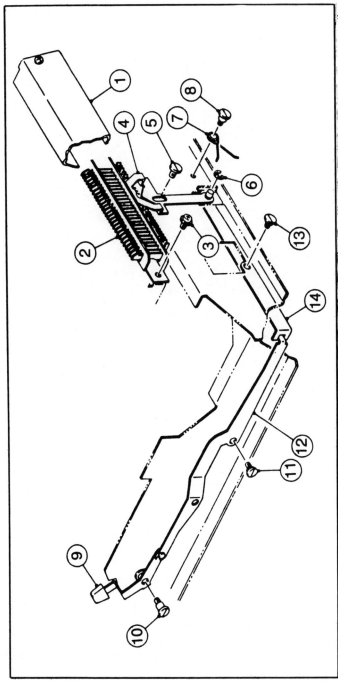

Fig. 5-54. If any mystery concerning the tab set-clear mechanism remains in your mind, this illustration, which shows how to remove the mechanism, should clear it up (courtesy of OLYMPIA USA INC.).

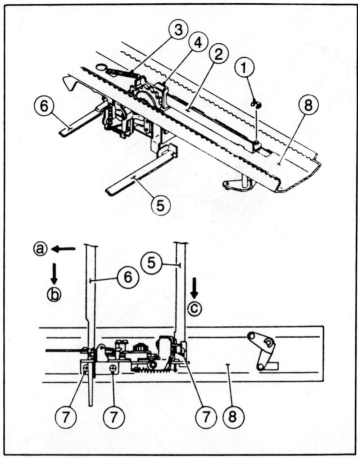

Fig. 5-55. To remove the escapement mechanism, study this drawing along with the text (courtesy of OLYMPIA USA INC.).

Removing the Back Frame

To remove the back frame (with various parts), refer to Fig. 5-56. Extract the margin link (9) while the carriage stopper (6) is pushed. Extract the tabulator link (8) while the tabulator main bar (11) is pushed. To remove the complete bell, remove screws (1—two in all) from the back frame (3).

After the complete bell is removed, you can remove the carriage stopper (6). First, remove the spring (7). Then remove screws (5—two in all) from the back frame (3). Remove the complete stopper bracket (4) from the back frame (3). Now the carriage stopper (6) can be removed.

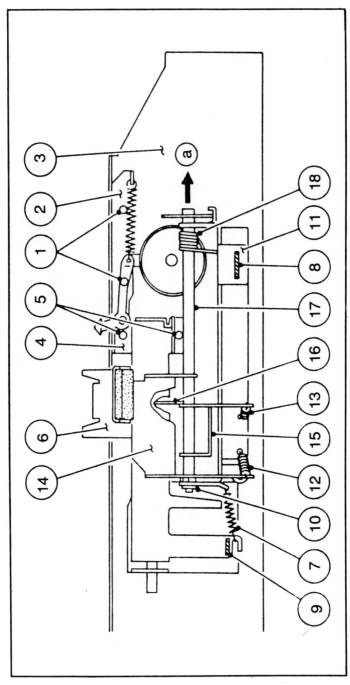

Fig. 5-56. To the back frame are attached mechanisms, or portions of mechanisms, as described in the text (courtesy of OLYMPIA USA INC.).

231

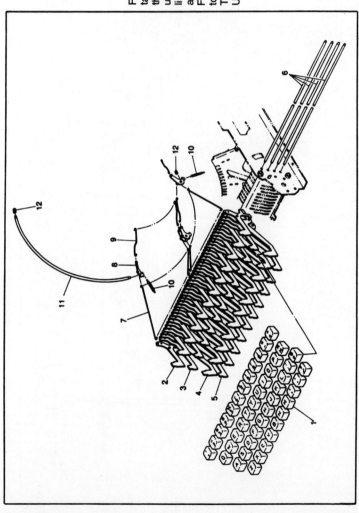

Fig. 5-57. In this drawing, numbers take on a different significance, in that they are *key numbers*, to be used in conjunction with the parts lists. The parts list for this, the key action mechanism, is in Table 5-1. Furthermore, to order parts relating to key numbers 7 and 8, refer to Table 5-2 (courtesy of OLYMPIA USA INC.).

Key No.	Parts No.	Description
1	(order by symbol)	Type and Key top
2	82010100	Key lever - A
3	82010110	Key lever - B
4	82010120	Key lever - C
5	82010130	Key lever - D
6	82010140	Key lever fulcrum shaft
7	82010360/790	Key lever link
8	82010810/1030	Sub lever
9	82020230	Typebar link
10	82010280	Sub lever spring
	82010320	Silent key spring
11	82010090	Sub lever sulcrum shaft
12	82010310	Sub lever fulcrum shaft stopper

To remove the stopper lift crank and brake arm, remove the following parts: springs (12 and 13) and E-ring (10). Then extract the main bar shaft (17) from the back frame (3) in the arrow direction (a). Now remove the brake arm (14), the complete stopper lift crank (15 and 16) and main bar spring (18). Finally you can remove the tabulator main bar (11).

BLOW-UP DRAWINGS WITH ACCOMPANYING PARTS NUMBERS AND NAME-NUMBER LISTS FOR THE OLYMPIA MODEL B-12

The following are parts blow-ups and parts names and numbers for the various mechanisms and other components of the Olympia Model B-12. See Fig. 5-57 and Table 5-1 for the key action mechanism and parts list.

Also see Table 5-2 for the parts numbers of the various key lever links (7) and sub levers (8), as they correspond to the various typebars. Note that the number "7" at the head of the column refers to the part number of the key lever link for the typeface across from it, and the number "8" refers to the corresponding sub lever.

See Fig. 5-58 and Table 5-3 for a blow-up and parts list of the Olympia Model B-12.

See Fig. 5-59 for the sequential arrangement of the typebars of the Model B-12. Order typebars by the name of the character or symbol.

See Fig. 5-60 and Table 5-4 for a parts blow-up and parts list for the space, back space and escapement mechanism of the Model B-12.

**Table 5-2. Parts Numbers of Various Key Lever
Links (7) and Sub Levers (8) (courtesy of OLYMPIA USA INC.).**

Pos. No.	(1)	(7) Part No.	(8) Part No.
1	! 1	82010360	82010812
2	Q q	82010370	82010820
3	A a	82010380	82010830
4	" 2	82010390	82010840
5	Z z	82010400	82010850
6	W w	82010410	82010860
7	S s	82010420	82010870
8	# 3	82010430	82010880
9	X x	82010440	82010890
10	E e	82010450	82010900
11	D d	82010460	82010910
12	S 4	82010470	82010920
13	C c	82010480	82010930
14	R r	82010490	82010940
15	F f	82010500	82010950
16	% 5	82010510	82010960
17	V v	82010520	82010970
18	T t	82010530	82010980
19	G g	82010540	82010990
20	— 6	82010550	82010000
21	B b	82010560	82011010
22	Y y	82010570	82011020
23	H h	82010580	82011020
24	& 7	82010590	82011010
25	N n	82010600	82011000
26	U u	82010610	82010990
27	J j	82010620	82010980
28	! 8	82010630	82010970
29	M m	82010640	82010960
30	I i	82010650	82010950
31	K k	82010660	82010940
32	(9	82010670	82010930
33		82010680	82010920
34	O o	82010690	82010910
35	L l	82010700	82010900
36	) O	82010710	82010890
37	. .	82010720	82010880
38	P p	82010730	82010870
39	: ;	82010740	82010860
40	* -	82010750	82010850
41	? /	82010760	82010840
42	¼ ½	82010770	82010830
43	@ ¢	82010780	82010820
44	+ =	82010790	82011030

The carriage mechanism in its entirety is shown in two blow-ups (Figs. 5-61 and 5-62).

Table 5-5 is the parts list for Fig. 5-61 and Table 5-6 is the parts list for Fig. 5-62.

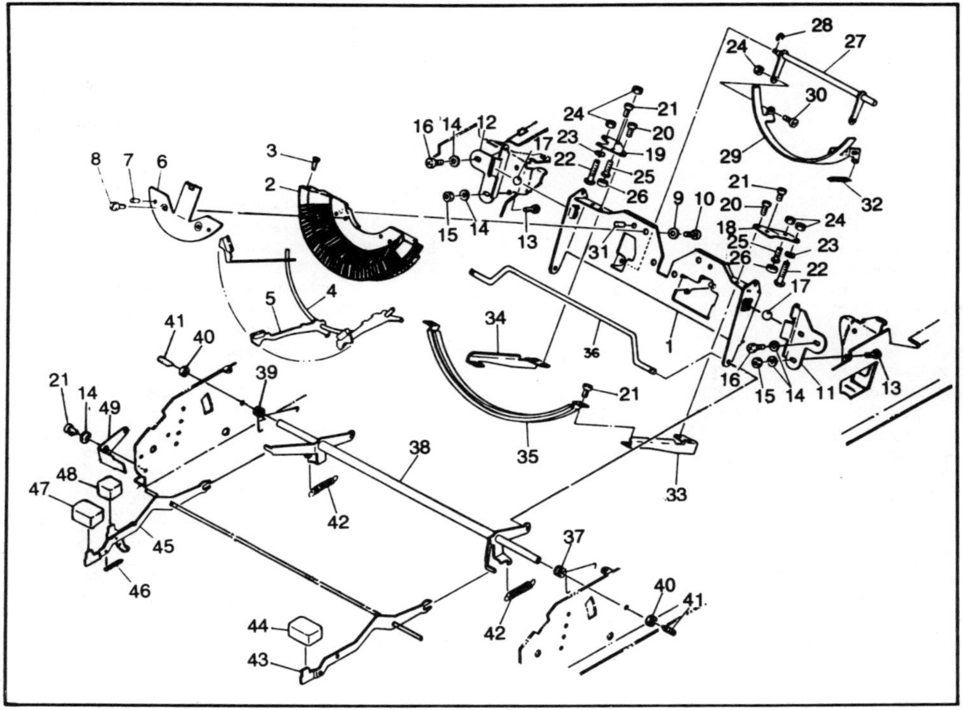

Fig. 5-58. This is the blow-up of the typebar and shift mechanisms, with key numbers (courtesy of OLYMPIA USA INC.).

235

Table 5-3. Parts List for Fig. 5-58 (courtesy of OLYMPIA USA INC.).

Key No.	Parts No.	Description	Key No.	Parts No.	Description
1	82020100	Segment base	31	82020090	Pin
2	82020010	Segment	32	01111100	Spring
3	82020680	Typebar fulcrum shaft stopper	33	82020070	Typebar rest support, right
4	82020020	Typebar fulcrum shaft	34	82020060	Typebar rest support, left
5	82020245/675	Typebar and Typeface	35	82020055	Typebar rest and rubber
6	82020030	Typebar guide	36	82020790	Segment base hanger shaft
7	82090060	Spring pin	37	82020820	Shift arm spring, right
8	01113110	Typebar guide fastening screw	38	82020785	Shift torsion bar
9	82090510	Washer (W-3.5)	39	82020810	Shift arm spring, left
10	82090220	Screw (+N3.5x5)	40	82090420	Nut (N-4)
11	82020860	Slide guide, right	41	82020800	Shift center
12	82020840	Slide guide, left	42	82020830	Segment lift spring
13	82090200	Screw (+N3x8)	43	82020710	Shift key lever, right
14	01007530	Washer (W-3)	44	01144560	Shift key
15	01003510	Nut (N-3)	45	82020715	Shift key lever, left
16	01100010	Screw (+N3-4)	46	01116050	Shift lock lever spring
17	01120050	1/4 steel ball	47	01144560	Shift key
18	82020180	Case stopper bracket, right	48	01144550	Shift lock key
19	82020170	Case stopper bracket, left	49	82020750	Shift lock plate
20	50170200	Screw (+N3-5)			
21	01100010	Screw (+N3-4)			
22	82020190	Shift upper stopper			
23	82020200	Rubber washer			
24	01003510	Nut (N-3)			
25	82020210	Shift lower stopper			
26	52100790	Stopper shoe			
27	82080135	Universal crank complete			
28	01102030	E-ring (E.2.5)			
29	82020110	Segment universal bar			
30	82020140	Universal bar setscrew			

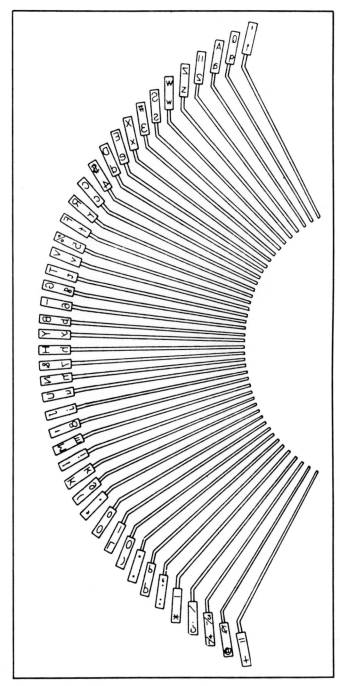

Fig. 5-59. This is the typebar arrangement of the Model B-12. If you care to count and number these from left to right, you will find that your numbers correspond to those under the column heading "Pos. No." of Table 5-2 (courtesy of OLYMPIA USA INC.).

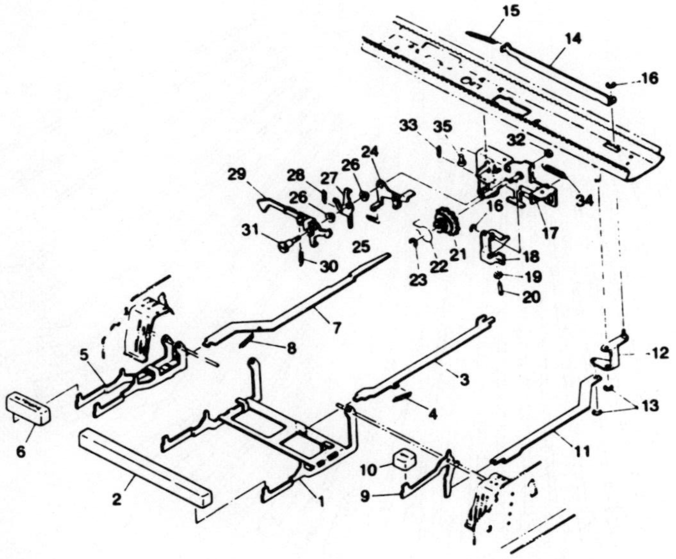

Fig.5-60. Here are the parts of the space, back space and escapement mechanism of the Model B-12. Take the key numbers to the list in Table 5-4 (courtesy of OLYMPIA USA INC.).

238

Table 5-4. Parts List for Fig. 5-60 (courtesy of OLYMPIA USA INC.).

Key No.	Parts No.	Description
1	82010150	Space key lever
2	82010290	Space bar
3	82010200	Space bar link
4	01111100	Space bar spring
5	82010160	Repeat space key lever
6	82010300	Repeat space key
7	82010210	Repeat space link
8	55102030	Repeat space key spring
9	82010180	Back key lever
10	01144500	Back space key
12	82030295	Back space crank complete
13	52100980	E-ring (E-3)
14	82030280	Back space pawl
15	82030330	Back space spring
16	01102030	E-ring (E-2.5)
17	82030015	Escapement base complete
18	82030160	Connection
19	01103510	Nut (N-3)
20	01118180	Trip adjust screw
21	82030025	Escapement wheel
22	82030050	Silencer spring
23	01102030	E-ring (E-2.5)
24	82030075	Loose dog complete
25	82030200	Loose dog spring
26	82030130	Loose dog color
27	82030060	Fixed dog
28	82030210	Fixed dog spring
29	82030095	Swing dog complete
30	82030220	Swing dog spring
31	82030120	Dog Pole
32	01003510	Nut (N-3)
33	82030230	Repeat controller spring
34	82030270	Margin lock spring
35	01100010	Screw (+N3-4)

See Fig. 5-63 and Table 5-7 for a blow-up and parts list of the tabulator and margin mechanism of the Model B-12. See Fig. 5-64 and Table 5-8 for a blow-up and parts list of the ribbon mechanism of the Model B-12. See Fig. 5-65 and Table 5-9 for the chassis and housing and accompanying parts list for the Olympia Model B-12.

SUMMARY

I have given adjustment, repair and parts removal procedures for the Olympia Model B-12, virtually in their entirety in this chapter. I have done this rather than to give a superficial treatment to an important subject namely, a thorough understanding of an

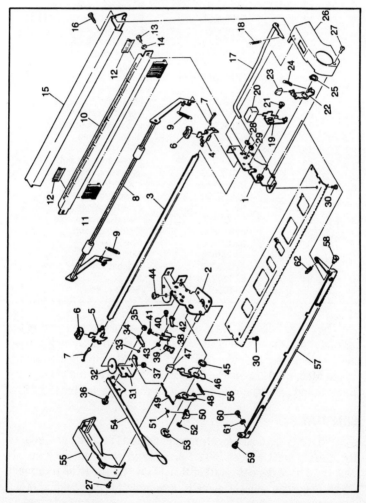

Fig. 5-61. Parts of the carriage mechanism (courtesy of OLYMPIA USA INC.).

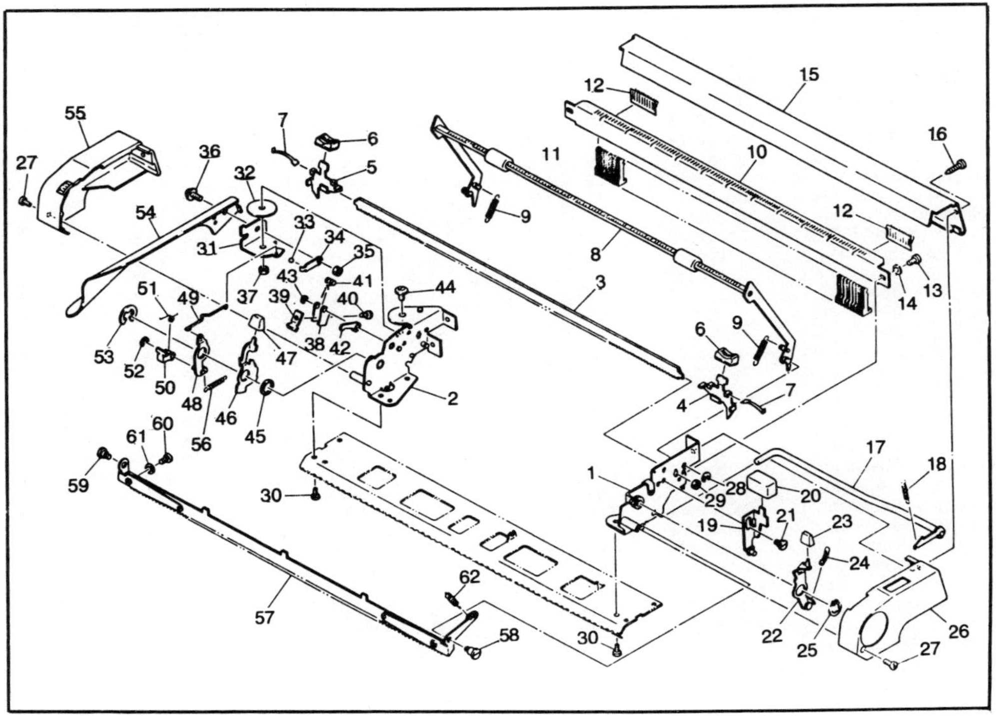

Fig. 5-62. More parts of the carriage mechanism in their entirety (courtesy of OLYMPIA USA INC.).

Table 5-5. Parts List for Fig. 5-61 (courtesy of OLYMPIA USA INC.).

Key No.	Parts No.	Description	Key No.	Parts No.	Description
1	82040125	Carriage side plate, right	33	82090600	Steel ball
2	82040115	Carriage side plate, left	34	82040360	Handle plate spring
3	82050340	Margin rack	35	50135100	Nut (N-3.5)
4	82050360	Margin stop, right	36	82040330	Lever setscrew
5	82050350	Margin stop, left	37	50135100	Nut (N-3.5)
6	82050380	Margin stop cap	38	82040410	Line space detent arm
7	82050370	Margin stop plate spring	39	82040400	Line space detent heel
8	82050395	Paper bail scale complete	40	82090240	Screw (-BA2.6-3)
9	01122070	Scale arm spring	41	82040430	Line space detent spring
10	82060260	Tab stop rack	42	82040420	Selector index
11	82060270	Tab chip	43	82040390	Carriage bracket setscrew
12	82060280	Tab chip spring	44	82040330	Spacer
13	01100010	Nut (+N3x4)	45	82040250	Line space selector
14	01107530	Washer (W-3)	46	30123040	Lever can
15	82080100	Carriage back cover	47	82040265	Line space feed arm
16	82090250	Carriage back cover set nut	48	82040300	Line space link
17	82050265	L-shaft arm complete	49	82040270	Line space feed pawl
18	01122070	Paper pan spring	50	82040290	Line space feed pawl spring
19	82040205	Carriage release lever complete	51	01102020	E-ring (E-2)
20	82040220	Carriage release button	52	82090010	E-ring (E-8)
21	82040180	Lever setscrew	53	82040340	Return handle
22	82050285	Paper release lever complete	54	82080080	Carriage slide cover, left
23	30123040	Lever cap	55	55102030	Line space spring
24	01115130	Paper release lever spring	56	82040155	Carriage rack complete
25	82090020	C-ring (C-9)	57	82040190	Lever setscrew
26	82080090	Carriage side cover, right	58	82040180	Lever setscrew
27	82090230	Carriage side cover fastening screw	59	01120180	Screw
28	01102030	E-ring (E-2.5)	60	01107530	Washer (W-3)
29	50135100	Nut (N-3.5)	62	82040240	Carriage rack spring
30	01100020	Screw (N+3-6)			
31	82040310	Return handle bracket			
32	82040320	Spacer			

Table 5-6. Pats List for Fig. 5-62 (courtesy of OLYMPIA USA INC.).

Key No.	Parts No.	Description
1	82050010	Platen
2	82050090	Metal Washer
3	50170500	E-ring (E-4)
4	82050080	Variable spring
5	52050070	Variable ratchet wheel
6	82050110	Push rod
7	82050035	Platen knob unit, left
8	82050105	Push button
9	82050060	Platen shaft
10	82050045	Platen knob, right
11	50170050	Socket screw
12	82050310	Eraser table
13	82050330	Table spring
14	82050320	Table shaft
15	82050190	Paper support plate
16	82050200	Paper support arm
17	01123550	Support arm fastening screw
18	01119310	Wave washer
19	82050120	Paper pan
20	82050140	Paper feed rear roller
21	82050150	Feed roller metal, right
22	82050160	Feed roller metal, left
23	52100980	E-ring (E-3)
24	82050130	Paper feed front roller
25	82040020	Upper carriage rail - 1
26	82040030	Upper carriage rail - 2
27	01120180	Carriage rail setscrew
28	30120050	Ball bearing retainer
29	01120050	Ball bearing
30	01120140	Ball bearing ratchet
31	82040015	Carriage base
32	82090260	Screw (-F3-5)
33	82020860	Eccentric nut
34	82040095	Main spring complete
35	82040100	Drawband
36	82090500	Washer (W-4)
37	82090410	Main spring fastening unit
38	01113110	Screw

excellent and representative manual, portable typewriter. Neither OLYMPIA USA INC., nor I, would recommend that you completely dismantle your Model B-12, as you have been shown how to do in this chapter. However, if you do so and reassemble it successfully, you can go on to repair manual typewriters, with the assurance that you have taken an important step in coming to terms with a rewarding profession.

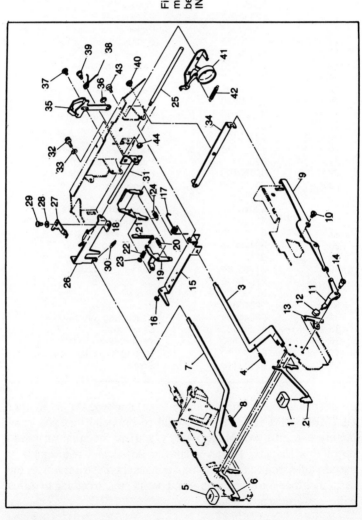

Fig. 5-63. Parts of the tabulator and margin mechanism, with key numbers (courtesy of OLYMPIA USA INC.).

Table 5-7. Parts List for Fig. 5-63 (courtesy of OLYMPIA USA INC.).

Key No.	Parts No.	Description
1	01144520	Tabulator key
2	82010190	Tabulator key lever
3	82010220	Tabulator link
4	01116050	Tabulator key spring
5	01144510	Margin key
6	82010180	Margin key lever
7	82010230	Margin link
8	01111100	Spring
9	82060240	Tab set/clear 1st crank
10	82040180	Lever setscrew
11	82060235	Tab set/clear lever
12	30123040	Lever cap
13	82070260	Fulcrum wire stopper, right
14	82070290	Lever setscrew
15	82060070	Tabulator main bar
16	01102030	E-ring (E-2.5)
17	82060080	Main bar spring
18	82060155	Brake arm and shoe
19	82060100	Stopper lift crank
20	01118270	Spring
21	82060115	Tabulator stopper
22	82060130	Stopper spring
23	01102010	E-ring (E-1.5)
24	82060350	Brake spring
25	82060090	Main bar shaft
26	82060020	Carriage stopper
27	82060050	Margin lock setter
28	01007530	Washer (W-3)
29	01100010	Screw (+N3-4)
30	01111030	Spring
31	82060035	Carriage stopper bracket
32	01120180	Hexagon screw
33	01107530	Washer (W-3)
34	82060255	Tab set/clear 2nd crank
35	82060170	Tab set/clear finger
36	52100980	E-ring (E-3)
37	01119130	Lever set screw
38	82060200	Neutral guide spring
39	82060220	Spring setscrew
40	82040180	Lever setscrew
41	82060315	Bell unit
42	01119050	Spring
43	01100010	Screw
44	01103510	Nut (N-3)

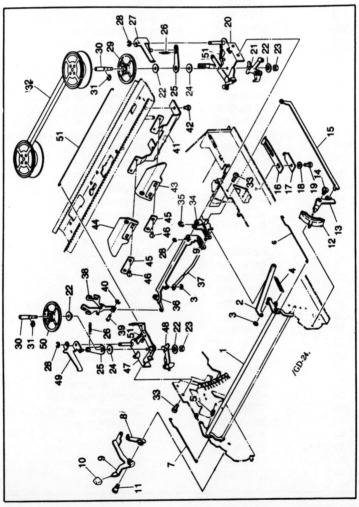

Fig. 5-64. Here are the parts of the ribbon mechanism, with key numbers (courtesy of OLYMPIA USA INC.).

Key No.	Parts No.	RIBBON MECHANISM / Description
1	82070055	Ribbon universal bar
2	82070090	Ribbon lift link
3	01102030	E-ring (E-2.5)
4	50111330	Ribbon universal bar spring
5	82070240	Touch control spring
6	82070800	Ribbon feed link, right
7	82070810	Ribbon feed link, left
8	82070250	Wire stopper, left
9	82070230	Touch control lever
10	30123040	Lever cap
11	82070290	Lever setscrew
12	82070280	Ribbon selector
13	82070200	Ribbon select lever
14	82040180	Lever setscrew
15	82070190	Color select link
16	82070130	Color select detent spring
17	82070140	Spring pad
18	00107530	Washer (W-3)
19	01100010	Screw (+N3-4)
20	82070515	Ribbon base complete, right
21	82070595	Ribbon feed lever complete, right
22	82070560	Lever metal
23	01103510	Nut (N-3)
24	82070580	Spacer
25	82070570	Spring hanger arm
26	82070770	Ribbon holding arm spring
27	82070735	Ribbon holding arm, right
28	01102030	E-ring (E-2.5)
29	82070530	Ribbon ratchet gear, right
30	82070550	Spool shaft
31	52100980	E-ring (E-3)
32		Ribbon lift link
33	82090210	Screw (+N3.5-4)
34	82070110	Cam lever
35	01102030	E-ring (E-2.5)
36	82070165	Ribbon lift crank
37	82070270	Ribbon lift bar
38	82070180	Ribbon viblator
39	82070170	Viblator set pin
40	01102010	E-ring (E-1.5)
41	82040490	Line locator support
42	01100010	Screw (+N3-4)
43	82040480	Line locator, right
44	82040470	Line locator, left
45	82040500	Line locator pad
46	01119260	Line locator setscrew
47	82070525	Ribbon base complete, right
48	82070605	Ribbon feed lever complete, left
49	82070745	Ribbon holding arm, left
50	82070540	Ribbon ratchet gear, left
51	82070720	Rivers spring

Table 5-8. Parts List for Fig. 5-64 (courtesy of OLYMPIA USA INC.).

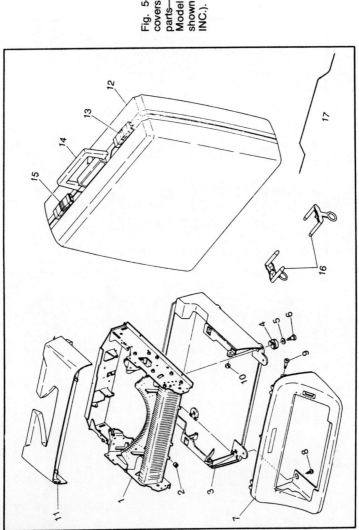

Fig. 5-65. Here are the chassis, covers, carrying case and various parts—without mechanisms—of the Model B-12. Key numbers are shown (courtesy of OLYMPIA USA INC.).

248

Table 5-9. Parts List for Fig. 5-65 (courtesy of OLYMPIA USA INC.).

CHASSIS and HOUSING		
Key No.	Parts No.	Description
1	82070015	Chassis complete
2	82010170	Fit rubber
3	82080020	Bottom plate
4	82080040	Rubber leg
5	82080070	Rubber leg washer
6	82080050	Bottom plate fastening screw
7	82080010	Front cover
8	82090270	Front cover set nut
9	82080060	Cover joint
10	50135100	Nut (N-3.5)
11	82080030	Top cover
12	82080150	Carring case
13	53110021	Carrying case latch, right
14	53110020	Carrying case latch, left
15	53110010	Carrying case handle
16	82080160	Carriage rail plugs
17	281/86	Typebar restraining wire

Finally, you should understand that everything presented in this chapter, including instructions and technical drawings, has been excerpted for the Olympia portable manual typewriter Model B-12 service manual. There has been just enough rewriting to clarify certain points for non-professionals.

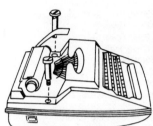

Chapter 6
Adjustment
And Repair
Procedures For The
The Brother Model JP8

The Brother International Corporation, which manufactures and distributes a variety of electrical and electronic business machines—as well as sewing machines—is a Japanese parented company, with American headquarters at 8 Corporate Place, Piscataway, NJ 08854.

The Brother Model JP8 electric typewriter can be further subdivided into Models 3,000, 1,000, XL-4,000 and 3500. The first three models mentioned here have several mechanisms which are activated through the continually rotating power roll, but the shift and carriage return mechanisms are activated manually. However, the Model 3500, a modified version of the Model JP8, has shift and carriage return mechanisms activated by the power roll. This chapter will cover both adjustment and repair procedures for the Brother 3,000, 1,000, and XL-4,000 and unmodified mechanisms of the 3500; and adjustment and repair procedures for the modified mechanisms of the JP8, as they appear in the model 3500. For a full view of the Brother Model JP8 (3500), see Fig. 6-1.

To clarify the information in this chapter, I should repeat that the modifications of the earlier JP8s resulted in powering of the shift mechanism and carriage return. Also, I should point out that, while shifting in some machines is accomplished through the lowering-raising of the typebar segment (or *sector*, as it is called in Brother terminology), shifting in the various models of the Brother JP8 is accomplished through the raising-lowering of the

Fig. 6-1. This is the Brother Model 3500 electric typewriter with electric power carriage return (courtesy of Brother International Corporation).

carriage—and thus the platen—while the typebars remain at a fixed elevation. I will now cover adjustment and repair procedures for the Brother 3,000, 1,000 and XL-4,000 as well as the unmodified mechanism in the 3500.

REMOVING THE COVERS

To remove the covers of the Brother 3,000, 1,000 and XL-4,000, refer to Fig. 6-2. To remove the top cover, simply pull it upward.

To remove the upper cover, set the right margin stop and left margin stop at their respective ends of the carriage. Push the

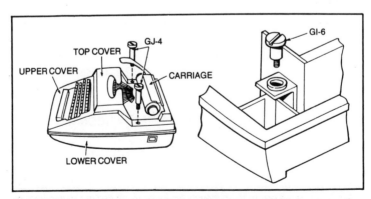

Fig. 6-2. Generally, the first task when repairing any machine is to remove the covers. This drawing shows how (courtesy of Brother International Corporation).

carriage lock lever to the rear to release the carriage. Shift-lock the carriage and then place it in the extreme right position. Remove the top cover. Remove screws (GJ-4). Remove the upper cover from the lower cover by applying force inward to the rear portion of the upper cover.

To remove the lower cover, remove four screws (GI-6) which secure the lower cover to the chassis unit. There is a slight difference, from that just outlined, for removing the covers of the Model 3500. This will be explained and illustrated fully in the section of this chapter dealing with the Model 3500.

Reinstalling the covers is done by reversing the procedure for removing them, but note the following precautions. Make sure the top cover and typebar rest do not interfere with each other. If necessary, bend the typebar rest downward. When installing the top cover onto the upper cover, push the top cover forcibly until it snaps into position. Incorrect installation of the covers may result in vibrating noises during operation.

See Fig. 6-3 for a schematic diagram of the electrical circuit of all Brother JP8 Models.

REMOVING THE MOTOR

To remove the motor of all Brother JP8 Models, refer to Fig. 6-4. Remove the covers. Remove the drive belt (GK-12). Remove the two clamp screws from the motor holder (the screws and holder are not shown; see these parts in Fig. 6-46 at the end of this chapter). Remove the lead wire from the motor. Remove the motor pulley (GK-4). Remove the three screws from the motor holder and then remove the motor.

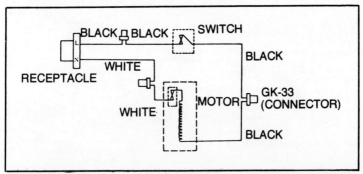

Fig. 6-3. Since the power to an electric typewriter mechanism is taken from a rotating roll, the electrical circuit is simplicity in itself (courtesy of Brother International Corporation).

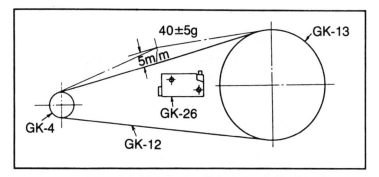

Fig. 6-4. Before immersing any typewriter in a cleaning solution, the motor and other electrical components should be removed. If the text, together with this illustration, doesn't clarify the procedure for you, look at the parts blow-ups at the end of this chapter (courtesy of Brother International Corporation).

ADJUSTING THE BELT TENSION

If the belt tension is too tight, the power roll (hereafter called the *snatch roll*) will not start satisfactorily, and the motor may run noisily. Conversely, if the belt tension is too loose, typing pressure will be too light and the actions of the repeat mechanisms will be erratic. To adjust the belt tension, refer again to Fig. 6-4. Loosen the three screws on the motor holder. Adjust the belt tension by sliding the motor holder along the elongated hole.

It would be desirable to have a gauge for measuring the amount of pressure necessary to deflect the belt a distance of 5 mm (see Fig. 6-4). However, if you can guess at this, the optimum pressure for the 5 mm deflection is 35-45 grams. Be sure to tighten the three screws when the adjustment is complete.

THE SWITCH MECHANISM

As shown in Fig. 6-5A, the switch lever (GK-18) is remote from the body of the switch itself, being connected through the switch operating wire (GK-22). When GK-18 is placed in the "on" position, GK-22 moves the switch operating lever (GK-23), causing the (1) portion of GK-23 to press down on the (2) portion of the switch (GK-21).

Removing the Entire Switch Mechanism

To remove all the parts of the switch mechanism, proceed as follows. Remove all the covers. Remove the drive belt and the snatch roll pulley.

Remove the stud screw. Then remove the switch lever (GK-18) and spring (GK-21). Remove the switch operating lever (GK-23) from its shaft. With these parts removed, the remaining parts of the switch can be removed. (When reinstalling the switch parts, make sure the on-off movement of the switch is positive and that the mechanism is stabilized in the on position.)

Adjusting the Switch Mechanism

Misadjustment of the switch mechanism may be indicated by either of two conditions. Moving the switch to the *off* position does not open the switch contacts, or moving the switch to the *on* position does not close the switch contacts.

The correct clearance between the (1) portion of GK-23 and the (2) portion of the switch itself (see Fig. 6-5B) should be 0.8-1.2 mm in the off position. In the on position, the portion (1) of GK-23 should push down on the (2) portion of GK-25, sufficiently to close the switch contacts. The above conditions can be met by bending the (1) portion of GK-23.

THE PRINTING MECHANISM

The printing mechanism is powered through the snatch roll. In the case of non-repeat typebars, the mechanism engages, prints once and disengages, even though the character key may be held down. In the case of repeat typebars, the mechanism engages when the character key is depressed and re-engages repeatedly for as long as the character key is held down. The non-repeat and repeat mechanisms will be described separately.

Gaining Easier Access to the Printing Mechanism

If certain parts of the printing mechanism, such as the dog shelf, bell crank, etc., need repairing, it will be easier to work on them if you remove the sub-chassis, with the key levers, as well as the sector plate with the typebars. To understand the procedure in detail, it is necessary to refer to several of the parts blow-ups and accompanying parts lists; therefore, to save you the trouble of leafing ahead through the pages of this chapter, I will give you that procedure in the latter part of this chapter, where the parts blow-ups are shown.

Understanding The Non-Repeat Mechanism

Refer to Figs. 6-6A and 6-6B. When the character key (Fig. 6-6A) is depressed, the key lever link (attached to the key lever)

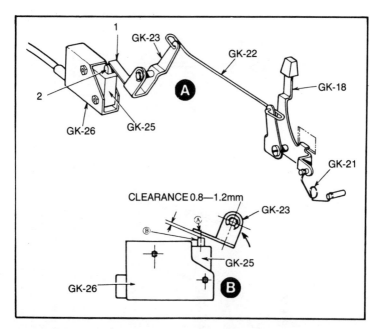

Fig. 6-5(A). The secret to positive on and off switching lies in the contact between (1) and (2) of this illustration (courtesy of Brother International Corporation). (B) When the switch is "off," the clearance between (1) and (2) should be 0.8-1.2 mm (courtesy of Brother International Corporation).

pushes the dog shelf down. The dog shelf engages with the snatch roll, which is shown rotating clockwise. Through its engagement with the snatch roll, the dog shelf is moved in the direction of arrow (1). Moving in the direction of (1), the dog shelf comes into contact with the dog shelf stopper and at the same time disengages from the snatch roll.

While making the just described movement, the dog shelf causes the bell crank to rotate around its fulcrum point (1b), in the arrow direction (2)—or counterclockwise. The rotation of the bell crank pulls the typebar wire, causing the typebar to rotate around its fulcrum point and move in the arrow direction (3) toward the platen.

Meanwhile, as you will remember, the dog shelf has become disengaged from the snatch roll. The tension of the spring (GB-56) pulls the dog shelf back to its original position. Likewise, the key lever and key lever link will return to home positions through spring tensions, thus pulling the typebar back to its original position.

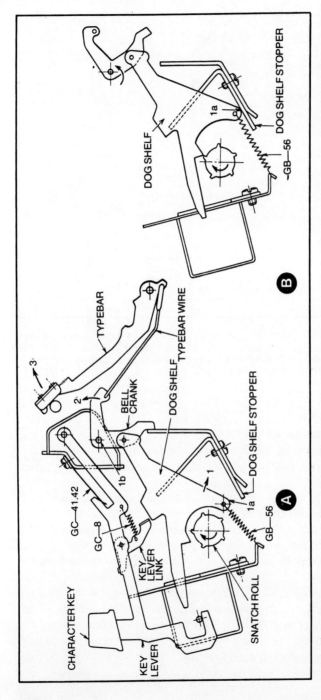

Fig. 6-6(A). Study this illustration carefully to understand the operation of the non-repeat printing mechanism. Note that the snatch roll engages with the dog shelf, pushes it to the stopper, and then disengages, so repeat printing isn't possible if adjustments are correct. (B) This illustration shows the position of the dog shelf just after it hits the stopper and disengages from the snatch, roll. Read the text to understand the function of the spring (GB-56) (courtesy of Brother International Corporation).

A close examination of the relationship between the tip of the key lever link and the dog shelf will show you why the mechanism will not repeat if the character key remains depressed (also see Fig. 6-6B).

Adjusting the Non-Repeat Mechanism

Conditions that indicate a misadjustment of the non-repeat mechanism are the typebar strikes the platen too hard, or the typebar strikes the platen too lightly.

To *reduce* the striking pressure, refer to Fig. 6-7. Use a screwdriver (driver) to bend the tip of the dog shelf stopper upward, thereby reducing the momentum of the dog shelf. Make this adjustment in small increments, as too much bending may result in a back pressure, which the typist would feel in the character key.

To *increase* the striking pressure, do not try to make any adjustment at the dog shelf stopper. Go instead to the typebar wire which, you will note, is bent (refer back to Fig. 6-6A). This bend to some extent determines the effective length of the typebar wire. If it is so long as to create a large amount of play between the typebar and typebar wire, the pressure will be decreased; thus, further

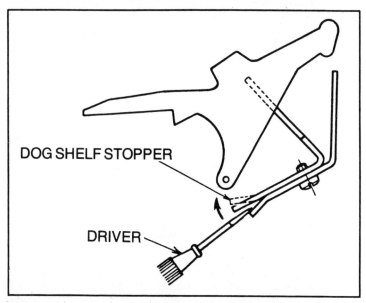

Fig. 6-7. Use a screwdriver to adjust the clearance between the dog shelf stopper and dog shelf (courtesy of Brother International Corporation).

bending of the typebar wire will increase the striking pressure of the typebar. Too much bending or repeated bending will weaken the typebar wire.

It may also be necessary to adjust the timing of the ribbon lift, as early timing of the ribbon lift may result in light printing. This adjustment will be explained later in this chapter.

Understanding the Repeat Mechanism

To understand the operation of the repeat mechanism, refer to Figs. 6-8A and 6-8B. Initial pressure on the character key will cause the character to print once, and further depressing will cause

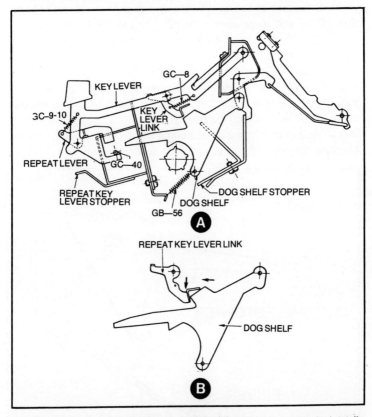

Fig. 6-8. (A) Study this illustration to note the differences in mechanical details between the repeat mechanism (of this drawing) and the non-repeat mechanism of Fig. 6-6. (B) Here, a difference in the design of the key lever link, from that of the non-repeat printing mechanism, doesn't allow the dog shelf to disengage from the snatch roll until the key is released by the typist (courtesy of Brother International Corporation).

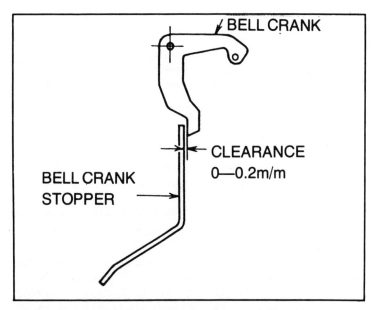

Fig. 6-9. For a better understanding of this illustration relate it to Fig. 6-8. Read the text to understand the adjustment procedure (courtesy of Brother International Corporation).

it to repeat. On the initial depression, the repeat lever (which is attached to the key lever) stops. Subsequently, depressing the character key farther extends the repeat lever movement, through the springs (GC-9 and 10).

If the repeat lever is extended until it hits the repeat key lever stopper, the dog shelf will go through the same movement as in the case of the non-repeat mechanism.

As the dog shelf activates the mechanism through one printing cycle and returns to its original position, it will again be lowered (Fig. 6-8B). Printing will be repeated for as long as the character key is held down.

Adjusting the Repeat Mechanism

Irregularity of the repeat mechanism may be adjusted as follows. While bending the repeat lever stopper (Fig. 6-8A) downward, depress the repeat character key deeply and observe the regularity. Adjust the repeat key lever stopper accordingly.

See Fig. 6-9. Adjust the clearance between the lower tip of the bell crank and the bell crank stopper to 0-0.2 mm, with the character key not depressed.

The beginning of the movement of the typebar wire and bell crank should be about simultaneous. To check this timing, depress the character key while rotating the snatch roll by hand (use the pulley). Incorrect timing can be corrected by bending the typebar wire; however, do it carefully so as not to damage the typebar wire.

Other Adjustments to the Printing Mechanism

Misadjustments in various points of the printing mechanism may cause such problems as no-printing when a key is touched quickly or lightly, or repeat printing in the non-repeat mechanism. For optimum performance, the following adjustments should be made.

See Figs. 6-10A and 6-10B. Adjust the clearance between the key lever link and dog shelf (Fig. 6-10A) to be 0.4-1.0 mm, when the character key is not depressed.

Adjust the contacted area between the key lever link and dog shelf (Fig. 6-10B) to 0.5-1.2 mm when the character key is depressed. A too-small contacted area here can cause non-printing at high-speed typing. Too much contacted area can cause repeat operation.

Refer to Fig. 6-11. Depress the character key while rotating the snatch roll manually. Observe the distance of the typeface from the platen when the dog shelf disengages from the snatch roll. Optimally, this distance would be 20-28 mm. To make this

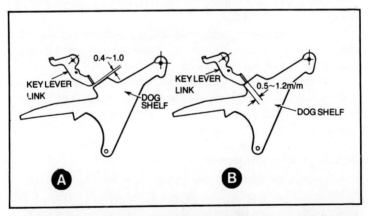

Fig. 6-10. (A) The clearance between the key lever link and dog shelf should be 0.4-1.0 mm, on the non-repeat mechanism, when the key is not depressed. (B) When the key is depressed, the contacted area between the key lever link and dog shelf should be within the shown tolerance, for correct printing (courtesy of Brother International Corporation).

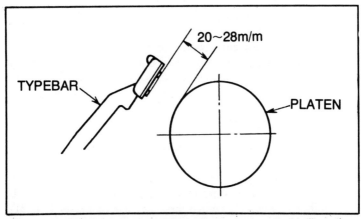

Fig. 6-11. Read the text to understand the adjustment shown in this illustration. Move the various mechanisms manually to note areas of engagement, etc. (courtesy of Brother International Corporation).

adjustment, slightly bend or extend the typebar. Moreover, if the play between the typebar wire, bell crank and typebar is minimized, the dog shelf will have more momentum. The disengagement of the dog shelf from the snatch roll will be slower. If, on the other hand, the dog shelf stopper is adjusted upward, the disengagement of the dog shelf from the snatch roll will be faster. This will result in lighter printing (i.e., a lighter stroke).

Refer to Fig. 6-12. As the typebar swings toward the platen and comes to rest (no clearance) at the (A) portion, the clearance

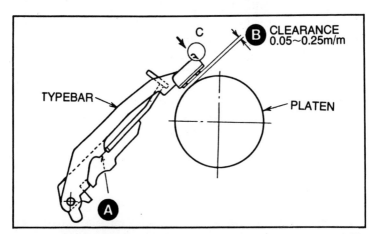

Fig. 6-12. Move the typebar manually and note the clearances at (A) and (B) (courtesy of Brother International Corporation).

between the typebar head and platen (B) should be 0.05-0.25 mm, except in the case of a small character, such as the period ("."), in which case the clearance should be 0.45-0.65 mm. Moreover, when the (C) portion is depressed until the (B) clearance just becomes zero, the clearance at (A) should also be zero. This adjustment can be made by smashing or grinding the (A) portion.

THE SPACE BAR MECHANISM

Spacing is accomplished manually, that is, without the help of the snatch roll. See Figs. 6-13A and 6-13B.

Depressing the space bar (GD-11) lowers the space crank (GD-15) through a rotating movement. The rotation of GD-15 transmits a movement through the space bar connector (GD-21), which rotates the space bar crank (GD-22).

The rotation of GD-22 is transmitted through the space bar wire (GD-24) to cause the rear escape crank (GF-30) to rotate. This causes the half space ratchet (GF-37) to be moved by the eccentric screw (GF-34).

The half space ratchet (GF-37) rotates the space ratchet (GF-36), resulting in the disengagement of GF-36 from the space ratchet wheel (GF-23). This accomplishes a one-half space movement.

After the half-space movement is accomplished, the remaining half space will be accomplished through the tension of the spring drum (the spring drum in an electric machine performs essentially the same function as in the manual machine—it provides the power for the leftward movement of the carriage), when the space bar returns to home position.

To adjust the space bar mechanism, refer to Fig. 6-13B. Adjust the clearance between the cushion rubber (GD-13) and the stopper portion of the chassis, when the space ratchet (GF-36 of Fig. 6-13A) is disengaged from the space ratchet wheel (GF-23) by slowly lowering the space bar (GD-11), until the clearance is more than 0.5 mm (Fig. 6-13B). Make this adjustment by bending the space bar wire (GD-24, Fig. 6-13A).

THE ESCAPEMENT MECHANISM

As you remember from previous descriptions, the escapement mechanism of a typewriter causes the carriage to move one pitch when a typebar is activated. On the Brother Models under discussion—as well as on most other typewriters—this is ac-

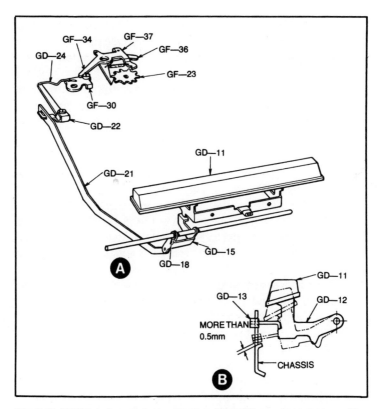

Fig. 6-13. (A) This is the spacing mechanism. You will be seeing lots more of the parts (GF-23, GF-36 and GF-37). (B) Study this illustration and the text to understand the function of part (GD-24) in the adjustment of the space mechanism (courtesy of Brother International Corporation).

complished by the motion of the typebar being transmitted through various linkages to the escapement mechanism.

Understanding the Escapement Mechanism

Refer to Fig. 6-14. When the typebar (not shown) pushes the escapement drive plate unit (GA-54, which in Fig. 6-14 is isolated from the rest of the mechanism) in the arrow direction, the universal bar (GA-57) is lowered, and the front escape crank (GF-26) is rotated.

The rotation of GF-26 will shift the half space ratchet (GF-37) to the place where it will engage with the space ratchet wheel (GF-23). This motion is transmitted through the rear space crank (GF-30).

As GF-37 is engaged with the space ratchet wheel, the space ratchet (GF-36) is simultaneously disengaged from the space ratchet wheel. In this condition, the carriage is shifted one-half pitch by the tension of the spring drum.

GF-37 and GF-36 return to their original positions through the tension of the associated springs. As the escapement drive plate unit returns to its original position, the carriage will move the remaining half pitch.

Adjusting the Escapement Mechanism

To adjust the escapement mechanism, proceed as follows. Still referring to Fig. 6-14, check that the area of engagement between the space ratchet (GF-36) and space ratchet wheel (GF-23) is 1.7-1.9 mm (See point A of Fig. 6-14). Also check that the clearance between the half space ratchet (GF-37) and the tip of the space ratchet wheel (GF-23) is 0.1-0.3 mm (see point B of Fig. 6-14).

If the above clearances are not correct, adjust the clearance between GF-34 and GF-37 (point C) by rotating the eccentric screw. If the clearances at (A) and (B) are not correct, but there is sufficient clearance at (C), the clearance at (B) can be adjusted by turning the eccentric screw for GF-36.

After making these adjustments, you can time the escapement by adjusting the eccentric screw at GF-34, so that escapement is accomplished when you move the typebar to within 1-10 mm from the surface of the platen by moving the typebar manually. If there is a significant difference between the timing of a center typebar and a right- or left-end typebar, you can decrease this difference by shifting GA-59 (the guide plate for GA-57) in either the E or F direction, as follows. When GA-59 is shifted in the E direction, the escapement as a function of the center typebars will be faster than that of the end typebars. When GA-59 is shifted in the F direction, the escapement as a function of the center typebars will be the slower. Shifting GA-59 too far may cause other escapement problems, such as failure to escape.

If the escapement timing is excessively fast or slow, or if the escapement fails to work when the space bar is depressed, you can adjust by lengthening or shortening the space bar wire (GD-24 of Fig. 6-14). The optimum adjustment for GD-24 is no clearance when GD-24 is engaged with the rear escape crank (point D of GF-34), when the carriage is shifted (there still may be approximately 1.5 mm of clearance under non-shift condition, but this is tolerable).

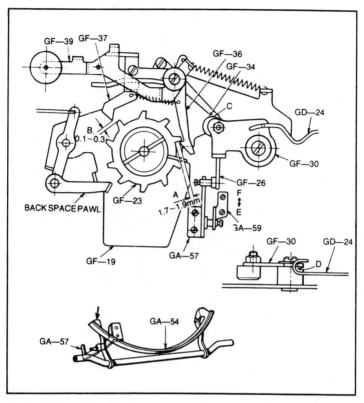

Fig. 6-14. This is the escapement mechanism of the Brother JP8 Models. Read the text to understand the points of adjustment (courtesy of Brother International Corporation).

BACK SPACE MECHANISM

The back space mechanism of the Brother Models under discussion is not powered by the snatch roll. Refer to Figs 6-15A and 6-15B.

Understanding the Back Space Mechanism

When the back space key (GB-102, Fig. 6-15A) is pushed down, the back space lever (GC-12) pulls the back space wire (GC-14) in the direction of the arrow.

The lateral movement of GC-14 rotates the back space link (GC-15), thus moving the back space pawl in the arrow direction. This rotates the space ratchet wheel (GF-23) in the arrow direction—i.e., clockwise. Since the rotation of GF-23 is one

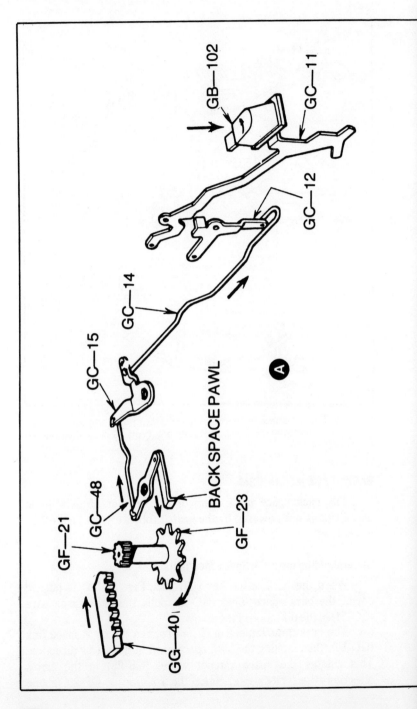

BACK SPACE PAWL

GB—102
GC—11
GC—12
GC—14
GC—15
GC—48
GF—23
GF—21
GG—40

Ⓐ

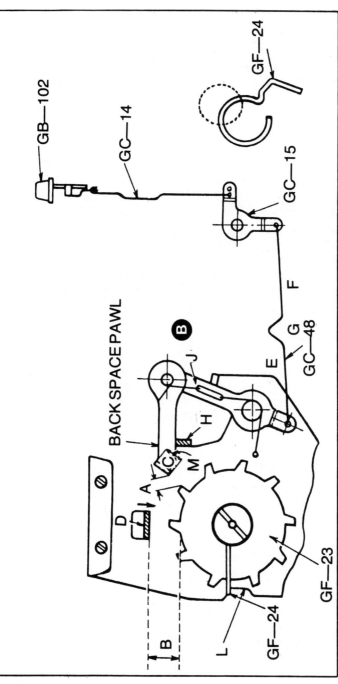

Fig. 6-15. (A) This drawing isolates the back space mechanism from the machine, making its operation readily understandable (be sure and read the text, however). (B) This illustration, together with the text, explains how to adjust the back space mechanism. The connecting wires (GC-48, GC-24 and GC-14) are bent for a purpose—as a means of adjusting their lengths; however, bend them only if necessary, and then as minimally as possible, to prevent damage to them (courtesy of Brother International Corporation).

pitch, this is transmitted to the carriage rack (GG-40) through the space pinion (GF-21).

If it should become necessary to remove any parts of the back space mechanism, information on this procedure will be given at the end of this chapter, where you can more easily refer to the parts blow-ups.

Adjusting the Back Space Mechanism

To adjust the back space mechanism, refer to Fig. 6-15B. The clearance at point (A) should be minimized. Do this by shortening the (G) portion of the rear back space wire (GC-48), under shifted condition, to obtain the minimum clearance, but without the (C) portion of the back space pawl touching the space ratchet wheel (GF-23). After this adjustment is made, the E and F sections of the rear back space wire (GC-48) should still be in alignment.

In case the carriage moves back more than one pitch when the back space key is forcibly and quickly pushed, bend the (D) portion, in the direction of the arrow, to be equal with the clearance (I). Do not bend the (D) portion too much. Optimally, the (J) portion of the back space pawl and the (H) portion of the pinion base should touch each other lightly.

When installing the ratchet release spring (GF-24) on GF-23, it should be installed from the dotted line side, as shown in Fig. 6-15B. The tip of the spring (GF-24) should be against the notched portion (L) of the pinion base. If the spring (GF-24) is not installed correctly, the carriage may not shift correctly or may not lock properly in place.

THE SHIFT MECHANISM

You will remember that the Brother Models 3,000, 1,000 and XL-4,000 shift manually, that is, not through the power of the snatch roll.

Understanding the Shift Mechanism

Refer to Fig. 6-16A. When the shift lever unit (GD-1) is lowered, the shift crank (GF-7) is rotated counterclockwise. Through the rotation of GF-7, the shift wire (GF-14) rotates the rear shift link (GF-15) counterclockwise. The rotation of GF-15 will raise the right and left side frames (the left side frame is shown as GF-4), thus shifting the carriage to the shift stopper (Fig. 6-16B). When the shift lock key lever (GD-5) is pushed down, the

Fig. 6-16. (A) The upper part of this illustration is a perspective view of the shift mechanism, and the lower part is a side view, showing the left-hand shift key, together with the shift-lock key. (B) The shift stoppers regulate the upper and lower limits of carriage travel as it shifts up and down. They should be set in such a manner that the carriage doesn't "float," so that it raises equally across the machine, and so that upper and lower case characters bottom on the same line. However, once you understand the principles involved, the adjustment is easier than it sounds. (C) In this illustration, part (GB-106) is the shift lock key. If it doesn't lock, read the text and study this illustration to learn how to adjust for positive locking (courtesy of Brother International Corporation).

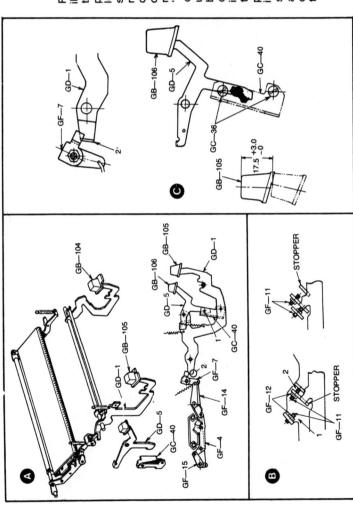

tip (I) of GD-5 is lowered until it hooks under the shift lock plate (GC-40), thus locking the carriage in the shift position.

The procedure for removing the parts of the shift mechanism will be given at the end of this chapter, where you can more easily refer to the parts blow-ups.

Adjusting the Shift Mechanism

Adjusting the shift mechanism means essentially to adjust the raising of the carriage so that the base of the small letters and capital letters remain even, that the carriage is raised evenly across its length, and that the shift lock maintains the carriage in a shifted-locked position. Refer to Fig. 6-16B.

To adjust for alignment of the capital and small letters, loosen the nuts (GF-12, two in all) and turn the shift adjusting screws (GF-11) up or down. Turning the (1) portion of GF-11 clockwise will lower the small letter; and turning the (1) portion counterclockwise will raise the small letter. Rotating the (2) portion of GF-11 clockwise will raise the capital letters; and rotating the (2) portion counterclockwise will lower the capital letters. In making the above adjustment, first make sure the curved face of the small letter or capital letter is fitted with the platen. Then adjust the position of the letter that does not fit.

You understand, of course, that the adjustment screws (GF-11) are found on both ends of the machine. They should be adjusted for carriage alignment across the paper.

At either shift or no-shift position, if there is a clearance between the tip of GF-11 and the stopper, either the shift motion or shift-lock may be adversely affected. Moreover, if there is clearance at these points, further adjustment of the mechanism will be difficult or impossible.

If the shift-lock is too easily released, the cause will probably be a clearance between GF-11 and the stoppers. If it is difficult to engage the shift-lock mechanism (through the lowering of GD-5 of Fig. 6-16A), you may find that the shift lock plate (GC-40) is too low. To move the shift lock plate, loosen the screw (GC-36, Fig. 6-16C) and move the plate. The adjustment can be made through the hole of the snatch roll pulley.

Further, make sure the stroke of the shift key (GB-105) is no less than 17.5 mm and no more than 17.8 mm, when the shift lock motion is adjusted. To make this adjustment, bend the shift lever unit (GD-1) to get the correct stroke.

270

THE TABULATOR MECHANISM

The tabulator mechanism is not powered through the snatch roll. It simply releases the carriage which, through the tension of the spring drum, travels a preset distance and stops at a preset tab stop.

Understanding the Tabulator Mechanism

Refer to Fig. 6-17A. When the tab key (GB-103) is pushed down, the various connecting linkages cause the tab operating crank to be rotated in the arrow direction (counterclockwise).

The rotation of the tab operating crank is transmitted through the rear tab operating wire (GC-46), thus rotating the tab operating lever in the arrow direction. The rotation of the tab operating lever first rotates the tab stopper in the arrow direction, engaging the tip of the tab stopper with the tab stop pawl (GH-16). Simultaneously, the tab operating lever pushes the space ratchet (GF-36), disengaging it from the space ratchet wheel (GF-23). Upon disengagement of GF-36 from GF-23, the carriage moves to the left under spring tension until the tab stopper contacts GH-16.

Adjusting the Tabulator Mechanism

To adjust the tabulator mechanism, refer to Fig. 6-17B. Some adjustment may be obtained by lengthening or shortening the rear tab operating wire (GC-46) to get 1.5-2.0 mm clearance at point (1), between the tab operating lever and the space ratchet (GF-36). Also, adjust the 0.8-1.3 mm clearance at point (2), between the tab stopper and the tab stop pawl (GH-16).

If GF-36 is excessively inclined (see the dotted lines in Fig. 6-17B), and if the clearance at point (1) is not 1.5-2.0 mm (and even if the (2) clearance is 0.8-1.3 mm), bend the (3) portion of the tab operating lever to get the clearance of 1.5-2.0 mm at (1). If, after obtaining the correct clearance at points (1) and (2), there is excessive play at the (4) portion (which might result in erratic release of GF-36 from GF-23), remove the play at (4—between GC-46 and the pin) by bending GC-46.

THE COLOR CHANGE AND THE RIBBON LIFTING MECHANISM

The color change and ribbon lifting mechanism establishes whether the upper or lower half of the ribbon is used. It causes the ribbon to be raised when ribbon typing is desired or not to be raised

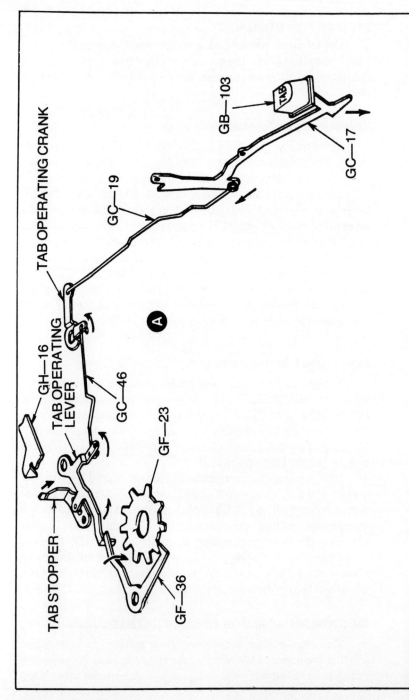

TAB OPERATING CRANK

GB—103

GC—17

GC—19

GH—16

TAB OPERATING LEVER

GC—46

GF—23

TAB STOPPER

GF—36

A

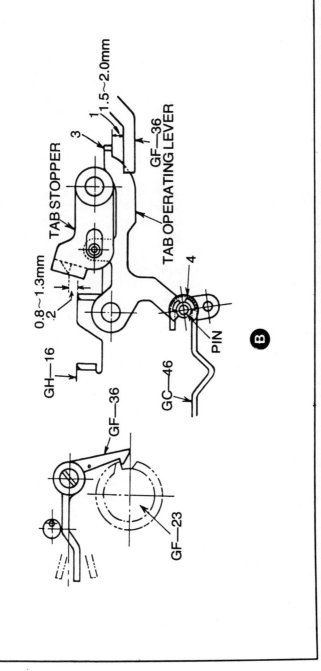

Fig. 6-17. (A) The tabulator mechanism of these Brother Models is quite conventional and easily understood. Remember that though the machine is electric, the tabbing operation is mechanical, with the leftward movement of the carriage "powered" by a spring drum. (B) The primary place to make an adjustment in the tabbing mechanism is at the bend of part (GC-46); however, be sure to read the text to fully understand the adjustments (courtesy of Brother International Corporation).

273

when ribbon typing is not desired (as in the case of typing a mimeograph stencil).

How the Black Color of the Ribbon is Obtained

To see how the black portion of the ribbon is put in place for typing, refer to Fig. 6-18. When the ribbon color selector (GD-32) is set for black, the color change lever (GD-37) rotates and places the front ribbon vibrator wire (GD-45) in the lowest groove of the ribbon vibrator operating lever (GD-39).

Likewise, the rotation of GD-32 for black typing will rotate the color change stopper—via the color change stop wire (GD-46)—to where it becomes the stopper for the ribbon operating link (GD-48). When a character key is pushed, the bell crank (the bell crank is a part of the typing mechanism, as you may remember) rotates, and the ribbon operating bar also rotates. Through the rotation of the ribbon operating bar, the rear color change link wire (GD-44) is pulled, rotating the color change link (GD-41) in the arrow direction.

The rotation of GD-41 pulls the front color change link wire (GD-43) in the arrow direction. The movement of GD-43 causes the ribbon vibration operating lever (GD-39) to rotate in the arrow direction. Since the ribbon color selector is set for black typing, GD-39 is moved only minimally.

GD-48 will rotate in the arrow direction, thus pulling the rear ribbon vibrator wire (GD-49). Through the movement of GD-49, the ribbon vibrator link (GD-53) will rotate and lift the ribbon vibrator (GD-56).

How the Mechanism Holds the Ribbon in Place for Stencil Cutting

In stencil cutting, the ribbon is not raised between the typebar face and platen. Therefore, the ribbon is not an impediment to cutting a clear opening through the stencil. Here is how no-ribbon lift is accomplished.

When the ribbon color selector (GD-32) is set for stencil cutting, the color change lever (GD-37) rotates and places the front ribbon vibrator wire (GD-45) into the middle position of the groove of the ribbon vibrator operating bar, etc., go through the same motions as described for black typing. However, when GD-39 is rotated, GD-45 remains motionless because of its position in the groove of GD-39. Consequently, no lifting motion is imparted to the ribbon vibrator (GD-56), and the ribbon remains stationary.

274

How the Mechanism Sets the Ribbon for Red Typing

The ribbon set for red typing is accomplished as follows. When the ribbon color selector (GD-32) is set for red, the color change lever (GD-37) rotates and places the front ribbon vibrator wire (GD-45) into the top groove of GD-39.

Through the rotation of GD-32 by making a red setting, the color change stopper rotates via GD-46 to the place where the ribbon operating link (GD-45) is not contacted, even though it moves. When a character key is pushed, the bell crank, ribbon operating bar, etc., go through the movements described in previous sections. The ribbon vibrator (GD-56) is lifted up until it contacts and is stopped by its stopper portion.

Adjustment of the Color Change and Ribbon Lifting Mechanism

The adjustment of the color change must satisfy the following conditions. With the ribbon color selector set on black, the ribbon must be completely lifted when the typebar face is manually placed 15-25 mm from the platen surface (use a typebar near the center of the sector for this trial). If the ribbon is lifted completely when the typebar face is farther than 25 mm from the platen surface, the impression will be too light. If, on the other hand, the ribbon does not lift completely before the typebar face is as close as 15 mm from the platen surface, the impression may be a mix of black and red, or part of the character will be cut off.

When a combination character, such as ½ or ¼, is manually moved toward the platen surface, under non-shift, the lower edge of the small character must be 1.5 mm higher than the edge of the red ribbon in the case of a black color selection. The upper edge of the small letter must be 1 mm lower than the edge of the black ribbon in the case of red color selection.

The adjustment of the conditions just described are as follows. Refer to Fig. 6-18B. If the timing of the ribbon lift is too early, lengthen the (3) portion of the front color change link wire (GD-43) or extend the front ribbon vibrator wire (GD-45).

If the timing of the ribbon lift is too late (the movement of GD-56 is too short), shorten the (3) portion of GD-43 or GD-45 (Fig. 6-18B). Then adjust the (G) portion until GD-45 is almost touched by the (5) end of the ribbon vibrator operating lever (GD-39). Yet another adjustment, which would increase the distance of movement of the ribbon, is to move the color change lever (GD-37) upward. When making adjustments, be careful not to

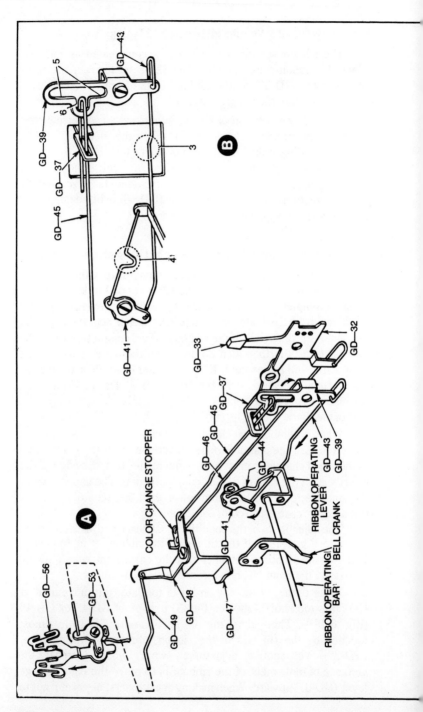

A

GD—56
GD—53
COLOR CHANGE STOPPER
GD—49
GD—48
GD—47
GD—41
GD—44
GD—46
GD—45
GD—37
GD—33
GD—32
GD—43
GD—39
RIBBON OPERATING LEVER
BELL CRANK
RIBBON OPERATING BAR

B

GD—43
5
6
GD—39
GD—37
GD—45
GD—41
3
41

276

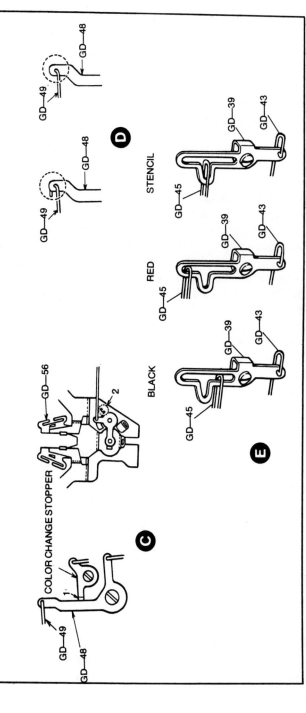

Fig. 6-18. (A) This is the color change and ribbon lift mechanism, which probably looks simpler in the machine than it does on paper. In the context of this discussion, "color" means black and red ribbon, black and black on an all black ribbon, and perhaps even black and "white" in the case of a correcting ribbon. Part (GD-56) is the ribbon vibrator, through which the ribbon is guided. It moves up and down (thus, "vibrates") during typing, except when GD-33 is set for "stencil," in which case GD-56 remains stationary. (B) Adjust the timing of the ribbon lift by bending GD-43 at point (3); however, do this with care. (C) A point at which the movement of the ribbon vibrator can be regulated is marked (1) in this illustration. Read the text. (D) If you're not sure what GD-49 represents in this illustration, refer back to Fig. 6-18A and, as always, read the text. (E) A glance at this illustration will reveal how and why the color change and ribbon lift mechanism works (courtesy of Brother International Corporation).

277

shorten the entire length of GD-45 or GD-43 too much. In the case of a stencil setting, note that the ribbon vibrator (GD-56) is moved up and down when the ribbon color selector (GD-32) is operated.

If a mix of black and red is printed, and/or portions of characters are cut off, adjust the distance that the ribbon vibrator moves. Bend the tip (point 1—see Fig. 6-18C) of the color change stopper so that the ribbon vibrator (GD-56) is stopped in the correct position.

As an example, if in black typing the lower portion of a character is printed red (as would be caused by excessive lifting of (GD-56), bend the (1) portion of the color change stopper (Fig. 6-18C) slightly, so as to limit the movement of GD-48.

As another example, if the upper portion of a character is cut off (as would be caused by insufficient ribbon lift), bend the (1) portion of the color change stopper so that GD-56 is lifted slightly higher.

If there is rough operation between the ribbon operating link (GD-48—refer to Fig. 6-18D) and rear ribbon vibrator wire (GD-49), the ribbon vibrator (GD-56) will not operate correctly and the printed impression will be affected. To correct this, adjust the radius of the curvature of GD-49 to make it smaller to insure a smoother operation (Fig. 6-18D).

The three positions of the ribbon vibrator wire (GD-45) in the grooves of the ribbon vibrator operating lever (GD-39) are shown in Fig. 6-18E. Note the position for *black* color selection, the position for *red* color selection and the position for *no-ribbon* or *stencil cutting*.

If the front ribbon vibrator wire (GD-45) does not return to its proper position when the ribbon color selector is changed from stencil to black, or stencil to red, the cause may be that either GD-43 or GD-45 is too short. GD-43 can be lengthened by adjusting the (3) portion of GD-43 (see Fig. 6-18B). The effective length of GD-45 can be increased by insuring that GD-39 is vertical, and that there is clearance, by adjusting the (4) portion (see Fig. 6-18B).

THE RIBBON FEED AND REVERSE MECHANISM

For a perspective view of the ribbon feed and reverse mechanism, see Fig. 6-19A.

Understanding the Ribbon Feed and Reverse Mechanism

Here's how the mechanism works. When a character key is pushed, the printing mechanism goes into operation, and ultimately the bell crank is rotated. The rotation of the bell crank rotates the ribbon operating bar. The movement of the ribbon operating bar is transmitted to the ribbon feed wire (GD-8), causing the ribbon feed pawl (GE-3) to rotate the right-hand ribbon feed wheel (GE-13).

With the ribbon being pulled off the right-hand spool, the eyelet of the ribbon (the eyelet is within inches of the end of the ribbon, as you will remember) will not pass through the slotted portion of the right ribbon reverse lever. Therefore, the pulling force of the ribbon rotates GE-7. At the same time, through the medium of the ribbon reverse wire (GE-32), the left ribbon reverse lever is pulled (the left ribbon reverse lever is part number GE-22 of Fig. 6-19B). Once the left and right ribbon reverse levers are rotated, they remain stabilized in that position through a reverse snap ring (GE-30, Fig. 6-19B).

The procedure for removing the complete ribbon spool holder will be given at the end of this chapter, where you can more easily refer to parts blow-ups and numbers.

Adjusting the Ribbon Feed and Reverse Mechanism

To adjust the ribbon feed and reverse mechanism, and insure positive ribbon reversing, see Fig. 6-19B. Adjust the position of the reverse snap ring (GE-30) by loosening the screw (GE-31), so that the (2) portion of GE-30 is at the center of the swing of the (1) portion of the ribbon reverse lever (GE-22), when GE-22 is moved from left to right by hand.

When the tip of (1) and (2) are together, the clearance (3) between the right ribbon feed wheel (GE-13) and the right wheel backlash stopper (GE-5), and between their counterparts on the left side, should be 0 and 2 mm, respectively.

If the amount of pull necessary to move either the right or left ribbon reverse levers (GE-7 or GE-22) is either too heavy or too light, adjust by bending the (4) portion of GE-30. However, before making this adjustment, be sure that rough movement of GE-7 or GE-22 is not caused by these parts themselves.

It should take only a light pull to operate either of the left or right ribbon feed pawls, and all should be aligned correctly in respect to each other. Whenever the feed pawls do not contact the ribbon reverse levers, they should contact the teeth of the ribbon feed wheels.

The foregoing steps describe how to insure ribbon reversal; the following steps describe how to insure positive ribbon feeding

(Fig. 6-19B). When the ribbon feed pawls do not contact their respective ribbon feed wheels, or when the ribbon is not being fed correctly, adjust the contact of the feed pawls and ribbon feed wheels by bending the ribbon feed wire (GD-8) to lengthen or shorten it. When operating normally, the ribbon feed wheels should be moved three or four teeth each time a typebar is activated.

When the movement of the ribbon reverse wire (GD-32) is sticky or incorrect because of being too short or too long, adjust the length by bending the (5) or (6) portions of GE-32. Note that the left and right spool holding arms (GE-25 and GE-10) do not rub against the ribbon spool. Note that the hole of the ribbon spool does not fit too tightly over the spool shafts of the right and left ribbon spool holders.

When the (1) portion of GE-22 and the (2) portion of GE-30 come into contact, the portion to release the ribbon feed pawls from the ribbon reverse levers should be located along the circumference of the left and right ribbon feed wheels (GE-28 and GE-13), respectively.

If all the adjustments are made, but ribbon reversing from the right side winding to the left side winding is difficult, the difficulty may be corrected if the roller of the (2) portion of GE-30 is made to roll smoothly. If ribbon feeding remains unsatisfactory, check the operation of GE-3, GE-5, GE-18 and GE-20. Make sure that GE-3 and GE-18 are engaged with GE-13 and GE-28 (also refer to Fig. 6-19C).

THE MARGIN RELEASE AND MARGIN STOP MECHANISM

When the preset right margin is reached during typing, the carriage will lock at the right margin. It will not move leftward until the margin release key is depressed.

Understanding the Right-hand Margin Stop Mechanism

Refer to Fig. 6-20A. During typing the carriage moves leftward. The right margin stop (GH-12) approaches the carriage stopper (GF-68) until farther movement of the carriage leftward results in GH-12 pushing GF-68 to the left. As GF-68 moves to the left, the margin release bar (GC-24) starts to rotate counterclockwise.

Because of the rotation of GC-24, the escape stop wire (GF-58) will pull the escape stopper (GF-54). The escape stop wire (GF-58) will move into the notched portion of the front escape crank (GF-26); thus, the movement of GF-26 will be stopped.

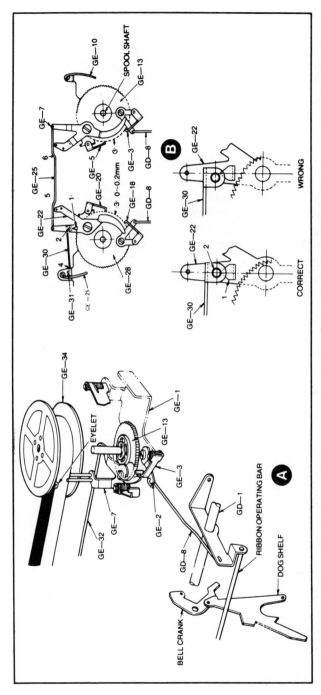

Fig. 6-19. (A) Herewith, the mystery of the feeding—as well as the reversing—of the ribbon is unveiled. By now you know that the little point marked "eyelet" has an important function in ribbon reversing. (B) As with any other mechanism, the ribbon feed and reverse may some time need adjustment; to learn how, read the text in conjunction with this illustration. (C) Having point (2) located at the apex of point (1) will probably solve ribbon feeding problems (courtesy of Brother International Corporation).

281

Understanding the Margin Release Mechanism

Still referring to Fig. 6-20A, the margin release works as follows. When the margin release key (GB-101) is pushed down, GC-24 is pushed rearward (arrow direction), through the movement of the various levers (namely GC-21 and GC-22). GC-24 pushes the pin of GF-68, inclining GF-68 forward, resulting in its disengagement from the margin stop GH-12.

Adjusting the Margin Stop and Margin Release Mechanism

Refer to Figs. 6-20A through 6-20C. Adjust the nut (GF-12) to obtain 2.0-2.5 mm movement of the carriage stopper (GF-68), as it is pushed by the right margin stop (GH-12). See Fig. 6-20B.

Adjust the clearance between the front escape crank (GF-26, Fig. 6-20C) and the escape stopper (GF-54) to 0.5-1.00 mm (Fig. 6-20C) through the adjusting screw of GF-54 and GF-58. The number of the adjusting screw is GF-55, if you wish to see it more clearly in the parts blow-ups at the end of this chapter.

THE SPRING DRUM

The spring drum is the power source for moving the carriage leftward during typing, tabbing, etc. To tension the spring drum, the main spring should have between 600 g and 700 g of tension when the carriage draw string is pulled 150 mm to the right, farther from the right end of the chassis unit. The number of windings for the spring drum is about seven or eight.

THE PAPER FEED MECHANISM

The feeding of the paper around the platen is accomplished through the grip of the platen with the feed rollers, which are located directly below the platen. This is a simple mechanism to understand—just look it over.

Adjusting the Paper Feed Mechanism

See Fig. 6-21A for an end view of the paper feed mechanism. The Brother technical department recommends some direct measurements to determine the condition of this mechanism; however, except in unusual conditions, you should be able to make adjustments without measuring gauges.

Still referring to Fig. 6-21A, the amount of pressure necessary to push the feed rollers away from the platen should be 350 g ± 150 g. You will note, moreover, that there are two sets of feed

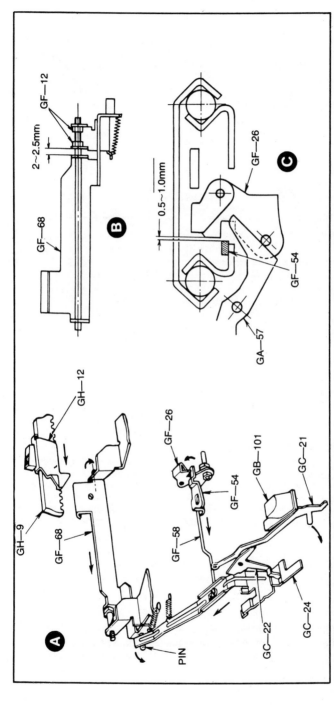

Fig. 6-20. (A) Study the text and this illustration to understand how the right margin stop works. (B) The clearance between GF-12 and GF-68 should be 2-2.5 mm, obtainable by turning the nut GF-12. (C) For the adjustment procedure illustrated by this Brother sketch, read the text (courtesy of Brother International Corporation).

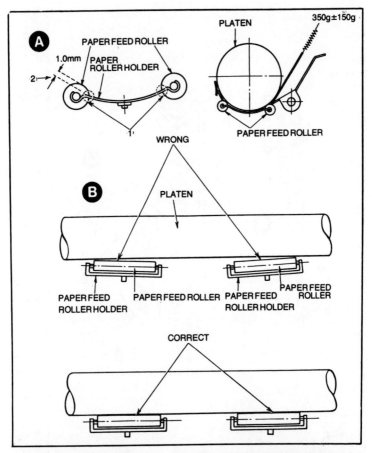

Fig. 6-21. (A) The drawings show why bending of the paper roller holder may solve paper feeding problems; however, do it carefully. (B) The drawing marked "WRONG" in this illustration is probably a somewhat exaggerated view of a poor relationship between the rollers and the platen. At any rate, the ideal relationship is for the rollers to contact the platen evenly all the way across, as shown in the drawing marked "CORRECT" (courtesy of Brother International Corporation).

rollers. The tension should be about the same on the two sets, within a tolerance of the aforementioned 150 grams.

If paper feeding indicates that some adjustment should be made, you can enlarge the clearance at (2), by 1.0 mm, by bending—or re-forming—the (1) portion of the feed roller holder. For a better view of the feed roller holder unit, see Fig. 6-43 at the end of this chapter; the parts number of the feed roller holder unit is GH-5.

In other words, the normal shape of the feed roller holder unit is bowed, as shown in the left-hand illustration of Fig. 6-21A. Straightening this bow through bending, just slightly, will increase the clearance between this unit and the platen, and will therefore effectively reduce the pressure exerted on the paper.

When either the right or left paper feed operation is unsatisfactory, first check the pressure at the problem point, remembering that 350 g ± 150 g is the amount of force needed to pull a tag from between the feed roller and platen, while holding the platen to keep it from rolling. If there is significantly more pressure on one side than the other (in this context, "side" means in-feed/out-feed sides), you must decide which side is correct. Then bend the (1) portion of the feed roller holder unit appropriately.

Note also that the platen should be parallel to the feed rollers; that is, the clearance between the feed rollers and platen should be equalized across the width of the feed rollers, as well as across the width of the platen (Fig. 6-21B). One indication of too much pressure between the feed rollers and platen is a carbon mark of the offending roller, in the case of carbon typing.

Removing the Platen

To remove the platen, refer to Fig. 6-22. Incline the paper release lever (GG-2) in the arrow direction. Swing the paper bail scale (GH-7) upward. Set the line space selector at "R."

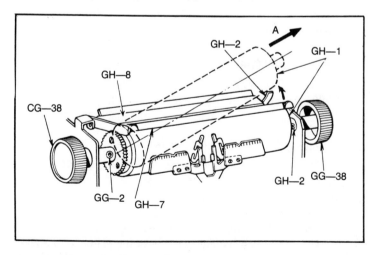

Fig. 6-22. Read the text and study this illustration to learn how to remove the platen (courtesy of Brother International Corporation).

Loosen the setscrews (GH-2, both ends) and remove both platen knobs. Set the left margin stop at the extreme left end, and move the carriage to the extreme right (against the left margin stop, that is). Now lift up the paper rest (GH-8) and remove the platen as shown in Fig. 6-22.

Reinstall the platen by reversing the above procedure. Be sure that GG-38 is tightened against the left carriage side plate, with zero clearance, when the set screws are tightened.

THE PAPER RELEASE MECHANISM

The paper release mechanism makes it possible for the typist to straighten the paper after it is fed into the machine or to remove it quickly without the need to rotate the platen. It accomplishes this by releasing the grip between the feed rollers and platen.

Understanding the Paper Release Mechanism

See Fig. 6-23. When the paper release lever (GG-2) is pushed rearward, the (A) portion of GG-2 pushes downward on the paper pan (the feed roller holder unit, that is). The clearance between the unit and the platen is enlarged.

Adjusting the Paper Release Mechanism

If the paper release lever has a tendency to return to its original position, even after being pushed rearward, bend the (A) portion of GG-2 until it operates correctly.

THE LINE SPACE MECHANISM

As you will remember, the Brother Models 3,000, 1,000 and XL-4,000 have manual carriage returns. Therefore, the handle by which the carriage is returned is also the line space lever.

Understanding the Line Space Mechanism

See Fig. 6-24A. When the line space and carriage return lever (GG-26) is pushed sideways, the line space lever holder (GG-20) pulls the line space ratchet unit (GG-8).

Through the above motion, the tip of GG-8 will engage with the line space ratchet wheel (GH-3—see Fig. 6-24B) and rotates the platen. The number of line spaces that the platen is rotated is determined by the step (1) of the line space selector (GG-11), which stops the movement of the line space ratchet unit (GG-8).

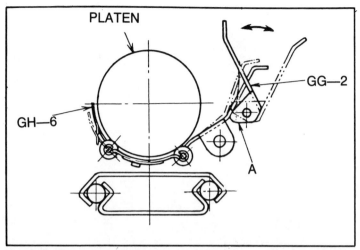

Fig. 6-23. This is the paper release mechanism—or more precisely, the mechanism that releases the grip of the paper feed rollers from the platen. It is adjustable in case of problems (courtesy of Brother International Corporation).

Adjustment of the Line Space Mechanism

To adjust the line space mechanism, refer to Fig. 6-24B. If, in the case of single line spacing, characters are aligned thus: HHH$_{HHH,}$ the line space ratchet wheel (GH-3) has not been rotated far enough by the line space ratchet. To correct this, loosen the screw (GH-34) and move the line space ratchet roller (GG-17) rearward.

If, on the other hand, line spacing produces character alignment like this: HHH^{HHH}, GH-3 is being rotated too far. To correct this, loosen the screw (GG-34) and move GG-17 frontward. The releaser (GG-16) should be set so there is no interference between the (1) portion of the line space ratchet and the circumference of GH-3.

THE CARRIAGE RELEASE

The carriage can be released from its normally locked-in position, to move leftward freely, by pulling the carriage release lever. To understand this fairly simple mechanism and its adjustment, refer to Fig. 6-25 and also to Fig. 6-42 (the latter illustration is a parts blow-up near the end of this chapter).

Understanding the Carriage Release Mechanism

The carriage release lever, which is a part of the space rack unit (GG-40) is pulled. The space rack unit swivels on the fulcrum

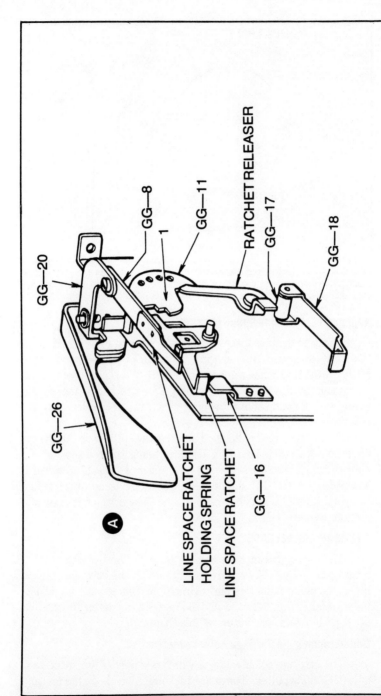

GG—20

GG—26

GG—8

1

GG—11

RATCHET RELEASER

GG—17

GG—18

LINE SPACE RATCHET
HOLDING SPRING

LINE SPACE RATCHET

GG—16

A

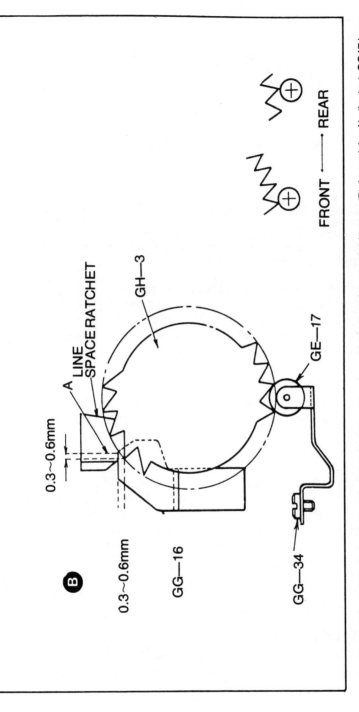

Fig. 6-24. (A) The line space mechanism is activated by the return lever (GG-26), as it pushed sideways. (B) As explained in the text, GG17 is an adjustment point in the line space mechanism, and the screw to loosen to make the adjustment possible is GG-34. Poor line spacing produces poor looking typed copy, but the problem is easy to correct (courtesy of Brother International Corporation).

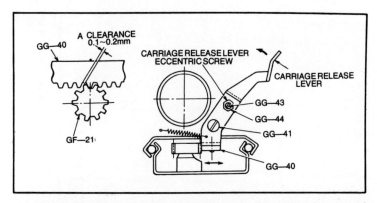

Fig. 6-25. On the Brother Models under discussion, the carriage is released from its normally locked-in position by moving the part marked carriage release lever, which transmits a movement that swings GG-40 of mesh with GF-21, allowing the carriage to "freewheel" until returned to normal operating mode (courtesy of Brother International Corporation).

point of the screw (GG-41), and in so doing the teeth of the space rack disengage from the teeth of the space pinion (GF-21). This allows the carriage to move freely leftward. The carriage release lever is returned to normal operating mode and the carriage is locked in.

Adjusting the Carriage Release Mechanism

Refer to Figs. 6-25 and 6-42, loosen the nut (GG-44) of the eccentric screw (GG-43), and turn the screw to obtain 0.1-0.2 mm clearance at point (A), between the space pinion (GF-21) and the space rack unit (GG-40).

To know whether this was effective, the following two conditions indicate a misadjustment. If the engagement between GF-21 and GG-40 is too deep, the carriage may bind or it may move noisily. If the engagement between GF-21 and GG-40 is too shallow, the carriage may run off to the left side when the machine is inclined more than 30 degrees, and at the same time the space bar and key are pushed.

A further check for the adjustment is that the space pinion (GF-21) can be moved slightly by hand without moving the space rack unit (GG-40).

ADJUSTMENT OF THE WARNING BELL

Refer to Fig. 6-26. The warning bell should sound about six to eight characters before the carriage line-locks at the right margin stop. Adjust the (A) portion of the bell hammer operating plate (this portion contacts the right margin stop) by bending it.

To adjust the tone of the warning bell, adjust the clearance between the bell hammer and warning bell, at the (B) portion, to obtain 0.3-0.6 mm, by bending the (C) portion of the bell hammer stopper.

THE REPEAT SPACE MECHANISM

When the repeat space key is depressed and held down, the carriage will repeat space until the key is released by the typist.

Understanding the Repeat Space Mechanism

See Fig. 6-27. When the repeat space key (GD-20) is pushed down, the repeat space crank (GD-15) is lowered. Through the movement of GD-15, the front repeat space crank (GD-26) is rotated, as shown by the arrow.

The rotation of GD-26 pulls the repeat space crank wire (GD-31), which rotates the rear repeat space (GF-51). The rotation of the rear repeat space (GF-51) pulls the spring (GF-48), thus rotating the repeat space operating lever (GF-39).

The rotation of GF-39 pushes the half space ratchet (GF-37), causing it to engage with the space ratchet wheel (GF-23), and at the same time the space ratchet (GF-36) is disengaged from the

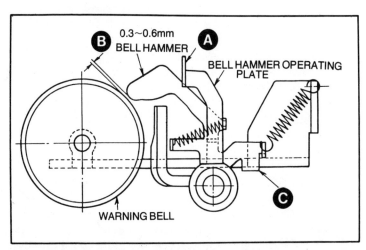

Fig. 6-26. Both the tone of the warning bell and the timing of its sound in relation to the proximity of the carriage to the right margin can be adjusted—read the text (courtesy of Brother International Corporation).

space ratchet wheel (GF-23). By the slope of the (1) portion of GF-37, the tooth-tip of GF-23 will tend to push GF-37 back to its original position, through the tension of the spring drum.

As GF-37 is pushed back by the tooth-tip of GF-23, it will alternately engage with GF-23, through the inertia of GF-48 and GF-39, under interlocking with GF-36. The end result is a repeat spacing operation.

Adjusting the Repeat Space Mechanism

For the adjustment procedure of the repeat space mechanism, still refer to Fig. 6-27A. If a light touch on the repeat space key (GD-20) does not result in repeat spacing, the cause is probably an insufficient movement of the repeat space operating lever (GF-39), causing the space ratchet (GF-36) not to be released from the space ratchet wheel (GF-23). Note the following adjustments.

☐ If there is excessive play in the repeat space crank wire (GD-31), shorten GD-31 by bending.

☐ If the tension of the spring (GF-48) is too weak, increase the tension by moving the repeat space adjusting plate (GF-53), after loosening the screw (GF-49, shown in Fig. 6-27B, also see this part in the parts blow-up of Fig. 6-41). When you make this adjustment, be sure that there is 0.3 mm clearance between GF-39 and GF-37.

☐ If the engagement between GF-36 and GF-23 is too deep, decrease it. However, be sure that after this adjustment is made the carriage does not skip when the space bar is depressed. This condition can be corrected by adjusting for slower timing of the escapement, as described earlier in this chapter.

If the carriage stops while the repeat space is being operated, the cause is probably too much tension of the spring (GF-48), which will not let GF-23 push GF-37, with the result that it only takes a slight resistance to stop the carriage. In this case, loosen the screw (GF-49) and move GF-53; or decrease the movement distance of the front repeat space crank (GD-26) by shifting the repeat space stopper (GD-50).

If these adjustments do not solve the problems of inoperative conditions, or moving-and-stopping of the carriage, loosen the stud screw (GD-27, Fig. 6-27B). Move GD-26 one way or the other to solve the problem. If the repeat space operation is not made smoothly, depress the repeat space key (GD-20). Push the carriage by hand through the entire operating range, noting that the spring (GF-48) is forcibly pulled.

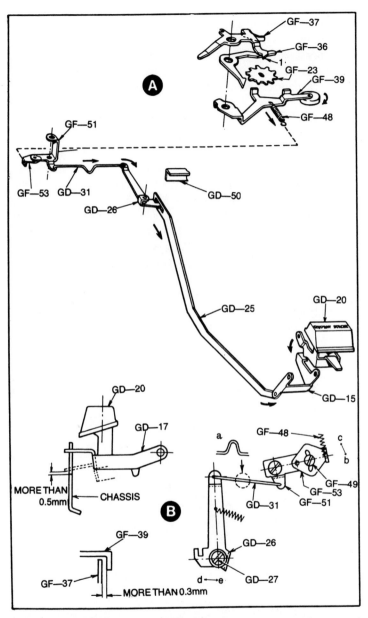

Fig. 6-27. (A) Repeat spacing creates the illusion of an electrically powered mechanism; however, it is accomplished—quite ingeniously—through purely mechanical means. It is a time-saver for the typist, and should be kept in adjustment. (B) Excessive play in the repeat space crank wire (GD-31) can be eliminated by bending at (1) (courtesy of Brother International Corporation).

293

After making all the adjustments, you can check for smooth and positive operation in all positions by lightly depressing the repeat space key (GD-20) until there is 0.5 mm clearance between GD-17 and the stopper of the chassis (see Fig. 6-27B). Note also that the carriage can start from any position.

REMOVING THE UPPER COVER AND LEFT PLATEN KNOB

As I said in the beginning of this chapter, the Brother Model 3500 is a modified version of the JP8, with both the carriage return and shift (for capitals, etc.) being powered through the snatch roll. The following repair and adjustment procedures apply to the modified mechanisms of the Brother Model 3500.

Refer to Fig. 6-28. To remove the upper cover (JL-1), first turn on the switch, depress the shift lock key to place the carriage in shift position, and then turn off the switch. Place the carriage at the extreme left, as in Fig. 6-28. Then remove the upper cover (JL-1).

Refer to Fig. 6-29. To remove the left platen knob (JG-47), insert a hex wrench through the hole for the line space indicator of the left carriage cover (JG-50). Loosen the screws (JH-2).

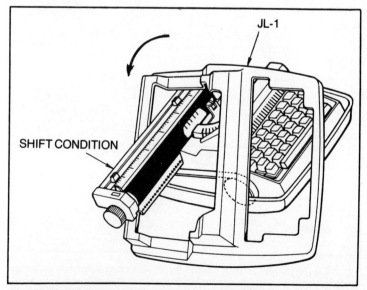

Fig. 6-28. Removing the top cover of the Brother Model 3500 is a bit more tricky than on earlier Models. Here, the mystery is removed (courtesy of Brother International Corporation).

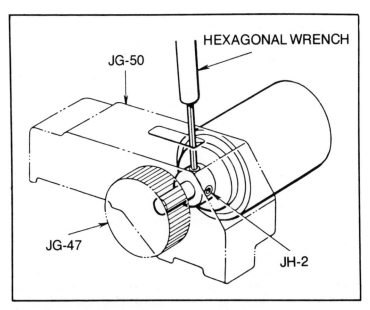

Fig. 6-29. This sketch shows how to remove the left platen knob (courtesy of Brother International Corporation).

THE SHIFT MECHANISM

Unlike the shift mechanism of the earlier Brother Models discussed in this chapter, the shift mechanism of the Brother Model 3500 is operated through the power of the snatch roll.

Understanding the Operation of the Shift Mechanism

Refer to Fig. 6-30A. When either of the shift keys (JB-105, for example) is depressed, the shift key lever unit (JI-5) rotates clockwise. The shift cam spring stop that is a part of the shift lever unit (JI-1) is lowered.

Through the disengagement of the (1) portion of the shift cam spring stop from the shift cam spring (JM-16), JM-16 will begin to rotate with the snatch roll (JM-14). Since one end of JM-16 is inserted into the hole of the shift cam (JM-17), JM-17 will be rotated counterclockwise with the snatch roll, until one end of the JM-16 contacts the (2) portion.

The roller (not to be confused with the snatch roll), which is installed on the shift operating lever unit (JI-17), comes into contact with JM-17, causing JI-17 to be rotated clockwise with the rotation of JM-17. The rotation of JI-17 rotates the shift crank (JI-8) counterclockwise through the spring (JI-21). Further, the shift crank adjusting screw (JI-14), which is secured on JI-8 by a nut, comes into contact with JI-17 by means of JI-21. Because of design, the moving distance of JI-17 is larger than the shift motion, causing JI-21 to be extended after the carriage stops, thereby separating JI-14 and JI-17.

The rotation of JI-8 will be transmitted through the shift wire (JI-12), causing the rear shift link (JF-11) to rotate counterclockwise.

The rotation of JF-11 will push the carriage frame (JF-4) upward, where it will remain for as long as the shift key (JB-105) is held down. Thus, the carriage is in shift position. You will note that this differs from some other typewriters, on which the sector-and-typebars are shifted.

When the shift key (JB-105) is released and returns to its home position, JM-16, being stopped at the (2) portion of the shift cam spring stop, will be rotated until the (1) portion, together with JM-17, and returned to their home position. Thus, each portion is in no-shift position.

Understanding the Shift Lock Mechanism

To understand the shift lock mechanism, still refer to Fig. 6-30A. When the shift lock key (JB-106) is depressed, the tip (3) portion of the shift key lock lever unit (JI-5) is lowered, contacting the surface of the shift lock plate (JC-39). Upon being lowered farther, it will engage and lock with JC-39. This locks the carriage in shift position until one of the shift keys is depressed.

Adjustment of the Shift Mechanism

To adjust the shift mechanism, refer to Fig. 6-30B. The shift crank (JI-8) is assembled by securing the shift crank adjusting screw (JI-14) at the center of the elongated hole of the shift crank (JI-8). When the carriage is in shift position, note that the curvature of the typeface matches the curvature of the platen.

If the carriage floats, without the adjusting screw (JF-8, Fig. 6-30C) contacting the stopper, under non-shift condition, loosen JI-14 and move it in the arrow direction until JF-8 contacts the stopper. To adjust the misalignment between capital and small letters, read the instructions in the adjusting the shift mechanism section earlier in the chapter.

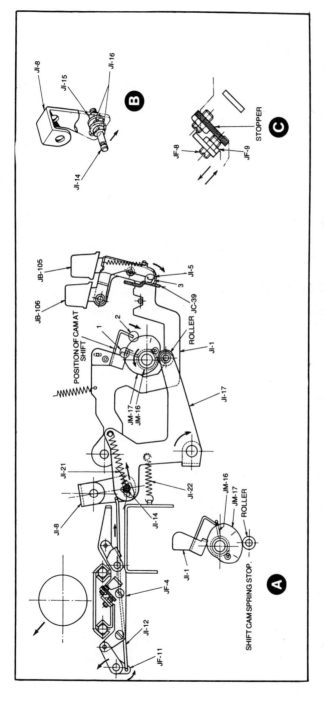

Fig. 6-30. (A) This side view shows how the shift mechanism is powered through the snatch roll. For your orientation, this mechanism is found on the left end of the machine. (B) Read the text to understand the adjustment made available at this point. (C) The stoppers, which regulate the raising and lowering of the carriage, are not unique to the Model 3500 but are found on earlier Models as well. They may turn out to be important adjustment points (courtesy of Brother International Corporation).

THE CARRIAGE RETURN MECHANISM

On the Brother Model 3500, the carriage is returned through the power of the snatch roll, which turns continuously. See Fig. 6-31A.

When the carriage return key (JB-107) is depressed, the (1) portion of the return key lever unit (JJ-1) depresses the (2) portion of the return key lever unit (JJ-1), causing it to rotate counterclockwise.

The rotation of JJ-7 causes it to engage with the snatch roll (JM-14), which rotates the link (3) portion of the clutch operating link unit (JJ-17). Simultaneously, JJ-7 contacts the eccentric stud for the dog shelf stop (JJ-12) and is operated until disengaged from the snatch roll (it is held by the dog shelf lock crank, JJ-36, Fig. 6-31B.)

The rubber on the (3) portion depresses the return collar (JM-23) and operates the clutch, which transfers the rotation of the snatch roll to the return gear (JM-25). The rotation of the return gear (JM-25) is transferred to the return drum gear (JJ-22). The return drum rotates clockwise and winds up the return belt unit (JJ-34).

Meanwhile, the line space mechanism comes into play as follows. The pull of the return belt (JJ-34) pulls downward on the line space operating lever, and line spacing is accomplished. Then the carriage returns. As the carriage reaches the right end, the left margin stop (JH-13) pushes the carriage stopper (JF-62, Fig. 6-31B).

The movement of JF-62 is transmitted through the return release link (JJ-39), through the center return release link (JJ-42), through the (4) portion of the return release connector (JJ-42 and JJ-43), and finally rotates the dog shelf lock crank (JJ-36), disengaging JJ-36 from JJ-6, allowing JJ-7 to return to its original position. The clutch is also released, and the rotation of the snatch roll is no longer transmitted to the return gear (JM-25).

THE RETURN CLUTCH

See Fig. 6-32 for an end view and profile view of the return clutch of the Brother Model 3500. One end of the return spring (JM-22) is inserted into the collar-A (JM-21), and the other end is inserted into the hole of the return collar (JM-23). JM-21 is secured to the snatch roll by the screw (JM-5, which can be seen in the parts blow-up of Fig. 6-57).

When the return mechanism is operated, the rubber (JJ-18) presses against JM-23, stopping its rotation. Because the collar-A (JM-21) is being rotated, JM-21 will tighten up against the collar-B (JM-24). Thus, the rotation of the snatch roll will be transmitted through the mechanism to the return gear (JM-25). While the clutch is in operation, the rubber (JJ-18) and JM-23 are slipping on each other.

THE RETURN JAMMING RELEASE

If, while the carriage is returning, the movement is stopped—such as forcibly by hand—and the motor is stopped, the carriage return can be disengaged. Thus, the motor can again be started without the load of the carriage return mechanism. The disengagement is accomplished by deeply depressing the tab keybutton. See Figs. 6-33A through 6-33G.

Understanding the Operation of the Return Jamming Release

The operation of the return jamming release is as follows. When the tab key (JB-103, Fig. 6-33A) is depressed, the tab key lever (JC-17) rotates counterclockwise, thus pushing the front tab operating wire (JC-19).

The movement of the tab operating wire rotates the tab operating crank counterclockwise and, as a result, the center return release link (JJ-42) also rotates counterclockwise. The rotation of JJ-42 is transmitted linearly through the return release connector (JJ-43), releasing the engagement between JJ-6 and JJ-36. This disengagement releases the return clutch. Simultaneously, tabulation is effectively accomplished. The carriage will move leftward until it contacts a tab stop pawl.

Adjustment of the Return Jamming Release

Adjust the return jamming release as follows. Bend the wire (JJ-8) so that the clearance (a) (see Fig. 6-33B) between the rubber (JJ-18) and the return collar (JM-23) is 0.3-1.5 mm (see JJ-8 in Fig. 6-31A).

Adjust the movement of the dog shelf as follows. Referring to Fig. 6-33C, adjust the eccentric stud for the dog shelf stop (JJ-12), up and down, so that the clearance is 0.1-0.8 mm, when JJ-7 has moved its maximum distance and is engaged with the snatch roll (rotate the snatch roll manually). Move JJ-12 upward for zero clearance, when JJ-7 is not locked, and move JJ-12 downward for

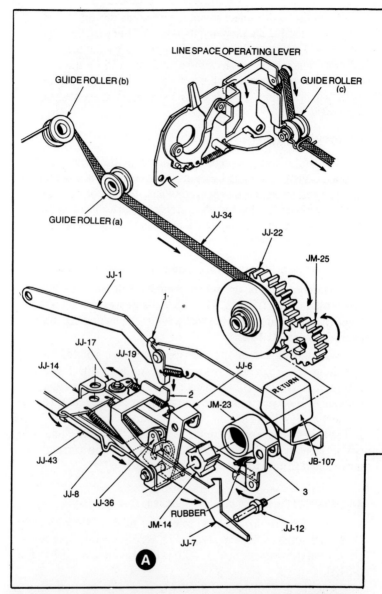

LINE SPACE OPERATING LEVER

GUIDE ROLLER (b)

GUIDE ROLLER (c)

GUIDE ROLLER (a)

JJ-34

JJ-22

JM-25

JJ-1

JJ-17

JJ-19

JJ-6

JJ-14

JM-23

JJ-43

RETURN

JB-107

JJ-8

JJ-36

3

RUBBER

JM-14

JJ-12

JJ-7

A

Fig. 6-31. (A) Powering the return of the carriage on the Model 3500 is accomplished by transmitting the rotation of the snatch roll to the return gears (JM-25 and JM-22), via a simple clutch arrangement. This ingenious mechanism is a fascinating study in motions. (B) Study this illustration and read the text to understand how the return of the carriage places mechanisms into motion that will ultimately disengage the mechanism from the snatch roll (courtesy of Brother International Corporation).

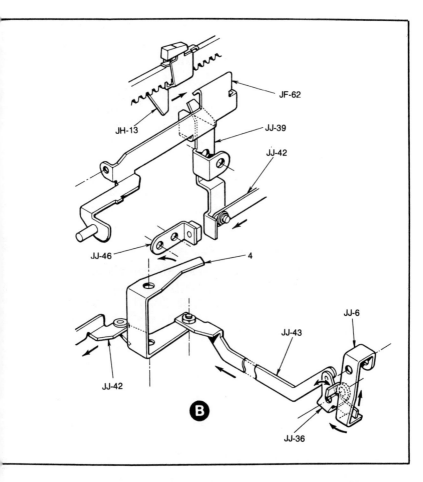

excessive clearance, so as to change the timing of the disengagement of JJ-7 from the snatch roll.

Adjust the return release crank stop plate (JJ-46, Fig. 6-33D), by moving it left/right until the clearance (c) between the return release link (JJ-39) and the cushion rubber (JJ-47) is 1.0-1.5 mm.

When the return release connector (JJ-43, Fig. 6-33E) is installed on the center return release link (JJ-42) by the stud screw (JJ-44), the clearance (d) should be less than 0.5 mm.

Adjust the clearance (e) between the return gear (JM-25, Fig. 6-33F) and snap ring (JM-26) to less than 0.3 mm, by loosening the screw (JM-5) of the collar-A (JM-21).

To adjust the tension of the return belt, shift the carriage to the right to wind the return drum spring (JJ-30), which is affixed to the large gear (JJ-22, of Fig. 6-31A), until the sag of the return belt is removed. Rotate the return drum flange approximately two rounds, so as to apply tension to the return belt. Then wind up the spring and secure the nut.

See Fig. 6-33G. Adjust the clearance (f) between the right margin stop and the carriage stopper (JF-62) to 0.1-0.5 mm. Make this adjustment by rotating the eccentric stud (JJ-40). JJ-40 can be seen in the parts blow-up of Fig. 6-54.

THE CARRIAGE RELEASE MECHANISM

The carriage release mechanism of the Brother Model 3500 works somewhat differently than that of the previously discussed, earlier Brother JP8 Models.

Understanding the Carriage Release Mechanism

See Fig. 6-34. When the carriage release lever is moved in the arrow direction, the carriage release bar (JG-5) pushes the pin, which is caulked on the space ratchet (JF-32). This causes the space ratchet (JF-32) to rotate clockwise, thereby disengaging it from the space ratchet wheel (JF-19).

Adjusting the Carriage Release Mechanism

The optimum clearance between the pin and the carriage release bar (JG-5) is 0.7 mm. To obtain this clearance, loosen the nut (JG-9) and rotate the eccentric screw (JG-8). After making this adjustment, note that the pin does not contact the carriage rail when the carriage release lever is fully pulled.

LINE SPACE MECHANISM

As you remember, the operation of the line space mechanism of the Brother Model 3500 results from the pull of the return belt when the carriage is returned.

Understanding the Line Space Mechanism

Refer to Fig. 6-35A. When the carriage return mechanism is operated, the return belt (JJ-34) tightens up, pulling down on the line space operating lever (JG-13). This causes the line space operating lever to rotate clockwise.

The line space ratchet is contacted by the line space selector through the spring (JG-12). If the line space selector is set on "1"

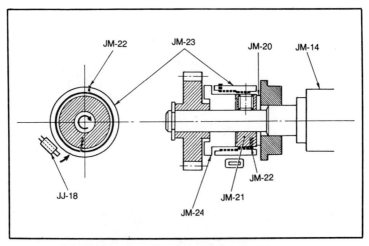

Fig. 6-32. The heart of the carriage return mechanism is the clutch, shown here in a cutaway view (courtesy of Brother International Corporation).

on the indicator, the line space ratchet will engage with the line space ratchet wheel (JH-3) at the (1) portion, shift JH-3 for a distance of two teeth, and then stop by contacting the line space ratchet stop. When the return mechanism is released, the line space operating lever returns to its original position through the pull of the spring (JG-15).

Adjusting the Line Space Mechanism

Refer To Fig. 6-35B. When the line space ratchet contacts the line space ratchet stop during its operation, the roller (JG-19) should equally contact the teeth of the line space ratchet wheel (JH-3). To make this adjustment, loosen the nut (JG-21) and rotate the eccentric stud (JG-20). If the above adjustment is not correct, the line of typing will be slanted.

Note the (1) portion of Fig. 6-35B. Just before the line space ratchet engages with the teeth of JH-3, the slanted portion of the tooth should be aligned with the slanted portion of the line space ratchet. To make this adjustment, move the spring (JG-16) back and forth, as shown by the double-ended arrow.

When JG-19 contacts the tip of the tooth of JH-3, JH-19 and JH-3 should be parallel with each other. If they are not parallel, the acutal number of line spaces achieved will be erratic or will differ from the number of line spaces selected. Adjust for parallelism by bending JG-18.

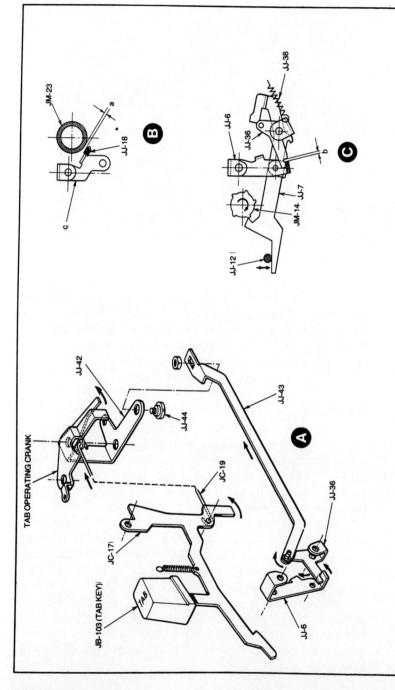

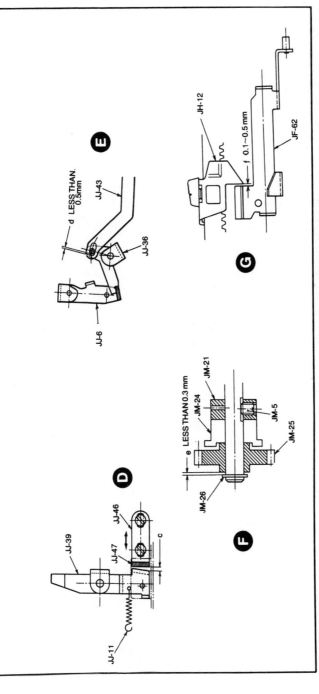

Fig. 6-33. (A) If the return of the carriage was inadvertently and forcibly stopped, restarting it would pose the problem of loading the motor, if some means of disengaging the mechanism were not provided. The mechanism in this illustration is that provision. (B) The clearance at (a) should be 0.3-1.5 mm. Read the text to learn how to obtain it. (C) Move JJ-12 up or down to get 0.1-0.8 mm clearance at (b). Read the text. (D) Move JJ-46 one way or the other to get 1.0-1.5 mm clearance at (c). (E) Read the text to understand the clearance at (d). (F) Loosen the screw (JM-5) to obtain less than 0.3 mm clearance at (e). (G) The clearance at (f) is as shown. Read the text to learn how to obtain it (courtesy of Brother International Corporation).

305

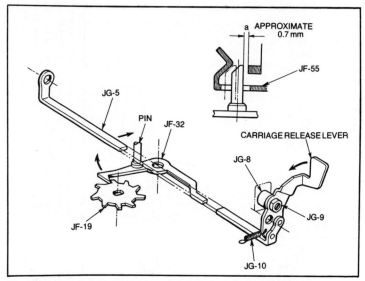

Fig. 6-34. The carriage release mechanism for the Model 3500 is easy to understand and adjust (courtesy of Brother International Corporation).

PARTS BLOW-UPS AND PARTS NAMES AND NUMBERS FOR THE BROTHER MODELS 3,000, 1,000 AND XL-4,000

Throughout this entire chapter I have, with a few exceptions, referred to parts by numbers, preceded by two capital letters. Quite conveniently for your ease of reference, these numbers are actual parts numbers for the parts of the Brother Models under discussion. Therefore, if you want to see any part that was previously referred to, in considerable detail in its relation to the rest of the mechanism, refer to the appropriate parts blow-up.

For Brother Models 3,000, 1,000, and XL-4,000, the parts blow-ups and corresponding parts numbers invariably contain the capital letter "G".

For the Brother Model 3500, the parts blow-ups and corresponding parts numbers invariably contain the capital letter "J." The capital letter that follows the letter "G" or "J" is a key letter to the mechanism, and all parts of that mechanism will also contain that capital letter.

As an example, Fig. 6-36 is the parts blow-up and Table 6-1 is the accompanying parts list for the typebar, sector plate and universal bar of Brother Models 3,000, 1,000 and XL-4,000. Any parts numbers for this mechanism, on these specific Brother Models, will be preceded by the capital letters "GA" (when

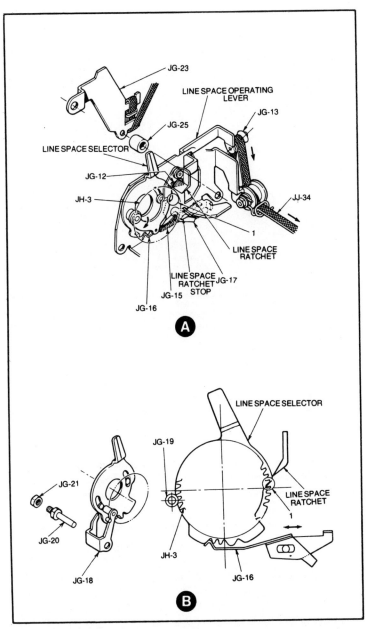

Fig. 6-35. (A) The line space mechanism of the Model 3500 works through the pull of the return belt (JJ-34). (B) Several adjustment points of the line space mechanism make it possible to keep the mechanism operating perfectly (courtesy of Brother International Corporation).

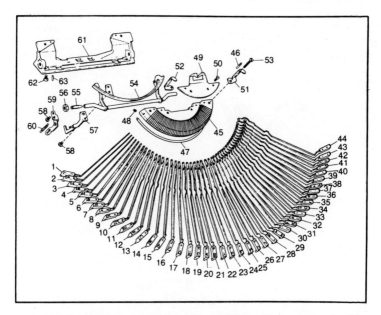

Fig. 6-36. The typebar, sector plate and universal bar. Parts numbers for this mechanism will be preceded by the letters GA (courtesy of Brother International Corporation).

ordering parts from Brother, ignore the illustration numbers, as they will have no meaning to the Brother parts department).

By way of further explanation, while many of the mechanisms of the Models 3,000, 1,000 and XL-4,000 are similar to many of those in the Brother Model 3500, and thus the procedures described in this chapter for the earlier Models will also apply to the Model 3500, you should understand that the Model 3500 is indeed a different machine than the earlier Models. As a consequence, a separate parts catalog has been compiled for all the mechanisms therein, with parts number generally (but not always) differing from those of the earlier Brother Models.

Now let's move on to other parts blow-ups and parts names and numbers for the Brother Models 3,000, 1,000 and XL-4,000. At the risk of being repetitious, I would again mention that the parts numbers of the Models 3,000, 1,000 and XL-4,000 are preceded by the capital letter "G," together with the key letter of the mechanism.

Figure 6-37 is the parts blow-up and Table 6-2 is the accompanying parts list of the typebar wire, bell crank and key. Figure 6-38 is the parts blow-up and Table 6-3 is the accompanying

Table 6-1. Parts List for Fig. 6-36 (courtesy of Brother International Corporation).

REF.NO.	PART NO.	PART NAME	QTY.	MEMO
GA-1		Typebar Unit (left 22)	1	
GA-2		Typebar Unit (left 21)	1	
GA-3		Typebar Unit (left 20)	1	
GA-4		Typebar Unit (left 19)	1	
GA-5		Typebar Unit (left 18)	1	
GA-6		Typebar Unit (left 17)	1	
GA-7		Typebar Unit (left 16)	1	
GA-8		Typebar Unit (left 15)	1	
GA-9		Typebar Unit (left 14)	1	
GA-10		Typebar Unit (left 13)	1	
GA-11		Typebar Unit (left 12)	1	
GA-12		Typebar Unit (left 11)	1	
GA-13		Typebar Unit (left 10)	1	
GA-14		Typebar Unit (left 9)	1	
GA-15		Typebar Unit (left 8)	1	
GA-16		Typebar Unit (left 7)	1	
GA-17		Typebar Unit (left 6)	1	
GA-18		Typebar Unit (left 5)	1	
GA-19		Typebar Unit (left 4)	1	
GA-20		Typebar Unit (left 3)	1	
GA-21		Typebar Unit (left 2)	1	
GA-22		Typebar Unit (left 1)	1	
GA-23		Typebar Unit (right 1)	1	
GA-24		Typebar Unit (right 2)	1	
GA-25		Typebar Unit (right 3)	1	
GA-26		Typebar Unit (right 4)	1	
GA-27		Typebar Unit (right 5)	1	
GA-28		Typebar Unit (right 6)	1	
GA-29		Typebar Unit (right 7)	1	
GA-30		Typebar Unit (right 8)	1	
GA-31		Typebar Unit (right 9)	1	
GA-32		Typebar Unit (right 10)	1	
GA-33		Typebar Unit (right 11)	1	
GA-34		Typebar Unit (right 12)	1	
GA-35		Typebar Unit (right 13)	1	
GA-36		Typebar Unit (right 14)	1	
GA-37		Typebar Unit (right 15)	1	
GA-38		Typebar Unit (right 16)	1	
GA-39		Typebar Unit (right 17)	1	
GA-40		Typebar Unit (right 18)	1	
GA-41		Typebar Unit (right 19)	1	
GA-42		Typebar Unit (right 20)	1	
GA-43		Typebar Unit (right 21)	1	
GA-44		Typebar Unit (right 22)	1	
GA-45	509397000	Sector Plate	1	
GA-46	509598001	Knock Pin for GA-45	2	
GA-47	500262000	Typebar Pivot Wire	1	
GA-48	011630413	Screw for GA-47	2	
GA-49	509396001	Typebar Guide	1	
GA-50	500750002	Screw for GA-49	2	
GA-51	516187001	Top Cover Prop : right	1	
GA-52	516188001	Top Cover Prop : left	1	
GA-53	009661603	Screw for GA-45, 51, 52	2	
GA-54	516121001	Escapement Drive Plate Unit	1	
GA-55	500278001	Center Screw for GA-55	2	
GA-56	106129001	Nut for GA-56	2	
GA-57	516125001	Universal Bar	1	
GA-58	402281002	Screw for GA-57, 59	3	
GA-59	501004001	Guide Plate for GA-57	1	
GA-60	507277001	Spring for GA-59	1	
GA-61	500801000	Sector Plate Holder	1	
GA-62	002670613	Screw for GA-61	4	
GA-63	507596001	Knock Pin for GA-61	2	

parts list of the key lever, sub frame, margin release, back space and tabulator.

Figure 6-39 is the parts blow-up and Table 6-4 is the accompanying parts list of the space bar, paper meter and color change. Figure 6-40 is the parts blow-up and Table 6-5 is the accompanying parts list for the ribbon feed and ribbon reversal. Figure 6-41 is the parts blow-up and Table 6-6 is the accompanying parts list of the carriage rail, pinion base, spring drum and warning bell.

Figure 6-42 is the parts blow-up and Table 6-7 is the accompanying parts list of the carriage side plate. Figure 6-43 is the parts blow-up and Table 6-8 is the accompanying parts list of the carriage. Figure 6-44 is the parts blow-up and Table 6-9 is the accompanying parts list of the chassis. Figure 6-45 is the parts blow-up and Table 6-10 is the accompanying parts list of the cover and case. Figure 6-46 is the parts blow-up and Table 6-11 is the accompanying parts list of the electrical components.

PARTS BLOW-UPS AND PARTS NAMES
AND NUMBERS FOR THE BROTHER MODEL 3500

Again at the risk of being repetitious, many of the mechanisms of the Brother Model 3500 are the same as those of the Models 3,000, 1,000 and XL-4,000; however in all cases, the parts numbers are preceded by the capital letter "J." In some cases the digit component of the parts number is the same in all Models, but in some other cases this is not true. To avoid duplicating illustrations, therefore, when parts numbers digits are the same for the Model 3500 as for the earlier Models, I will so indicate, with the suggestion that you precede the number with the appropriate letters.

The parts blow-up for the typebar, sector plate and universal bar of the Model 3500 is identical to that of the earlier JP8 Models. Therefore, refer back to Fig. 6-36. If ordering parts, precede the parts numbers by "JA."

Figure 6-47 is the parts blow-up and Table 6-12 is the accompanying parts list of the typebar wire, bell crank and key. Figure 6-48 is the parts blow-up and Table 6-13 is the accompanying parts list of the key lever, sub frame, margin release, back space and tabulator.

Figure 6-49 is the parts blow-up and Table 6-14 is the accompanying parts list of the space bar, paper meter and color change. For the parts blow-up and parts list of the ribbon feed and

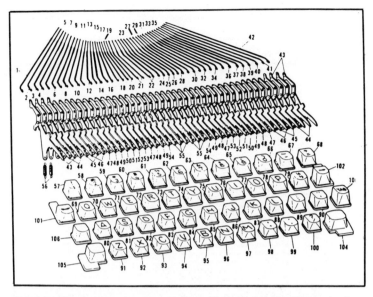

Fig. 6-37. The typebar wire, crank and key. Parts numbers for this mechanism will be preceded by the letters GB (courtesy of Brother International Corporation).

reversal, refer back to Fig. 6-40 and Table 6-5; when ordering parts precede all the parts numbers by the letters "JE."

Figure 6-50 is the parts blow-up and Table 6-15 is the accompanying parts list of the carriage rail, pinion base, spring drum and warning bell. Figure 6-51 is the parts blow-up and Table 6-16 is the accompanying parts list of the carriage side plate.

Figure 6-52 is the parts blow-up and Table 6-17 is the accompanying parts list of the carriage. Figure 6-53 is the parts blow-up and Table 6-18 is the accompanying parts list of the shift. Figure 6-54 is the parts blow-up and Table 6-19 is the accompany parts list of the carriage return.

Figure 6-55 is the parts blow-up and Table 6-20 is the accompanying parts list of the chassis. Figure 6-56 is the parts blow-up and Table 6-21 is the accompanying parts list of the cover and case. Figure 6-57 is the parts blow-up and Table 6-22 is the accompanying parts list of the electrical components and snatch roll.

MECHANISM REMOVAL PROCEDURES

As promised earlier in this chapter, here are the procedures for removing certain parts and mechanisms from the JP8 Models.

Table 6-2. Parts List for Fig. 6-37 (courtesy of Brother International Corporation).

REF.NO.	PART NO.	PART NAME	QTY.	MEMO
GB- 1	51625700	Typebar Wire(left 22)	1	
GB- 2	51625600	Typebar Wire(left 21)	1	
GB- 3	500174001	Typebar Wire (left 20)	1	
GB- 4	500173001	Typebar Wire (left 19)	1	
GB- 5	500172 001	Typebar Wire (left 18)	1	
GB- 6	500171001	Typebar Wire (left 17)	1	
GB- 7	500170001	Typebar Wire (left 16)	1	
GB- 8	500169001	Typebar Wire (left 15)	1	
GB- 9	500168001	Typebar Wire (left 14)	1	
GB-10	500167001	Typebar Wire (left 13)	1	
GB-11	500166001	Typebar Wire (left 12)	1	
GB-12	500165001	Typebar Wire (left 11)	1	
GB-13	500164001	Typebar Wire (left 10)	1	
GB-14	500163001	Typebar Wire (left 9)	1	
GB-15	500162001	Typebar Wire (left 8)	1	
GB-16	500161001	Typebar Wire (left 7)	1	
GB-17	500160001	Typebar Wire (left 6)	1	
GB-18	500159001	Typebar Wire (left 5)	1	
GB-19	500158001	Typebar Wire (left 4)	1	
GB-20	500157001	Typebar Wire (left 3)	2	
GB-21	500156001	Typebar Wire (left 1, 2)	2	
GB-22	500134001	Typebar Wire (right 1, 2)	1	
GB-23	500135001	Typebar Wire (right 3)	1	
GB-24	500136001	Typebar Wire (right 4)	1	
GB-25	500137001	Typebar Wire (right 5)	1	
GB-26	500138001	Typebar Wire (right 6)	1	
GB-27	500139001	Typebar Wire (right 7)	1	
GB-28	500140001	Typebar Wire (right 8)	1	
GB-29	500141001	Typebar Wire (right 9)	1	
GB-30	500142001	Typebar Wire (right 10)	1	
GB-31	500143001	Typebar Wire (right 11)	1	
GB-32	500144001	Typebar Wire (right 12)	1	
GB-33	500145001	Typebar Wire (right 13)	1	
GB-34	500146001	Typebar Wire (right 14)	1	
GB-35	500147001	Typebar Wire (right 15)	1	
GB-36	500148001	Typebar Wire (right 16)	1	
GB-37	500149001	Typebar Wire (right 18)	1	
GB-38	500150001	Typebar Wire (right 18)	1	
GB-39	500151001	Typebar Wire (right 19)	1	
GB-40	500152001	Typebar Wire (right 20)	1	
GB-41	500153001	Typebar Wire (right 21)	1	
GB-42	500154001	Typebar Wire (right 22)	2	
GB-43	516026001	Bell Crank Unit (L: 22, R: 22)		
GB-44	516024001	Bell Crank Unit (L: 19,20,21,R:19,20,21)	6	
GB-45	516022001	Bell Crank Unit (L: 16, 18, R: 1, 18)	4	
GB-46	516020001	Bell Crank Unit(L: 14, 15, 17, R: 14, 15, 17)	6	
GB-47	516010001	Bell Crank Unit (L: 7,R: 7)	2	
GB-48	516008001	Bell Crank Unit (L: 6,13,R: 6,13)	4	
GB-49	516006001	Bell Crank Unit (L: 5,12,R: 5,12)	4	
GB-50	516018001	Bell Crank Unit (L: 11,R: 11)	2	
GB-51	516016001	Bell Crank Unit (L: 10,R: 10)	2	
GB-52	516014001	Bell Crank Unit (L: 9,R: 9)	2	
GB-53	516012001	Bell Crank Unit (L: 8,R: 8)	2	
GB-54	516004001	Bellcrankunit (L: 4, R, 4)	2	
GB-55	516001001	Bell Crank Unit (L:1, 2, 3, R:1, 2, 3)	6	
GB-56	500404001	Spring for Bell Crank Unit	44	
GB-57		Key (1 • !)	1	
GB-58		Key (2 • (α)	1	
GB-59		Key (3 • #)	1	
GB-60		Key (4 • $)	1	
GB-61		Key (5 • %)	1	
GB-62		Key (6 • c)	1	
GB-63		Key (7 • &)	1	
GB-64		Key (8 • *)	1	
GB-65		Key (9 • ()	1	
GB-66		Key (0 •))	1	
GB-67		Key (- • -)	1	
GB-68		Key (= • +)	1	
GB-69		Key (Q)	1	
GB-70		Key (W)	1	
GB-71		Key (E)	1	
GB-72		Key (R)	1	
GB-73		Key (T)	1	

Table 6-2. Parts List for Fig. 6-37 (courtesy of
Brother International Corporation) **(continued from page 312).**

GB- 74		Key (Y)	1
GB- 75		Key (U)	1
GB- 76		Key (I)	1
GB- 77		Key (O)	1
GB- 78		Key (P)	1
GB- 79		Key ('₂ • ¼)	1
GB- 80		Key (A)	1
GB- 81		Key (S)	1
GB- 82		Key (O)	1
GB- 83		Key (F)	1
GB- 84		Key (G)	1
GB- 85		Key (H)	1
GB- 86		Key (J)	1
GB- 87		Key (K)	1
GB- 88		Key (L)	1
GB- 89		Key (: • :)	1
GB- 90		Key (• • • .)	1
GB- 91		Key (Z)	1
GB- 92		Key (X)	1
GB- 93		Key (C)	1
GB- 94		Key (V)	1
GB- 95		Key (B)	1
GB- 96		Key (N)	1
GB- 97		Key (M)	1
GB- 98		Key (. . .)	1
GB- 99		Key (• • •)	1
GB-100		Key (/ • ?)	1
GB-101	516087	Margin Release Key	1
GB-102	516091	Back Space Key	1
GB-103	516118	Tabulator Key	1
GB-104	516078	Shift Key (right)	1
GB-105	516079	Shift Key (left)	1
GB-106	516083	Shift Lock Key	1

To see the mechanisms or parts blown up, take the part number to the appropriate blow-up. The part designated as "snap ring (GD-18)" will be found in Fig. 6-39, and the part itself will be annotated with the number "18." In this particular case, the number in the *quantity* column is 8; therefore, this particular part will be found eight times in the blow-up.

Removing the Sub-Chassis and Sector Plate With the Typebar

When a dog shelf, bell crank, etc., become defective, they can be repaired or adjusted more easily if the following parts are removed:

☐ Remove two each of fastening screws (GA-58), which secure the guide plate for GA-57 (GA-59), from the bottom side of the machine.

☐ Remove two snap rings (GD-18) of the space and repeat space crank (GD-15). Then remove the space bar connector (GD-21) and the repeat space bar connector (GD-25).

☐ In removing GD-21 and GD-25, note that they must be removed from the space bar crank (GD-22) and the front repeat space crank (GD-26).

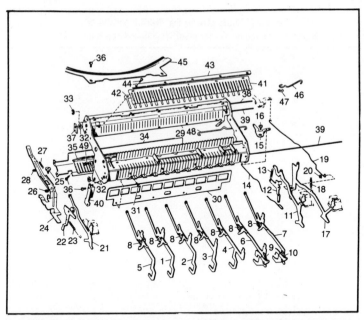

Fig. 6-38. The key lever, sub frame, margin release, back release and tabulator. Parts numbers for this mechanism will be preceded by the letters GC (courtesy of Brother International Corporation).

☐ Remove the snap rings (GD-18), first from the holder for GD-12 and GD-17 (which is welded on GC-29). Then remove GD-11 and GD-12, and GD-17 and GD-20.

☐ Remove four each of screws (GC-31) of the bell crank stopper (GC-34) from each direction of both left and right of the chassis (GI-1). Remove GC-34 from the machine.

☐ Remove the snap ring (GC-20, one only) from the tab key lever (GC-17), which will allow you to remove the front tab operating wire (GC-19) from the pin of GC-17.

☐ Remove the front back space wire (GC-14) from the back space lever (GC-12).

☐ Remove the color change stop wire (GD-46) from the ribbon color selector (GD-32).

☐ Remove the stud screw for GD-37 (GD-38) from the right side of GI-1.

☐ Remove the driving belt (GK-12).

☐ Remove the snatch roll pulley (GK-13).

☐ Remove the spring for GC-21 (GK-23) from the shift lock plate (GC-40).

314

☐ Remove two each of GC-36, from the left side of GI-1, and then remove GC-40.

☐ Remove the spring for GD-5 (GD-6) from the shift lever unit (GD-1), at the left of GI-1; and then remove the stud screw for GD-5 (GD-7). Then remove the shift lock key lever (GD-5).

Table 6-3. Parts List for Fig. 6-38 (courtesy of Brother International Corporation).

REF.NO.	PART NO.	PART NAME	QTY.	MEMO
GC- 1	516028001	Key Lever Unit (right,2,6,10,14,22)	10	
		(left: 3,7,11,15,19)		
GC- 2	516033001	Key Lever Unit (right: 4,8,12,16,20)	11	
		(left: 1,5,9,13,17,21)		
GC- 3	516035001	Key Lever Unit (right: 1,5,9,13,17,21)	11	
		(left, 4,8,12,16,20)		
GC- 4	516037001	Key Lever Unit (right: 3,7,11,19)	8	
		(left: 2,6,10,18)		
GC- 5	516031001	Key Lever Unit (left: 22)	1	
GC- 6	516043001	Repeat Key Lever for Top Line Keys		
GC- 7	516039001	Repeat Key Lever for Lowest Line Keys		
GC- 8	550814001	Spring for GC-1,2,3,4,5,6,7		
GC- 9	516207001	Spring for GC-6		
GC-10	516206001	Spring for GC-7		
GC-11	516092001	Back Space Key Lever	1	
GC-12	516093001	Back Space Lever	1	
GC-13	512463001	Spring for GC-11	1	
GC-14	516094001	Back Space Wire (front)	1	
GC-15	500289001	Back Space Link	1	
GC-16	500283001	Stud Screw for GC-15	1	
GC-17	516116001	TAB key Lever	1	
GC-18	511091001	Spring for GC-17	1	
GC-19	516119001	TAB Operating Wire (front)	1	
GC-20	048025346	Snap Ring for GC-19	1	
GC-21	516088001	Margin Release Key Lever	1	
GC-22	516089001	MR Operating Lever	1	
GC-23	516208001	Spring for GC-21	1	
GC-24	516090001	Margin Release Bar	1	
GC-25	507481001	Stud Screw for GC-24	1	
GC-26	500296001	Nut for GC-25	1	
GC-27	500677001	Spring for GC-24	1	
GC-28	04802346	Snap Ring for GC-24	1	
GC-29	516045001	Sub Chassis Unit	1	
GC-30	516173001	Dog Shelf Adjusting Plate	1	
GC-31	001679413	Screw for GC-29, 30, 34	12	
GC-32	510909001	Washer for GC-29	6	
GC-33	500379001	Snap Ring for GC-38	2	
GC-34	516066001	Bell Crank Stopper	1	
GC-35	516067001	Dog Shelf Stopper	1	
GC-36	401881003	Screw for GC-34, 40, 45	8	
GC-37	516062001	Stop Plate for GC-39	2	
GC-38	510669001	Key Lever Pivot Wire	1	
GC-39	500251001	Key Lever & Bell Crank Stop Wire	2	
GC-40	516085001	Shift Lock Plate	1	
GC-41	516063001	Key Lever Return Spring (A)	1	
GC-42	516064001	Key Lever Return Spring (B)	1	
GC-43	516065001	Fastening Plate for GC-41, 42	1	
GC-44	402281002	Screw for GC-43	5	
GC-45	500943001	Typebar Rest with Rubber	1	
GC-46	507557001	TAB Operating Wire (rear)	1	
GC-47	500379001	Snap Ring for GF-63	1	
GC-48	500291001	Back Space Wire (rear)	1	
GC-49	001679413	Screw for GC-29	2	

315

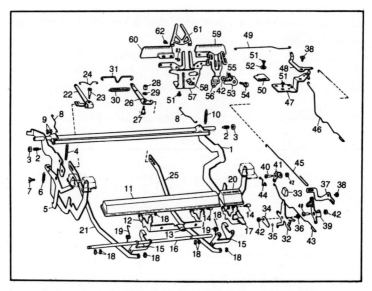

Fig. 6-39. The space bar, paper meter and color change. Parts numbers for this mechanism will be preceded by the letters GD (courtesy of Brother International Corporation).

☐ Remove the snap ring for GK-14 (GK-17) from the right of GI-1; then remove GK-15 from the right end of the snatch roll.

☐ Remove the snatch roll (GK-14) by pulling it out to the right.

☐ Remove two each of the screws for GA-45 (GA-53).

☐ From both the left and right of GI-1, remove two each on each left and right side respectively, washers (GC-32), of the screws (GC-49).

The sub-chassis, with key lever, as well as the sector plate with typebars, can be removed as an assembly.

Removing the Back Space Parts

To remove the back space parts, proceed as follows:

☐ Most of the removal and replacement can be done by only removing the cover; however, the job will be made easier by removing the sub-chassis (this procedure has just been described).

☐ Remove the screws (GF-50 and GF-63) of the right and left carriage holder (GF-3 and GF-6) and carriage rail (GF-59).

☐ Remove the stud screw for GC-15 (GC-16).

☐ After removing the carriage rail (GF-59), remove the front back space wire (GC-14) and rear back space wire (GC-48).

Table 6-4. Parts List for Fig. 6-38 (courtesy of Brother International Corporation).

REF.NO.	PART NO.	PART NAME	QTY.	MEMO
GD- 1	516071001	Shift Lever Unit	1	
GD- 2	500498001	Center Screw for GD-1	2	
GD- 3	106129001	Nut for GD-2	2	
GD- 4	500685001	Spring for GD-1	1	
GD- 5	516082001	Shift Lock Key Lever	1	
GD- 6	511091001	Spring for GD-5	1	
GD- 7	516084001	Stud Screw for GD-5	1	
GD- 8	516080001	Ribbon Feed Wire	2	
GD- 9	048040346	Snap Ring for Ribbon Operating Bar	2	
GD-10	512125001	Spring for Ribbon Operating Bar	1	
GD-11	512974	Space Bar	1	
GD-12	516096001	Space Bar Lever Unit	1	
GD-13	500315001	Cushion Rubber for GD-12	1	
GD-14	516171001	Stud Screw for GD-12, 17	2	
GD-15	516172001	Space & Repeat Space Crank	2	
GD-16	516101001	Shaft for GD-15	1	
GD-17	516104001	Repeat Space Lever	1	
GD-18	048025346	Snap Ring for GD-12, 15,17,21,25	8	
GD-19	516102001	Spring for GD-15	2	
GD-20	512975	Repeat Space Key	1	
GD-21	516100000	Space Bar Connector	1	
GD-22	500973001	Space Bar Crank	1	
GD-23	500422001	Stud Screw for GD-22	1	
GD-24	500974001	Space Bar Wire	1	
GD-25	516107000	Repeat Space Bar Connector	1	
GD-26	509969001	Repeat Space Crank (front)	1	
GD-27	516108001	Stud Screw for GD-26	1	
GD-28	516109001	Nut for GD-27	1	
GD-29	503090001	Washer for GD-27	1	
GD-30	512189001	Spring for GD-26	1	
GD-31	509971001	Repeat Space Crank Wire	1	
GD-32	516111001	Ribbon Color Selector	1	
GD-33	503643	Tip for GD-32	1	
GD-34	500322001	Spring Plate for GD-32	1	
GD-35	071030050	Steel Ball	1	
GD-36	505951001	Stud Screw for GD-32	1	
GD-37	500693001	Color Change Lever	1	
GD-38	500283001	Stud Screw for GD-37, 48	2	
GD-39	500329001	Ribbon Vibrator Operating Lever	1	
GD-40	500422001	Stud Screw for GD-39, 41	2	
GD-41	500694001	Color Change Link	1	
GD-42	500296001	Nut for GD-36, 40, 54	4	
GD-43	516113001	Color Change Link Wire (front)	1	
GD-44	516114001	Color Change Link Wire (rear)	1	
GD-45	500331001	Ribbon Vibrator wire (front)	1	
GD-46	516115001	Color Change Stop Wire	1	
GD-47	507749001	Holder for GD-48	1	
GD-48	500332001	Ribbon Operating Link	1	
GD-49	500982001	Ribbon Vibrator Wire (rear)	1	
GD-50	516110001	Repeat Spacer Stopper	1	
GD-51	402281002	Screw for GD-47,50,57	5	
GD-52	500986001	Washer for GD-50	1	
GD-53	507306001	Ribbon Vibrator Link	1	
GD-54	507308001	Stud Screw for GD-53	1	
GD-55	507309001	Washer for GD-53	1	
GD-56	500658001	Ribbon Vibrator	1	
GD-57	507440001	Paper Meter Holder	1	
GD-58	507494001	Cushion Rubber for GD-53	1	
GD-59	507020001	Paper Meter (right)	1	
GD-60	507021001	Paper Meter (left)	1	
GD-61	505478001	Card Holder	1	
GD-62	505165001	Screw for GD-54,60,61	6	

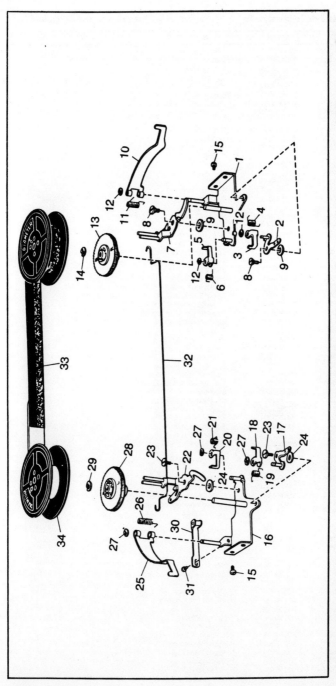

Fig. 6-40. The ribbon feed and ribbon reverse. Parts numbers for this mechanism will be preceded by the letters GE (courtesy of Brother International Corporation).

Table 6-5. Parts List for Fig. 6-40 (courtesy of Brother International Corporation).

REF.NO.	PART NO.	PART NAME	QTY.	MEMO
GE-1-14	(500983001)	Ribbon Spool Holder Complete (right)	1	
GE- 1	509590001	Ribbon Spool Holder (right)	1	
GE- 2	509592001	Lever for GE-3	1	
GE- 3	500371001	Ribbon Feed Pawl (right)	1	
GE- 4	500378001	Spring for GE-3	1	
GE- 5	500373001	Wheel Backlash Stopper (right)	1	
GE- 6	500710001	Spring for GE-5	1	
GE- 7	500984001	Ribbon Reverse Lever (right)	1	
GE- 8	500283001	Stud Screw for GE-2,7	2	
GE- 9	500986001	Washer for GE-2,7	2	
GE-10	505472001	Spool Holding Arm (right)	1	
GE-11	510725001	Spring for GE-10	1	
GE-12	500379001	Snap Ring for GE-2,5,10	3	
GE-13	504597001	Ribbon Feed Wheel (right)	1	
GE-14	500357001	Snap Ring for GE-13	1	
GE-15	402281002	Screw for GE-1,16	4	
GE-16-31	(500987001)	Ribbon Spool Holder Complete (left)		
GE-16	509591001	Ribbon Spool Holder (left)	1	
GE-17	509593001	Lever for GE-18	1	
GE-18	500372001	Ribbon Fed Pawl (left)	1	
GE-19	500376001	Spring for GE-18	1	
GE-20	500374001	Wheel Backlash Stopper (left)	1	
GE-21	500711001	Spring for GE-20	1	
GE-22	505484001	Ribbon Reverse Lever (left)	1	
GE-23	500283001	Stud Screw for GE-17,22	2	
GE-24	500986001	Washer for GE-17,22	2	
GE-25	505473001	Spool Holder Arm (left)	1	
GE-26	510726001	Spring for GE-25	1	
GE-27	500379001	Snap Ring for GE-18,21,25	3	
GE-28	504598001	Ribbon Feed Wheel (left)	1	
GE-29	500357001	Snap Ring for GE-28	1	
GE-30	505457001	Reverse Snap Spring	1	
GE-31	402281002	Screw for GE-30	1	
GE-32	516242001	Ribbon Reverse Wire	1	
GE-33	504594001	Ribbon Red/Black with Spool	1	
GE-34	500725001	Ribbon Spool	1	

This procedure might be clarified by referring back to Figs. 6-15A and 6-15B.

Reverse the procedure above for reinstalling the parts. Before fastening the carriage rail (GF-59), be sure both back space wires are hooked to GC-15. When this is completed, the final test is to try the back space to see that it works properly.

Removing the Parts of the Shift Mechanism

To remove the parts of the shift mechanism, proceed as follows:

☐ Remove the sub-chassis and typebar unit.

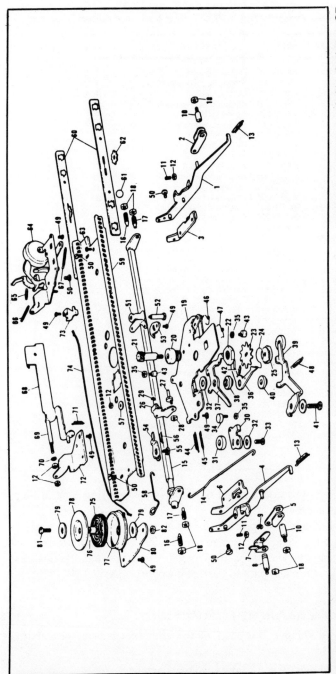

Fig. 6-41. The carriage rail, pinion base, spring drum and warning bell. Parts numbers for this mechanism will be preceded by the letters GF (courtesy of Brother International Corporation).

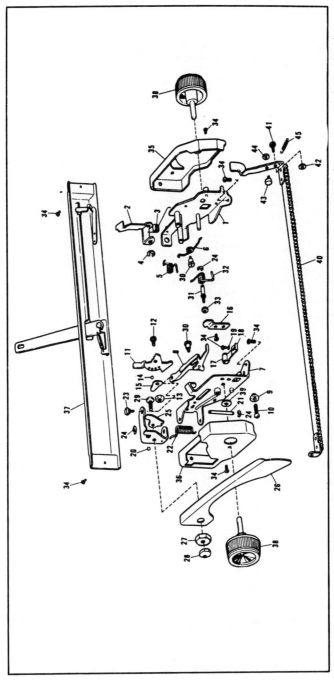

Fig. 6-42. The carriage side plate. Parts numbers for this mechanism will be preceded by the letters GG (courtesy of Brother International Corporation).

Table 6-6. Parts List for Fig. 6-41 (courtesy of Brother International Corporation).

REF.NO.	PART NO.	PART NAME	QTY.	MEMO
GF- 1	500990001	Carriage Frame (right)Unit	1	
GF- 2	500815001	Carriage Link(right)	1	
GF- 3	500400001	Carriage Holder(right)	1	
GF- 4	500993001	Carriage Frame(left)Unit	1	
GF- 5	500816001	Carriage Link(left)	1	
GF- 6	500401001	Carriage Holder(left)	1	
GF- 7	507466001	Shift Crank	1	
GF- 8	507473001	Stud for GF-7	1	
GF- 9	500357001	Snap Ring for GF-7	1	
GF-10	500784001	Stud Screw for GF-2,5	2	
GF-11	500405001	Shift Adjusting Screw	4	
GF-12	500296001	Nut for GF-11,55,72	7	
GF-13	500685001	Shift Balance Spring	2	
GF-14	507485001	Shift Wire	1	
GF-15	507830001	Shift Link(rear)Unit	1	
GF-16	500278001	Center Screw for GF-15	2	
GF-17	500498001	Stud for GF-15	2	
GF-18	106129001	Nut for GF-8,10,16,17	7	
GF-19-47	(520020001)	Pinion Base Complete	1	
GF-19	501009001	Pinion Base Unit	1	
GF-20	501010001	Pinion Boss	1	
GF-21	501012001	Space Pinion	1	
GF-22	501011001	Nut for GF-20	1	
GF-23	500430001	Space Ratchet Wheel	1	
GF-24	500431001	Ratchet Release Spring	1	
GF-25	500432001	Nut for GF-21	1	
GF-26	516164001	Escape Crank(front)	1	
GF-27	516241001	Eccentric Stud for GF-26	1	
GF-28	500683001	Nut for GF-27	1	
GF-29	048015346	Snap Ring for GF-26	1	
GF-30	501016001	Escape Crank(rear)	1	
GF-31	501017001	Stud Collar for GF-30	1	
GF-32	501018001	Washer for GF-30,37,39	3	
GF-33	100137003	Screw for GF-30	1	
GF-34	501019001	Eccentric Screw for GF-30	1	
GF-35	500296001	Nut for GF-34,43	3	
GF-36	507538001	Space Ratchet	1	
GF-37	509980001	Half Space Ratchet	1	
GF-38	501022001	Stud Collar for GF-36	1	
GF-39	509975001	Repeat Space Operating Lever	1	
GF-40	509974001	Stud Collar for GF-39	1	
GF-41	403857001	Screw for GF-39	1	
GF-42	500680001	Spring for GF-36	1	
GF-43	501023001	Eccentric Screw for GF-36,37	2	
GF-44	501406001	Spring for GF-37	1	
GF-45	503158001	Spring (A) for GF-39	1	
GF-46	501027001	Spring (A) for Back Space Pawl	1	
GF-47	500259001	Spring (B) for Back Space Pawl	1	
GF-48	520202001	Spring (B) for GF-39	1	
GF-49	402281001	Screw for GF-19,53,75,76	9	
GF-50	001660413	Screw for GF-1,4,59,64	10	
GF-51	509972001	Repeat Space Crank(rear)	1	
GF-52	509973001	Stud for GF-51	1	
GF-53	509977001	Repeat Space Adjusting Plate	1	

REF.NO.	PART NO.	PART NAME	QTY.	MEMO
GF-54	516174001	Escape Stopper Unit	1	
GF-55	505951001	Stud Screw for GF-54	1	
GF-56	512048001	Spring for GF-54	1	
GF-57	500986001	Washer for GF-54	1	
GF-58	516128001	Escape Stop Wire	1	
GF-59-62	(516237001)	Carriage Rail Complete	1	
GF-59	516165001	Carriage Rail	1	
GF-60-62 &CH-15	(500634001)	Carriage Retainer Unit	1	
GF-60	500635001	Carriage Retainer	2	
GF-61	105090001	Steel Ball	8	
GF-62	500396001	Sprocket Wheel	2	
GH-15	507569001	Carriage	1	
GF-63	507658001	Tapping Screw for GF-59	2	
GF-64	507578001	Warning Bell Complete	1	
GF-65	500413001	Spring (A) for GF-64	1	
GF-66	500680001	Spring (B) for GF-64	1	
GF-67	510688001	Spring (C) for GF-64	1	
GF-68	501043001	Carriage Stopper	1	
GF-69	501045001	Shaft for GF-71	1	
GF-70	502131001	Washer for GF-71	1	
GF-71	500404001	Spring for GH-71	1	
GF-72	506994001	Carriage Stopper Holder	1	
GF-73	500643001	Hook for GF-78	1	
GF-74	500470001	Carriage Draw String	1	
GF-75-82	(500465001)	Spring Drum Complete	1	
GF-75	500471001	Main Spring	1	
GF-76	500468001	Stud for GF-78	1	
GF-77	500467001	Spring Drum	1	
GF-78	500466001	Lid for GF-80	1	
GF-79	500469001	Lock Plate for GF-79	2	
GF-80	500473001	Spring Drum Holder	1	
GF-81	500472001	Spring Drum Screw	1	
GF-82	402230001	Nut for GF-84	1	

☐ Remove the complete ribbon spool holder, both right and left (this procedure will be explained in the section immediately following).

☐ Remove the color change link (GD-41). Then remove the rear color change link wire (GD-44) from the shift lever (GD-1).

☐ Remove the spring (GD-10).

☐ Remove two each of left and right nuts (GD-3), of the center screws (GD-2), and then remove the shift lever unit (GD-1).

The above procedure might be clarified by referring to Figs. 6-16A through 6-16C. Reinstall the parts by reversing the procedure for removing them.

Removing the Complete Ribbon Spool Holder

To remove the ribbon spool holders, proceed as follows:

☐ Remove the covers.

Table 6-7. Parts List for Fig. 6-42 (courtesy of Brother International Corporation).

REF.NO.	PART NO.	PART NAME	QTY.	MEMO
GG- 1	500590001	Carriage Side Plate (right) Unit	1	
GG- 2	500504001	Paper Release lever	1	
GG- 3	500595001	Spring for GG-2	1	
GG- 4	500357001	Snap Ring for GG-2	1	
GG- 5	500503001	Spring for GH-6	1	
GG- 6	500516001	Spring for GH-7	1	
GG- 7	500591001	Carriage Side Plate (left) Complete	1	
GG- 8	520109001	Line Space Ratchet Unit	1	
GG- 9	501028001	Stud Collar for GG-8	1	
GG-10	500654001	Screw for GG-8	1	
GG-11	500491001	Line Space Selector	1	
GG-12	50446001	Stud Screw for GG-11	1	
GG-13	40223001	Nut for GG-12	1	
GG-14	402104001	Steel Boal for GG-11,26	1	
GG-15	500492001	Plate Spring for GG-14	1	
GG-16	500489001	Release for GG-8	1	
GG-17	500495001	Line Space Ratchet Roller	1	
GG-18	500494001	Plate Spring for GG-17	1	
GG-19	500636001	Washer for GG-18	1	
GG-20	500483001	Line Space Lever Holder	1	
GG-21	500484001	Shaft for GG-20	1	
GG-22	500485001	Line Space Lever Reverse Spring	1	
GG-23	500460001	Stud Screw for GG-20	1	
GG-24	500379001	Snap Ring for GG-22,32	3	
GG-25	507993001	Plate Spring for GG-26	1	
GG-26	500479002	Line Space & Carriage Return Lever	1	
GG-27	506243001	Nut (A) for GG-26	1	
GG-28	506242001	Nut (B) for GG-26	1	
GG-29	501449001	Bolt for GG-26	1	
GG-30	500368001	Stud Screw for GG-6,GH-8	2	
GG-31	500500001	Bolt for GH-6	1	
GG-32	500501001	Spring for GH-6	1	
GG-33	500296001	Nut for GG-31	1	
GG-34	402281001	Screw for GG-1,7,16, 18,35,36,37	12	
GG-35	500543	Carriage Cover (right)	1	
GG-36	500544	Carriage Cover (left	1	
GG-37	501344	Carriage Cover (rear) Unit	1	
GG-38	507685	Platen Knob	2	
GG-39	102707001	Washer for GG-38	1	
GG-40	500457001	Space Rack Unit	1	
GG-41	500323001	Stud Screw for GG-40	1	
GG-42	101397001	Washer for GG-40	1	
GG-43	500461001	Eccentric Screw for GG-40	1	
GG-44	500683001	Nut for GG-43	1	
GG-45	500463001	Spring for GG-40	1	

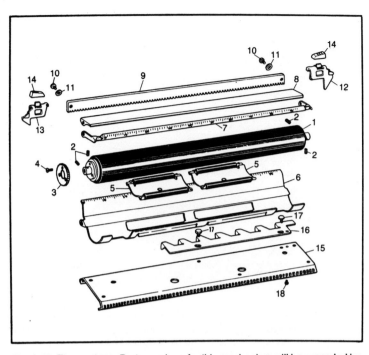

Fig. 6-43. The carriage. Parts numbers for this mechanism will be preceded by the letters GH (courtesy of Brother International Corporation).

Table 6-8. Parts List for Fig. 6-43 (courtesy of Brother International Corporation).

REF.NO.	PART NO.	PART NAME	QTY.	MEMO
GH-1	500517002	Platen	1	
GH-2	014679322	Screw for GH-1	4	
GH-3	500497001	Line Space Ratchet Wheel	1	
GH-4	512335001	Screw for GH-3	3	
GH-5	500592001	Paper Feed Roller Unit	2	
GH-6	500499	Paper Pin	1	
GH-7	500512001	Paper Bail Scale	1	
GH-8	500509	Paper Rest	1	
GH-9	500531001	Margin Rack	1	
GH-10	101531003	Screw for GH-9	2	
GH-11	500341001	Washer for GH-10	2	
GH-12	507267001	Margin Stop (right)	1	
GH-13	507268001	Margin Stop (left)	1	
GH-14	500542	Tip for GH-12,13	2	
GH-15	507569001	Carriage	1	
GH-16	507571001	Tap Stop Pawl	1	
GH-17	507573001	Screw for GH-16	2	
GH-18	104336001	Tapping Screw for GH-16	1	

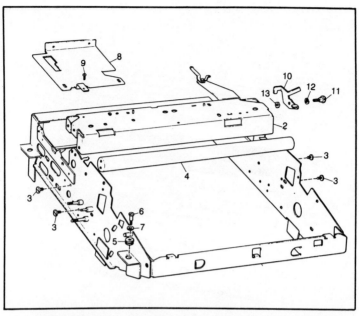

Fig. 6-44. The chassis. Parts numbers for this mechanism will be preceded by the letters GI (courtesy of Brother International Corporation).

☐ From both sides of the chassis unit (GI-1), remove two each of screws (GE-15) from the left and right, respectively.
☐ Remove the ribbon reverse wire (GE-32).

Table 6-9. Parts List for Fig. 6-44 (courtesy of Brother International Corporation).

REF.NO.	PART NO.	PART NAME	QTY.	MEMO
GI-1	516129001	Chassis Unit	1	
GI-2	516238001	Chassis Reinforce Block	1	
GI-3	001679413	Screw for GI-2,4	10	
GI-4	516175001	Chassis Reinforce Bar	1	
GI-5	511342001	Cushion Rubber	4	
GI-6	512281001	Screw for GI-1	4	
GI-7	510909001	Washer for GI-5	4	
GI- 8	516176001	Motor Cover	1	
GI- 9	500654001	Screw for GI-8	3	
GI-10	500559001	Carriage Lock Lever	1	
GI-11	507191001	Stud Screw for GI-10	1	
GI-12	500341001	Spring Washer for GI-10	1	
GI-13	500296001	Nut for GI-11	1	

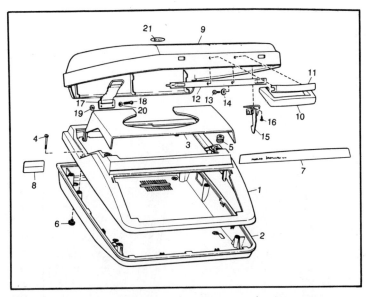

Fig. 6-45. The cover and case. Parts numbers for this mechanism will be preceded by the letters GJ (courtesy of Brother International Corporation).

Table 6-10. Parts List for Fig. 6-45 (courtesy of Brother International Corporation).

REF.NO.	PART NO.	PART NAME	QTY.	MEMO
GJ- 1	516182	Upper Cover	1	
GJ- 2	516183	Lower Cover	1	
GJ- 3	516184	Top Cover	1	
GJ- 4	516202001	Screw for GJ-1,2	2	
GJ- 5	516245001	Top Cover Fitting Rubber	2	
GJ- 6	512141001	Rubber Foot	4	
GJ- 7		Name Plate	1	
GJ- 8		Rating Plate	1	
GJ-9~21	516210	Lid Case Complete	1	
GJ- 9	516186	Lid Case	1	
GJ-10	507936	Carrying Handle	1	
GJ-11	520707	Handle Holder	1	
GJ-12	516197	Lock Operating Plate	1	
GJ-13	105205001	Screw for GJ-12	2	
GJ-14	025350333	Washer for GJ-13	2	
GJ-15	516191001	Lid Case Lock Unit	2	
GJ-16	401881003	Screw for GJ-15	4	
GJ-17	516203001	Supply Cord Hanger	2	
GJ-18	002660812	Screw for GJ-17	4	
GJ-19	402230001	Nut for GJ-18	4	
GJ-20	402287002	Washer for GJ-18	4	
GJ-21		Ornamental Plate	1	

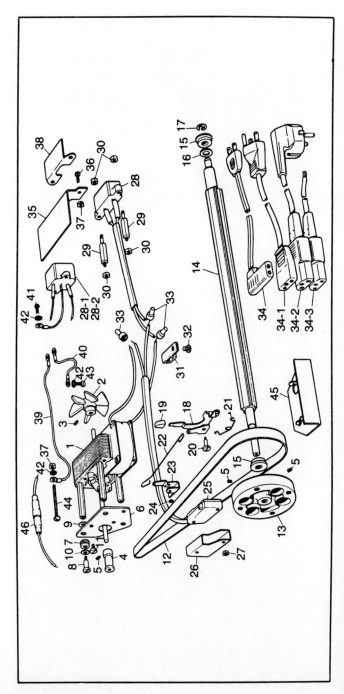

Fig. 6-46. The electrical components. Parts numbers for this mechanism will be preceded by the letters GK (courtesy of Brother International Corporation).

Table 6-11. Parts List for Fig. 6-46 (courtesy of Brother International Corporation).

REF NO.	PART NO.	PART NAME	QTY	MEMO
GK-1	516160001	Motor for 110V-125V (UL, CSA, etc.)	1	
GK-1-1	516216001	Motor for 220V-240V (VDE, SEV, etc.)	1	
GK-2	516199001	Motor Fan	1	
GK-3	011660512	Screw for GK-2	1	
GK-4	516153001	Motor Pulley (60 HZ)	1	
GK-4-1	516271001	Motor Pulley (50 HZ)	1	
GK-5	014679322	Screw for GK-4, 13	3	
GK-6	516157001	Motor Holder	1	
GK-7	513342001	Motor Cushion Rubber	3	
GK-8	516158001	Stud Screw for GK-1	3	
GK-9	403332001	Washer (A) for GK-1	3	
GK-11	402447001	Washer (B) for GK-1	3	
GK-11	001679413	Screw for GK-6	3	
GK-12	516156000	Driving Belt (60HZ)	1	
GK-12-1	516270000	Driving Belt (50HZ)		
GK-13	516154000	Snatch Roll Pulley	1	
GK-14	516068001	Snatch Roll	1	
GK-15	516009001	Snatch Roll Metal	2	
GK-16	516155000	Washer for GK-14	1	
GK-17	048050346	Snap Ring for GK-14	1	
GK-18-19	(516148001)	Switch Lever Unit	1	
GK-18	516149001	Switch Lever	1	
GK-19	503643	Tip for GK-18	1	
GK-20	509635001	Stud Screw for GK-18	1	
GK-21	503113001	Snap Spring	1	
GK-22	516152001	Switch Operating Wire	1	
GK-23	516151001	Switch Operating Lever	1	
GK-24	0408020346	Snap Ring for GK-23	1	
GK-25	516161001	Power Switch with Lead Wire for U.1. CSA	1	
GK-25-1	516161002	Power Switch with Lead Wire for BS and Others	1	
GK-25-2	5162200001	Power Switch with Lead Wire for VDE	1	
GK-25-3	5162650001	Power Switch with Lead Wire for SEV, NEMKO	1	
GK-26	551443001	Switch Cover	1	
GK-27	021260103	Nut for GK-25	2	
GK-28	516189001	Receptacle with Lead Wire for 100V-125V(UL)	1	
GK-28-1	516217001	Receptacle with Lead Wire for CSA.	1	
GK-28-2	516219001	Receptacle with Lead Wire for 220V-240V(VDE, SEV,etc.)	1	
GK-29	516159001	Bolt for GK-28 (100V - 125V)	2	
GK-29-1	516214001	Bolt for GK-28-1 (CSA)	2	
GK-29-2	516215001	Bolt for GK-28-2 (220V-240V)	2	
GK-30	021660103	Nut for GK-28, 29	4	
GK-31	120679001	Wire Holder	1	
GK-31-1	516267001	Wire Holder for BS Only	1	
GK-32	400298002	Screw for GK-31	1	
GK-33	207216000	Wire Conector	3	
GK-34	207553001	Power Supply Cord for 100V-125V	1	
GK-34-1	512901001	Power Supply Cord for CSA	1	
GK-34-2	550856001	Power Supply Cord for VDE	1	
GK-34-3	550980001	Power Supply Cord for 220V-240V	1	
GK-35	516248001	Receptacle Cover for VDE, SEV, NEMKO, BS	1	
GK-36	402659001	Screw for GK-35	1	
GK-37	021660103	Nut for GK-36, 44		
GK-38	516347001	Insulating Paper for VDE SEV, NEMKO, BS	1	
GK-39	516218001	Earthing Wire (A)	1	
GK-40	516249001	Earthing Wire (B)	1	
GK-41	105123002	Screw for Earthing Wire	1	
GK-42	550719001	Toothed Lock Washer		
GK-43	400298001	Screw for GK-40	1	
GK-44	516234001	Screw for GK-39	1	
GK-45	516246000	Motor Cover for CSA only	1	
GK-46	516266001	Fuse Unit for BS only	1	

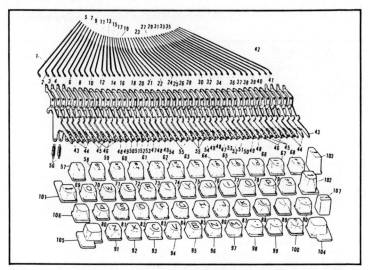

Fig. 6-47. The typebar wire, bell crank and key for the Brother Model 3500. Parts numbers for this mechanism will be preceded by the letters JB (courtesy of Brother International Corporation).

Table 6-12. Parts List for Fig. 6-47 (courtesy of Brother International Corporation).

REF. NO.	PART NO.	PART NAME	Q'TY
JB- 1	516257001	Typebar Wire (left 22)	1
JB- 2	516256001	Typebar Wire (left 21)	1
JB- 3	500174002	Typebar Wire (left 20)	1
JB- 4	500173002	Typebar Wire (left 19)	1
JB- 5	500172002	Typebar Wire (left 18)	1
JB- 6	500171002	Typebar Wire (left 17)	1
JB- 7	500170002	Typebar Wire (left 16)	1
JB- 8	500169002	Typebar Wire (left 15)	1
JB- 9	500168002	Typebar Wire (left 14)	1
JB-10	500167002	Typebar Wire (left 13)	1
JB-11	500166002	Typebar Wire (left 12)	1
JB-12	500165002	Typebar Wire (left 11)	1
JB-13	500164002	Typebar Wire (left 10)	1
JB-14	500163002	Typebar Wire (left 9)	1
JB-15	500162002	Typebar Wire (left 8)	1
JB-16	500161002	Typebar Wire (left 7)	1
JB-17	500160002	Typebar Wire (left 6)	1
JB-18	500159002	Typebar Wire (left 5)	1
JB-19	500158002	Typebar Wire (left 4)	1
JB-20	500157002	Typebar Wire (left 3)	1
JB-21	500156002	Typebar Wire (left 1, 2)	2
JB-22	500134002	Typebar Wire (right 1, 2)	2
JB-23	500135002	Typebar Wire (right 3)	1
JB-24	500136002	Typebar Wire (right 4)	1
JB-25	500137002	Typebar Wire (right 5)	1
JB-26	500138002	Typebar Wire (right 6)	1
JB-27	500139002	Typebar Wire (right 7)	1
JB-28	500140002	Typebar Wire (right 8)	1
JB-29	500141002	Typebar Wire (right 9)	1
JB-30	500142002	Typebar Wire (right 10)	1
JB-31	500143002	Typebar Wire (right 11)	1
JB-32	500144002	Typebar Wire (right 12)	1
JB-33	500145002	Typebar Wire (right 13)	1
JB-34	500146002	Typebar Wire (right 14)	1
JB-35	500147002	Typebar Wire (right 15)	1
JB-36	500148002	Typebar Wire (right 16)	1

REF. NO.	PART NO.	PART NAME	Q'TY
JB-37	500149002	Typebar Wire (right 17)	1
JB-38	500150002	Typebar Wire (right 18)	1
JB-39	500151002	Typebar Wire (right 19)	1
JB-40	500152002	Typebar Wire (right 20)	1
JB-41	516254001	Typebar Wire (right 21)	1
JB-42	516255001	Typebar Wire (right 22)	1
JB-43	516026001	Bell Crank Unit (L:22, R:22)	2
JB-44	516024001	Bell Crank Unit (L:19, 20, 21, R:19, 20, 21)	6
JB-45	516022001	Bell Crank Unit (L: 16, 18, R: 1, 15, 18)	5
JB-46	516020001	Bell Crank Unit (L:14,15,17,R:14,17)	5
JB-47	516010001	Bell Crank Unit (L:7, R:7)	2
JB-48	516008001	Bell Crank Unit (L:6, 13, R: 6, 13)	4
JB-49	516006001	Bell Crank Unit (L: 5,12,R:5,12)	4
JB-50	516018001	Bell Crank Unit (L:11, R:11)	2
JB-51	516016001	Bell Crank Unit (L:10, R:10)	2
JB-52	516014001	Bell Crank Unit (L: 9,R:9)	2
JB-53	516012001	Bell Crank Unit (L: 8,R:8)	2
JB-54	516004001	Bell Crank Unit (L:4,R;4)	2
JB-55	516001001	Bell Crank Unit (L:1,2,3R:1,2,3)	6
JB-56	500404001	Spring for Bell Crank Unit	44
JB-57		Key (1.!)	1
JB-58		Key (2.)	1
JB-59		Key (3.#)	1
JB-60		Key (4 . $)	1
JB-61		Key (5 .. %)	1
JB-62		Key (6 . c)	1
JB-63		Key (7 . &)	1
JB-64		Key (8 . *)	1
JB-65		Key (9 ()	1
JB-66		Key (0-))	1
JB-67		Key (- . -)	1
JB-68		Key (= . +)	1
JB-69		Key (Q)	1
JB-70		Key (W)	1
JB-71		Key (E)	1
JB-72		Key (R)	1
JB-73		Key (T)	1
JB-74		Key (Y)	1
JB-75		Key (U)	1
JB-76		Key (I)	1
JB-77		Key (O)	1
JB-78		Key (P)	1
JB-79		Key (½ . ¼)	1
JB-80		Key (A)	1
JB-81		Key (S)	1
JB-82		Key (D)	1
JB-83		Key (F)	1
JB-84		Key (G)	1
JB-85		Key (H)	1
JB-86		Key (J)	1
JB-87		Key (K)	1
JB-88		Key (L)	1
JB-89		Key (: . ;)	1
JB-90		Key (. . . .)	1
JB-91		Key (Z)	1
JB-92		Key (X)	1
JB-93		Key (C)	1
JB-94		Key (V)	1
JB-95		Key (B)	1
JB-96		Key (N)	1
JB-97		Key (M)	1
JB-98		Key (, . ,)	1
JB-99		Key (. . .)	1
JB-100		Key (/ . ?)	1
JB-101	516087	Margin Release Key	1
JB-102	516336	Back Space Key	1
JB-103	516341	Tabulator Key	1
JB-104	516078	Shift Key (right)	1
JB-105	516079	Shift Key (left)	1
JB-106	516083	Shift Lock Key	1
JB-107	516343	Carriage Return Key	1

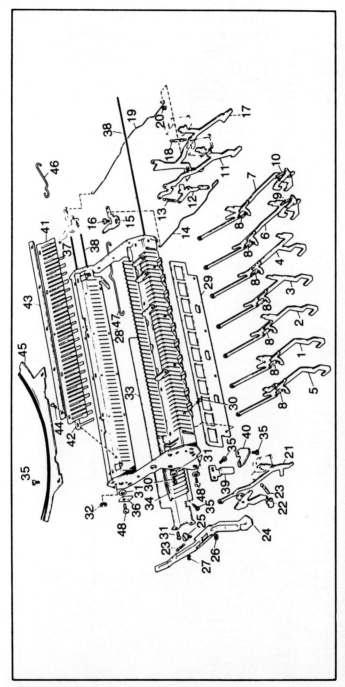

Fig. 6-48. The key lever, sub frame, margin release, back space and tabulator for the Brother Model 3500. Parts numbers for this mechanism will be preceded by the letters JC (courtesy of Brother International Corporation).

Table 6-13. Parts List for Fig. 6-48 (courtesy of Brother International Corporation).

REF. NO.	PART NO.	PART NAME	QTY	MEMO
JC- 1	516028001	Key Lever Unit (right:2,6,10,14,22)	10	
		(left:3,7,11,15,19)		
JC- 2	516033001	Key Lever Unit (right: 4,8,12,16,20)	11	
		(left: 1,5,9,13,17,21)		
JC- 3	516035001	Key Lever Unit (right: 1,5,9,13,17,21)	11	
		(left: 4,8,12,16,20)		
JC- 4	516037001	Key Lever Unit (right: 3,7,11,19)	8	
		(left: 2,6,10,18)		
JC- 5	516031001	Key Lever Unit (left: 22)	1	
JC- 6	516043001	Repeat Key Lever for Lowest Row Keys		
JC-7	516039001	Repeat Key Lever for Top Row Keys		
JC- 8	516272001	Spring for JC-1,2,3,4,5,6,7		
JC- 9	516207001	Spring for JC-6		
JC-10	516206001	Spring for JC-7		
JC-11	516337001	Back Space Key Lever	1	
JC-12	516093001	Back Space Lever	1	
JC-13	512463001	Spring for JC-11	1	
JC-14	516094001	Back Space Wire (front)	1	
JC-15	500289001	Back Space Link	1	
JC-16	500283001	Stud Screw for JC-15	1	
JC-17	516339001	TAB Key Lever	1	
JC-18	511091001	Spring for JC-17	1	
JC-19	516119001	TAB Operating Wire (front)	1	
JC-20	048025346	Snap Ring for JC-19	1	
JC-21	516088001	Margin Release Key Lever	1	
JC-22	516327001	MR Operating Lever	1	
JC-23	500677001	Spring for JC-21, 24	2	
JC-24	516334001	Margin Release Bar	1	
JC-25	507481001	Stud Screw for JC-24	1	
JC-26	500296001	Nut for JC-25	1	
JC-27	048020346	Snap Ring for JC-58	1	
JC-28	516045001	Sub Chassis Unit	1	
JC-29	516173001	Dog Shelf Adjusting Plate	1	
JC-30	001679413	Screw for JC-28, 29, 33	9	
JC-31	510909001	Washer for JC-28	6	
JC-32	500379001	Snap Ring for JC-37, JF-63	3	
JC-33	516066001	Bell Crank Stopper	1	
JC-34	516067001	Dog Shelf Stopper	1	
JC-35	401881003	Screw for JC-34,39,40,45	10	
JC-36	516062001	Stop Plate for JC-38	2	
JC-37	510669001	Key Lever Pivot Wire	1	
JC-38	500251001	Bell Crank Pivot Wire & Key	2	
		Lever Stop Wire		
JC-39	516312001	Shift Lock Plate	1	
JC-40	516313001	Shift Key Lever Stop Plate	1	
JC-41	516063001	Key Lever Return Spring (A)	1	
JC-42	516064001	Key Lever Return Spring (B)	1	
JC-43	516065001	Fastening Plate for JC-41,42	1	
JC-44	402281002	Screw for JC-43	5	
JC-45	500943001	Typebar Rest with Rubber	1	
JC-46	507577001	Tab Operating Wire (rear)	1	
JC-47	500291001	Back Space Wire (rear)	1	
JC-48	105123002	Screw for GC-29	5	

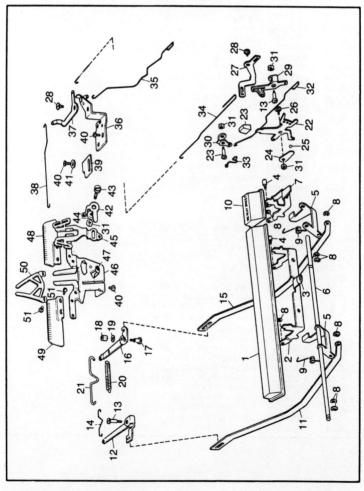

Fig. 6-49. The space bar, paper meter and color changer for the Brother Model 3500. Parts numbers for this mechanism will be preceded by the letters JD (courtesy of Brother International Corporation).

Table 6-14. Parts List for Fig. 6-49 (courtesy of Brother International Corporation).

REF. NO.	PART NO.	PART NAME	QTY	MEMO
JD-1	512974	Space Bar	1	
JD-2	516096001	Space Bar Lever Unit	1	
JD-3	500315001	Cushion Rubber for JD-2	1	
JD-4	516171001	Stud Screw for JD-2, 7	2	
JD-5	516172001	Space & Repeat Space Crank	2	
JD-6	516101001	Shaft for JD-5	1	
JD-7	516104001	Repeat Space Lever Unit	1	
JD-8	048025346	Snap Ring for JD-2,5,7,11,15	8	
JD-9	516102001	Spring for JD-5	2	
JD-10	512975	Repeat Space Key	1	
JD-11	516100001	Space Bar Connector	1	
JD-12	500973001	Space Bar Crank	1	
JD-13	500422001	Stud Screw for JD-12,29,30	3	
JD-14	516332001	Space Bar Wire	1	
JD-15	516107000	Repeat Space Bar Connector	1	
JD-16	509969001	Repeat Space Crank (front)	1	
JD-17	516108001	Stud Screw for JD-16	1	
JD-18	515109001	Nut for JD-17	1	
JD-19	503090001	Washer for JD-16	1	
JD-20	512189001	Spring for JD-16	1	
JD-21	509971001	Repeat Space Crank Wire	1	
JD-22	516111001	Ribbon Color Selector	1	
JD-23	503643	Tip for JD-22	1	
JD-24	500322001	Spring Plate for JD-22	1	
JD-25	071030050	Steel Ball	1	
JD-26	505951001	Stud Screw for JD-22	1	
JD-27	500693001	Color Change Lever	1	
JD-28	500283001	Stud Screw for JD-27, 37	2	
JD-29	500329001	Ribbon Vibrator Operating Lever	1	
JD-30	500694001	Color Change Link	1	
JD-31	500296001	Nut for JD-13, 26, 43	4	
JD-32	516113001	Color Change Link Wire (front)	1	
JD-33	516114001	Color Change Link Wire (rear)	1	
JD-34	500331001	Ribbon Vibrator wire (front)	1	
JD-35	516115001	Color Change Stop Wire	1	
JD-36	507749001	Holder for JD-37	1	
JD-37	500332001	Ribbon Operating Link	1	
JD-38	500982001	Ribbon Vibrator Wire (rear)	1	
JD-39	516110001	Repeat Spacer Stopper	1	
JD-40	402881002	Screw for JD-36, 39, 46	5	
JD-41	500986001	Washer for JD-39	1	
JD-42	507306001	Ribbon Vibrator Link	1	
JD-43	507308001	Stud Screw for JD-42	1	
JD-44	507309001	Washer for JD-42	1	
JD-45	500658001	Ribbon Vibrator	1	
JD-46	507440001	Paper Meter Holder	1	
JD-47	507494001	Cushion Rubber for JD-42	1	
JD-48	507020001	Paper Meter (right)	1	
JD-49	507021001	Paper Meter (left)	1	
JD-50	505478001	Card Holder	1	
JD-51	505165001	Screw for JD-48, 49, 50	6	

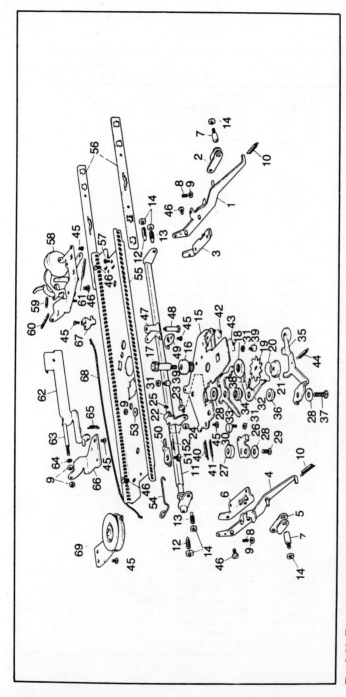

Fig. 6-50. The carriage rail, pinion base, spring drum and warning bell for the Brother Model 3500. Parts numbers for this mechanism will be preceded by the letters JF (courtesy of Brother International Corporation).

Table 6-15. Parts List for Fig. 6-50 (courtesy of Brother International Corporation).

REF. NO.	PART NO.	PART NAME	QTY	MEMO
JF-1	516388001	Carriage Frame (right) Unit	1	
JF-2	500815001	Carriage Link (right)	1	
JF-3	500400001	Carriage Holder (right)	1	
JF-4	516391001	Carriage Frame (left) Unit	1	
JF-5	500816001	Carriage Link (left)	1	
JF-6	500401001	Carriage Holder (left)	1	
JF-7	500784001	Stud Screw for JR-2, 5	2	
JF-8	516398001	Shift Adjusting Screw	4	
JF-9	516399001	Nut for JF-8, 51, 66	4	
JF-10	500685001	Shift Balance Spring	2	
JF-11	516294001	Shift Link (rear) Unit	1	
JF-12	500278001	Center Screw for JF-11	2	
JF-13	500498001	Stud for JF-1,4	2	
JF-14	106129001	Nut for JF-7, 12, 13	6	
JF-15~43	(516284001)	Pinion Base Complete	1	
JF-15	521439001	Pinion Base Unit	1	
JF-16	501010001	Pinion Boss	1	
JF-17	501012001	Space Pinion	1	
JF-18	501011001	Nut for JF-16	1	
JF-19	500430001	Space Ratchet Wheel	1	
JF-20	500431001	Ratchet Release Spring	1	
JF-21	500432001	Nut for JF-17	1	
JF-22	516164001	Escape Crank (front)	1	
JF-23	516241001	Eccentric Stud for JF-22	1	
JF-24	500683001	Nut for JF-23	1	
JF-25	048015346	Snap Ring for JF-22	1	
JF-26	501016001	Escape Crank (rear)	1	
JF-27	501017001	Stud Collar for JF-26	1	
JF-28	501018001	Washer for JF-26, 33, 35	3	
JF-29	100137003	Screw for JF-26	1	
JF-30	501019001	Eccentric Screw for JF-26	1	
JF-31	500296001	Nut for JF-30, 39, 51, 63	6	
JF-32	516405001	Space Ratchet	1	
JF-33	50998001	Half Space Ratchet	1	
JF-34	501022001	Stud Collar for JF-32	1	
JF-35	509975001	Repeat Space Opening Lever	1	
JF-36	509974001	Stud Collar for JF-35	1	
JF-37	403857001	Screw for JF-35	1	
JF-38	500680001	Spring for JF-32	1	
JF-39	501023001	Eccentric Screw for JF-32,33	2	
JF-40	501406001	Spring for JF-33	1	
JF-41	503158001	Spring (A) for JF-35	1	
JF-42	501027001	Spring (A) for Back Space Pawl	1	
JF-43	500259001	Spring (B) for Back Space Pawl	1	
JF-44	520202001	Spring (B) for JF-35	1	
JF-45	402281001	Screw for JF-15,49,58,66,67	9	
JF-46	001660413	Screw for JF-1, 4, 55, 58	10	
JF-47	509972001	Repeat Space Crank (rear)	1	
JF-48	509973001	Stud for JF-47	1	
JF-49	509977001	Repeat Space Adjusting Plate	1	
JF-50	516174001	Escape Stopper Unit	1	
JF-51	505951001	Stud Screw for JF-50	1	
JF-52	512048001	Spring for JF-50	1	
JF-53	500986001	Washer for JF-50	1	
JF-54	516128001	Escape Stop Wire	1	
JF-55,56 & JH-15	(516385001)	Carriage & Carriage Rail Unit		
JF-55	516165001	Carriage Rail	1	
JF-56	500634001	Carriage Retainer Unit	2	
JF-57	507658001	Tapping Screw for JF-55	2	
JF-58	507578001	Warning Bell Complete	1	
JF-59	500413001	Spring (A) for JF-58	1	
JF-60	500413001	Spring (B) for JF-58	1	
JF-61	510688001	Spring (C) for JF-58	1	
JF-62	516394001	Carriage Stopper	1	
JF-63	501045001	Shaft for JF-62	1	
JF-64	502131001	Washer for JF-62	1	
JF-65	500404001	Spring for JF-62	1	
JF-66	516396001	Carriage Stopper Holder	1	
JF-67	500643001	Hook for JF-68	1	
JF-68	500470001	Carriage Draw String	1	
JF-69	516412001	Spring Drum Complete	1	

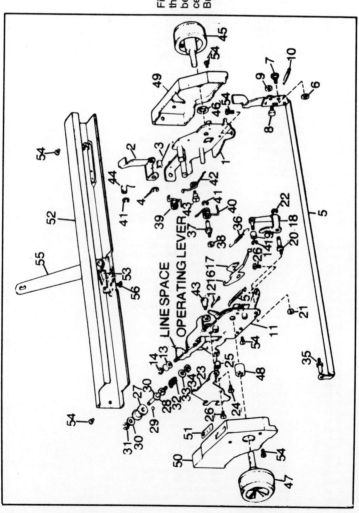

Fig. 6-51. The carriage side plate for the Brother Model 3500. Parts numbers for this mechanism will be preceded by the letters JG (courtesy of Brother International Corporation).

338

Table 6-16. Parts List for Fig. 6-51 (courtesy of Brother International Corporation).

REF	PART NO.	PART NAME	Q'TY	MEMO
JG-1	516474001	Carriage Side Plate (right) Unit	1	
JG-2	500504001	Paper Release Lever	1	
JG-3	500595001	Spring for JG-2	1	
JG-4	500357001	Snap Ring for JG-2	1	
JG-5	516407001	Carriage Release Lever Unit	1	
JG-6	101397003	Washer for JG-5	1	
JG-7	500323001	Stud Screw for JG-5	1	
JG-8	516411001	Eccentric Screw for JG-5	1	
JG-9	500683001	Nut for JG-8	1	
JG-10	500463001	Spring for JG-5	1	
JG11 ~ 35	516418001	Carriage Side Plate (left) Complete	1	
JG-11	516419001	Carriage Side Plate (left) Unit	1	
JG-12	509383001	Spring for Line Space Ratchet	1	
JG-13	516426001	Line Space Operating Lever Roller	1	
JG-14	048015346	Snap Ring for JG-13, 19	2	
JG-15	516429001	Line Space Operating Lever Spring	1	
JG-16	516430001	Spring for Line Space Selector	1	
JG-17	516431001	Washer for JG-16	1	
JG-18	512964001	Ratchet Roller Holder Unit (incl. JG-14, 19)	1	
JG-19	512966001	Ratchet Roller	1	
JG-20	508589001	Eccentric Stud for JG-18	1	
JG-21	402230001	Nut for JG-20	1	
JG-22	048025346	Snap Ring for JG-18	1	
JG-23	516432001	L.S. Operating Lever Guide	1	
JG-24	001660413	Screw for JG-23	1	
JG-25	516434001	Collar for JG-23	1	
JG-26	403863001	Screw for JG-11, 23, 25	3	
JG-27	516401001	Belt Guide Roller	1	
JG-28	516402001	Stud for JG-27	1	
JG-29	402104001	Steel Ball for JG-27	14	
JG-30	516368001	Washer for JG-27, 29	2	
JG-31	048020346	Snap Ring for JG-27	1	
JG-32	516435001	Belt Guide Wire	1	
JG-33	402887001	Washer for JG-32	1	
JG-34	500683001	Nut for JG-28	1	
JG-35	516465001	Stud for JG-5	1	
JG-36	513199001	Spring for JG-18	1	
JG-37	500500001	Stud for JH-6	1	
JG-38	500296001	Nut for JG-37	1	
JG-39	500503001	Spring for JH-6 (right)	1	
JG-40	500501001	Spring for JH-6 (left)	1	
JG-41	500379001	Snap Ring for JG-40, 44, JH-7, 8	2	
JG-42	500516001	Spring for JH-7	1	
JG-43	500368001	Stud Screw for JG-42, JH-6, 7	2	
JG-44	500511001	Spring for JH-7, 8	1	
JG-45	507686	Platen Knob (right)	1	
JG-46	102707001	Washer for JG-45	1	
JG-47	516440	Platen Knob (left)	1	
JG-48	516442001	Collar for JG-47	1	
JG-49	516433	Carriage Cover (right)	1	
JG-50	516458	Carriage Cover (left)	1	
JG-51	505479001	Line Space Indicator	1	
JG-52	588202001	Carriage Cover (rear) Unit	1	
JG-53	501406001	Spring for Paper Support Arm	1	
JG-54	402281002	Screw for JG-1, 16, 49, 50, 52	11	
JG-55	588203001	Paper Holder Unit	1	
JG-56	002639303	Screw for JG-55	1	

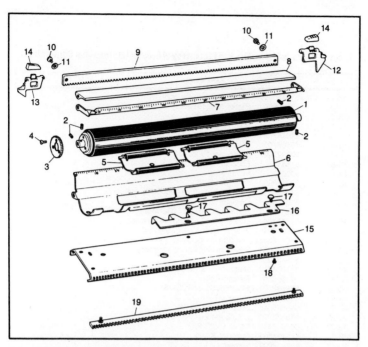

Fig. 6-52. The carriage for the Brother Model 3500. Parts numbers for this mechanism will be preceded by the letters JH (courtesy of Brother International Corporation).

Table 6-17. Parts List for Fig. 6-52 (courtesy of Brother International Corporation).

REF. NO.	PART NO.	PART NAME	QT'Y	MEMO
JH-1	516437001	Platen	1	
JH-2	014679322	Screw for JG-45, 47	4	
JH-3	500497001	Line Space Ratchet Wheel	1	
JH-4	51235001	Screw for JH-3	3	
JH-5	500592001	Paper Feed Roller Unit	2	
JH-6	500499	Paper Pan	1	
JH-7	500512001	Paper Bail Scale	1	
JH-8	500509	Paper Rest	1	
JH-9	500531001	Margin Rack	1	
JH-10	009670413	Screw for JH-9	2	
JH-11	500341001	Washer for JH-10	2	
JH-12	507267001	Margin Stop (right)	1	
JH-13	507268001	Margin Stop (left)	1	
JH-14	500542	Tip for JH-12, 13	2	
JH-15	516386001	Carriage	1	
JH-16	507571001	Tab Stop Pawl	1	
JH-17	507573001	Screw for JH-16	2	
JH-18	402281002	Screw for JH-16	1	
JH-19	516387001	Space Rack	1	

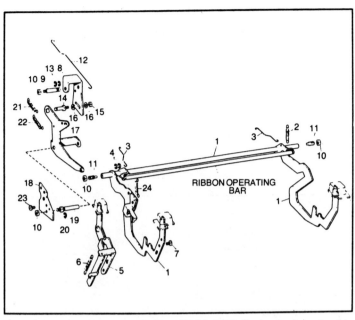

Fig. 6-53. The shift for the Brother Model 3500. Parts numbers for this mechanism will be preceded by the letters JI (courtesy of Brother International Corporation).

Table 6-18. Parts List for Fig. 6-53 (courtesy of Brother International Corporation).

REF. NO.	PART NO.	PART NAME	Q'TY	MEMO
JI-1	516302001	Shift Lever Unit	1	
JI-2	512125001	Spring for Ribbon Operating Bar	1	
JI-3	516080001	Ribbon Feed Wire	2	
JI-4	048040346	Snap Ring for Ribbon Operating Bar	2	
JI-5	516308001	Shift Key Lock Lever Unit	1	
JI-6	507303001	Spring for JI-5	1	
JI-7	516311001	Scew for JI-6	1	
JI-8	516314001	Shift Crank	1	
JI-9	516315001	Stud for JI-8	1	
JI-10	106129001	Nut for JI-9, 11, 19	4	
JI-11	500498001	Center Screw for JI-1	2	
JI-12	507485001	Shift Wire	1	
JI-13	500357001	Snap Ring for JI-8	2	
JI-14	516316001	Shift Crank Adjusting Screw	1	
JI-15	102853001	Nut for JI-14	1	
JI-16	402447001	Washer for JI-15	2	
JI-17	516317001	Shift Operating Lever Unit	1	
JI-18	516322001	Holder for JI-17	1	
JI-19	516321001	Stud for JI-17	1	
JI-20	048050346	Snap Ring for JI-17	1	
JI-21	516320001	Spring for JI-8, 17	1	
JI-22	516323001	Spring for JI-17	1	
JI-23	105123002	Screw for JI-18	2	
JI-24	511198001	Spring for JI-1	1	

341

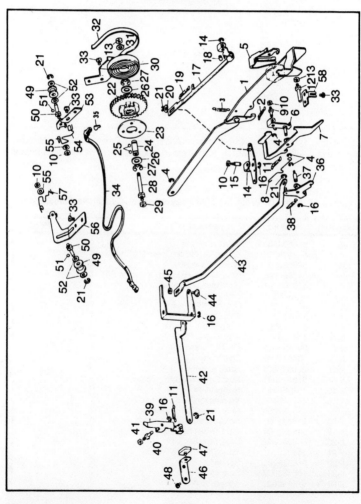

Fig. 6-54. The carriage return for the Brother Model 3500. Parts numbers for this mechanism will be preceded by the letters JJ (courtesy of Brother International Corporation).

Table 6-19. Parts List for Fig. 6-54 (courtesy of Brother International Corporation).

REF. NO.	PART NO.	PART NAME	Q'TY	MEMO
JJ-1	516344001	Return Key Lever Unit	1	
JJ-2	516272001	Spring (A) for JJ-1	1	
JJ-3	503153001	Spring (B) for JJ-1	1	
JJ-4	048025346	Snap Ring for JJ-1,6,8,15,17	6	
JJ-5	516347001	Return Key Lever Guide	1	
JJ-6	516348001	Holder for JJ-7	1	
JJ-7	516351001	Dog Shelf for Return	1	
JJ-8	516352001	Wire for JJ-14	1	
JJ-9	516353001	Stud for JJ-6	1	
JJ-10	402230001	Nut for JJ-9,15,50	4	
JJ-11	500597001	Spring for JJ-7, 39	2	
JJ-12	516354001	Eccentric Stud for Dog Shelf Shop	1	
JJ-13	021670403	Nut for JJ-12,28	2	
JJ-14	516355001	Clutch Operating Crank	1	
JJ-15	516357001	Stud for JJ-14	1	
JJ-16	048030346	Snap Ring for JJ-14,36,39,42	4	
JJ-17	516358001	Clutch Operating Link Unit	1	
JJ-18	500336002	Rubber for JJ-17	1	
JJ-19	504669001	Spring for JJ-17	1	
JJ-20	550951001	Washer for JJ-17	1	
JJ-21	048020346	Snap Ring for JJ-17,42,43,49	5	
JJ-22	516364001	Return Drum	1	
JJ-23	516366001	Return Drum Flange	1	
JJ-24	516367001	Collar for JJ-22	1	
JJ-25	071031850	Steel Ball for JJ-22	18	
JJ-26	516403001	Washer for JJ-22	2	
JJ-27	048050346	Snap Ring for JJ-22	2	
JJ-28	516369001	Stud for JJ-22	1	
JJ-29	402959001	Nut for JJ-28	1	
JJ-30	516478001	Return Drum Spring & Lid	1	
JJ-31	400806002	Washer for JJ-30	1	
JJ-32	516371001	Return Belt Cover	1	
JJ-33	001660413	Screw for JJ-32, 49, 58	5	
JJ-34	516372001	Return Belt Unit	1	
JJ-35	516466001	Stop Rubber for JJ-34	1	
JJ-36	516374001	Dog Shelf Lock Crank	1	
JJ-37	516376001	Stud for JJ-36	1	
JJ-38	515074001	Spring for JJ-36	1	
JJ-39	516377001	Return Release Link	1	
JJ-40	516379001	Eccentric Stud for JJ-39	1	
JJ-41	102853001	Nut for JJ-40	1	
JJ-42	516380001	Return Release Link (center)	1	
JJ-43	516383001	Return Release Connector	1	
JJ-44	516084001	Stud Screw for JJ-43	1	
JJ-45	500296001	Nut for JJ-44	1	
JJ-46	516384001	Return Release Crank Stop Plate	1	
JJ-47	510397001	Cushion Rubber for JJ-46	1	
JJ-48	001679413	Screw for JJ-46	2	
JJ-49-55 & JJ-10,21	516469001	Belt Guide Holder Unit (A)	1	
JJ-49	516401001	Belt Guide Roller	2	
JJ-50	516402001	Stud for JJ-49	2	
JJ-51	402104001	Steel Ball for JJ-49	28	
JJ-52	516368001	Washer for JJ-51	4	
JJ-53	516451001	Belt Guide Holder (A)	1	
JJ-54	516452001	Belt Guide Wire (A)	1	
JJ-55	503092001	Washer for JJ-54	2	
JJ-49-52 & JJ-10,21 56,57	516470001	Belt Guide Holder Unit (B)	1	
JJ-56	516400001	Belt Guide Holder (B)	1	
JJ-57	516404001	Belt Guide Wire (B)	1	
JJ-58	516361001	Dog Shelf (Return) Guide	1	

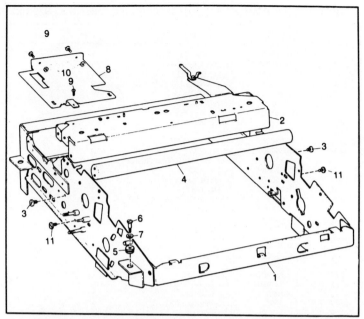

Fig. 6-55. The chassis for the Brother Model 3500. Parts numbers for this mechanism will be preceded by the letters JK (courtesy of Brother International Corporation).

After removing these parts, the ribbon spool holders can be removed. Remove the parts numbered GE-1 through GE-14 to remove the right ribbon spool holder. Remove the parts numbered GE-16 through GE-31 to remove the left ribbon spool holder.

Reinstallation of the parts can be done by reversing the procedure for removal. Be sure that when the covers are replaced,

Table 6-20. Parts List for Fig. 6-55 (courtesy of Brother International Corporation).

REF. NO.	PART NO.	PART NAME	Q'TY	MEMO
JK-1	516443001	Chassis Unit	1	
JK-2	516450001	Chassis Reinforce Block	1	
JK-3	002670613	Screw for JK-2	6	
JK-4	516175001	Chassis Reinforce Bar	1	
JK-5	511342001	Cushion Rubber	4	
JK-6	516296001	Screw for JK-1	4	
JK-7	510909001	Washer for JK-6	4	
JK-8	516176000	Motor Cover	1	
JK-9	500654001	Screw for JK-8	3	
JK-10	500296001	Nut for JK-9	2	
JK-11	001679413	Screw for JK-4	4	

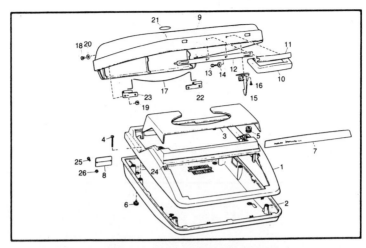

Fig. 6-56. The cover and case for the Brother Model 3500. Parts numbers for this mechanism will be preceded by the letters JL (courtesy of Brother International Corporation).

Table 6-21. Parts List for Fig. 6-56 (courtesy of Brother International Corporation).

REF. NO.	PART NO.	PART NAME	Q'TY	MEMO
JL-1	516182	Upper Cover	1	
JL-2	516490	Lower Cover (U.L.)	1	
JL-2-1	516224	Lower Cover (CSA)	1	
JL-2-2	516225	Lower Cover (VDE)	1	
JL-3	516184	Top Cover	1	
JL-4	516202001	Screw for JL-1,2	2	
JL-5	516245001	Top Cover Fitting Rubber	2	
JL-6	512141001	Rubber Foot	4	
JL-7		Name Plate	1	
JL-8		Rating Plate	1	
JL-9~21	516210	Lid Case Complete	1	
JL-9	516186	Lid Case	1	
JL-10	507936	Carrying Handle	1	
JL-11	520707	Handle Holder	1	
JL-12	516197	Lock Operating Plate	1	
JL-13	512701001	Screw for JL-12	2	
JL-14	503091001	Washer for JL-13	2	
JL-15	516191001	Lid Case Lock Unit	2	
JL-16	401881003	Screw for JL-15	4	
JL-17	516479001	Supply Cord Hanger	1	
JL-18	002660812	Screw for JL-22	4	
JL-19	402230001	Nut for JL-18	4	
JL-20	402287002	Washer for JL-18	4	
JL-21		Ornamental Plate	1	
JL-22	516480001	Holder for JL-17 (right)	1	
JL-23	516481001	Holder for JL-17 (left)	1	
JL-24	516244001	Switch Indicator (UL only)	1	
JL-25	009630813	Screw for JL-8 (CSA only)	2	
JL-26	500296001	Nut for JL-8 (CSA only)	2	

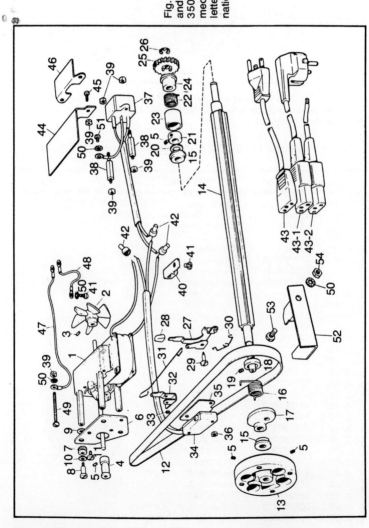

Fig. 6-57. The electrical components and snatch roll for the Brother Model 3500. Parts numbers for this mechanism will be preceded by the letters JM (courtesy of Brother International Corporation).

346

REF. NO.	PART NO.	PART NAME	Q'TY	MEMO
JM-1	516472001	Motor for 110V~125V (UL, CSA, etc.)	1	
JM-1-1	516479001	Motor for 220V~240V (VDE,SEV,etc.)	1	
JM-2	516473001	Motor Fan	1	
JM-3	011660512	Screw for JM-2	1	
JM-4	516453001	Motor Pulley (60 Hz)	1	
JM-4-1	516456001	Motor Pulley (50 Hz)	1	
JM-5	014679322	Screw for JM-4, 13, 21	5	
JM-6	516157001	Motor Holder	1	
JM-7	511342001	Motor Cushion Rubber	3	
JM-8	516158001	Stud Screw for JM-1	3	
JM-9	403332001	Washer (A) for JM-1	3	
JM-10	402447001	Washer (B) for JM-1	3	
JM-11	001679413	Screw for JM-6	3	
JM-12	516454001	Driving Belt	1	
JM-13	516154000	Snatch Roll Pulley	1	
JM-14	516329001	Snatch Roll	1	
JM-15	516069001	Snatch Roll Metal	2	
JM-16	516324001	Shift Cam Spring	1	
JM-17	516325001	Shift Cam	1	
JM-18	516326001	Collar for JM-16	1	
JM-19	011660312	Screw for JM-18	2	
JM-20	513200000	Washer for JM-14	1	
JM-21	513317001	Collar (A) for JM-22	1	
JM-22	513318001	Return Spring	1	
JM-23	513319001	Return Collar	1	
JM-24	513320001	Collar (B) for JM-22	1	
JM-25	516362001	Return Gear	1	
JM-26	048040346	Snap Ring for JM-25	1	
JM-27	516149001	Switch Lever	1	
JM-28	503643	Tip for JM-27	1	
JM-29	509635001	Stud Screw for JM-27	1	
JM-30	503113001	Snap Spring for JM-27	1	
JM-31	516152001	Switch Operating Wire	1	
JM-32	516151001	Switch Operating Lever	1	
JM-33	048020346	Snap Ring for JM-32	1	
JM-34	516483001	Power Switch with Lead Wire for UL CSA	1	
JM-34-1	516488001	Power Switch with Lead Wire for VDE, etc.	1	
JM-35	514172000	Insulating Paper for JM-34	1	
JM-36	021260103	Nut for JM-34	2	
JM-37	516402001	Receptacle with Lead Wire for 100~125V	1	
JM-37-1	516219001	Receptacle with Lead Wire for 220~240V	1	
JM-38	516214001	Bolt for JM-37 (100~125V)	2	
JM-38-1	516215001	Bolt for JM-37-1 (220~240V)	2	
JM-39	021660103	Nut for JM-37, 38, 45	7	
JM-40	120679001	Wire Holder	1	
JM-41	400298002	Screw for JM-40, 48	2	
JM-42	207216000	Wire Connector		
JM-43	512901001	Power Supply Cord for CSA, UL (100~125V)	1	
JM-43-1	550856001	Power Supply Cord for VDE	1	
JM-43-2	550980001	Power Supply Cord for 220~240V	1	
JM-44	516248001	Receptacle Covr for VDE, etc.	1	
JM-45	516298001	Screw for JM-44	2	
JM-46	516247000	Insulating Paper for VDE, etc.	1	
JM-47	516218001	Earthing Wire (A)	1	
JM-48	516249001	Earthing Wire (B) for VDE, SEV	1	
JM-49	516498001	Screw for JM-47, 52	1	
JM-50	502673001	Washer for JM-41, 49, 51	3	
JM-51	105123001	Screw for JM-37, 47, 48	1	
JM-52	516497001	Motor Cover for CSA only	1	
JM-53	001670603	Screw for Earthing Wire (CSA only)	1	
JM-54	106129001	Nut for JM-53 (CSA only)	1	

the top cover does not interfere with the ribbon spools. Moreover, immediately check ribbon reversing.

SUMMARY

In this chapter I have presented everything that you will need to know to adjust and repair the Brother Models 3,000, 1,000, XL-4,000 and Model 3500 of the JP8 group. I should like to thank Brother International Corporation for making all this information available to me, and ultimately to the reading public. Without the cooperation of Brother International Corporation, a major portion of this book would not have been possible.

Appendix: Typewriter Manufacturers and/or Distributors

Adler Business Machines
1600 Route 22
Union, NJ 07083

Brother International Corp.
Eight Corporate P1
Piscataway, NJ 08854

Facit-Addo, Inc.
66 Field Point Rd.
Greenwich, Conn. 06830

Hermes Products, Inc.
1900 Lower Road
Linden, NJ 07036

International Business Machines Corporation
Old Orchard Rd.
Armonk, NY 10504

Olivetti Corporation of America
500 Park Avenue
New York NY 10022

Olympia USA, Inc.
P.O. Box 22
Somerville, NJ 08876

Royal Typewriter Co.
150 New Park Ave.
Hartford, Conn. 06106

SCM Corporation
299 Park Ave.
New York NY 10017

Sperry Remington
P.O. Box 1000
Blue Bell, PA 19422

Index

A

Air compressor 136

B

Back space keybutton 39
   mechanism 51, 108, 265
Brother typewriter, adjusting belt tension 253
   escapement mechanism 262
   parts 306
   printing mechanism 254
   removing covers 251
   removing motor 252
   space bar mechanism 262
   switch mechanism 253

C

Carbon ribbons 23
   numbering system 165
Carriage 30
Carriage release 81, 287
   control button 37
   mechanism 128, 302
Carriage return 112
   control button 34
   mechanism 298
Cleaning a typewriter 135
Cleaning process 138
Cleaning solutions 136
Clear control button 36

Communications 12
Control buttons 32
Correction mechanism 130
Cotton ribbons 162

D

Driving mechanism 87

E

Electrical system 87
Electric typewriters 13
Elite 22
Escapement, malfunctions 179
Escapement mechanism 20, 46, 98, 262

F

Fabric ribbons 23, 163

H

Half space mechanism 105
High yield correctable film ribbon 25

I

IBM Selectric II, controls 41
   typewriters, old 156
Impression regulator 39

K

Keybuttons   14, 41
Keys   14

L

Levers   32
Line space lever   35
Line space mechanism   126, 286, 302
Line space
   selector lever   40
Lubricating   139
   a typewriter   135
Lubrication solutions   136

M

Manual typewriters   13
Margin release keybutton   37
   mechanism   57, 280
   set control button   36
   stop mechanism   52, 280
   stops   114
Multiply copy control lever   40
Mylar ribbons   164

N

Nylon ribbons   162

O

Olympia typewriter,
   adjustments   198-215
   cleaning   176
   oiling   176
   parts   172-176
   removing of
     components   215-233
     removing of covers   215-233
     removing of mechanisms   215-233
On-off control button   34

P

Paper bail   32
Paper feed   62
   malfunctioning   186
   mechanism   282
   release mechanism   127
Paper pan   31
Paper release   31
   lever   40
   mechanism   66, 286
Paper table-feed rolls   31
Parts catalogs   151
Pica   22
Pitch, of a typewriter   20
Platen   29
   reconditioning   158

Platen parts, removing   294
Platen release   131
   knob   40
   mechanism   83
Polyethylene ribbons   164
Power roll   86
Proportional spacing   20

R

Repeat space mechanism   107, 291
Return clutch   298
Return jamming release   299
Ribbon cartridge mechanism   126
Ribbon color change mechanism   123, 271
Ribbon feed mechanism   66, 123
Ribbon feed/reverse mechanism   278
Ribbon lift mechanism   74, 123
Ribbon lifting mechanism   271
Ribbon position control button   38
Ribbons, cotton   162
   fabric   163
   fails to reverse   196
   feed mechanism   194
   helpful tips   24
   mylar   164
   nylon   162
   problems   28
   polyethylene   164
   silk   162
   stocking an assortment   162
   typewriter   23
Rinsing   139
Rinsing solutions   136
Rolls, paper table-feed   31

S

Service manuals   12, 151
Shift control buttons   34
Shift lock, control buttons   34
   mechanism   60
Shift mechanism   59, 100, 268, 295
Silk ribbons   162
Single element typewriter   16
Single space mechanism   107
Space bar   32
   mechanism   262
Space mechanism   106
Spacing mechanism   45
Spacing problem   193
Spacing, proportional   20
Spring drum   282
Standard typewriter   18
Switch mechanism   87

T

Tab control button 36
Tab set 36
Tab set/clear key 188
Tab set-clear mechanism 80, 122
Tabulation mechanism 75
Tabulator 189
   mechanism 118, 271
Tech III ribbon 25
Tools 142
Touch control lever 39
Typebars 14
   adjusting pressure 158
   heads 14
   malfunctioning 190
   typewriter 16
Typebasket 16
Typewriter covers, removing 161
Typewriter ribbons 23
Typewriters, cleaning 135
   electric 13

   lubricating 135
   manual 13
   old IBM 156
   pitch 20
   proportional spacing 22
   securing information on 150
   single element 16
   standard 18
   sticky & dirty 134
   typebar 16
Typing mechanism 44, 89
Typing pressure regulation 39

V

Variable line spacer 197
Vertical line
   spacing mechanism 60

W

Warning bell, adjustment 290
Workshop, designing 148

DEMCO